™

SLATCOFF AND COMPANY LLC
Publishing Services

OTHER LITERARY WORKS

by
THOMAS SLATCOFF

Novels

Operation Red X
SLATCOFF AND COMPANY LLC, 2015

Atrocity in the Nave
SLATCOFF AND COMPANY LLC, 2017

Short Story

The Respondent: A Person Bewitched
SLATCOFF AND COMPANY LLC, 2017

Author Page
Amazon.com/author/ThomasSlatcoff

On the third worst day of his life, Gheorghi tightly closed his blue eyes, optimistic that when he opened them, the nightmare would be over. The tighter he clenched his eyes, and the more he desired closure, the more brilliant became the vision of SATAN. The image did not display a mythical two-horned man, dressed in a red suit, with a black goatee and holding a three-pointed rod. It revealed the reality of a human beast. A cruelly rapacious person, just as the dictionary defined a beast. Excessively greedy and grasping, true to the definition of rapacious. The vision displayed the Petitioner and her smirk.

The Respondent: A Person Bewitched
by Thomas Slatcoff

A short story prelude to the novel

The Respondent: A Person of Interest
by Thomas Slatcoff

Thomas Slatcoff

The Respondent:
A Person of Interest

A Novel

The Respondent: A Person of Interest   2019-5 F3

Description

A missing person investigation to find the petitioner to a six-year procrastinated divorce cracked open the respondent's mental conflict from voodoo dreams and the local police corruption that abetted a homegrown terrorist plot.

About the Author

Thomas Slatcoff returned to private business after he served twenty-three years in Federal law enforcement and retired as a Senior Criminal Investigator.

Thomas is the author of two novels, *Operation Red X*, his debut novel and *Atrocity In The Nave*, and a short story, *The Respondent: A Person Bewitched*, a prelude to *The Respondent: A Person of Interest*.

He uses his diverse experiences, knowledge, and observations from private business, global government service, federal law enforcement, public safety, and life to create literary works to *Entertain, Inform,* and *Inspire.* Thomas spends his time in Florida and Pennsylvania and traveling.

Visit Slatcoff.com for more about Thomas and SLATCOFF AND COMPANY.

Enjoy the reads and stay in touch.

Twitter
THOMAS SLATCOFF@SLATCOFFANDCO

Facebook
SLATCOFFANDCOMPANYLLC@SLATCOFFANDCOMPANY

LinkedIn
THOMAS SLATCOFF

Editor
Anne-Marie Rutella

Cover Art
Adrijus Guscia

The Respondent: A Person of Interest is a work of fiction.

The names, characters, and events in the book are the product of the author's imagination and are used fictitiously and not intended as accurate representations of real incidents or people, living or dead.

The places, cities, towns, organizations, and entities are used fictitiously and not intended as accurate representations of real places, cities, towns, organizations, and entities or anyone, in any manner, associated with the same.

Published by:

SLATCOFF AND **COMPANY** LLC

Florida, USA
Contact@Slatcoff.com
www.Slatcoff.com

First Print Edition: May 2019

ISBN-13: 978-0-9971506-5-0

Acknowledgments

To those who continue to support me in my literary journey, thank you.

Steve Gauding, thank you for the cop humor.

Mary, Samantha, Lauren, Bethany

Your support and enthusiasm motivate me.

Your love for me and belief in me inspires me.

Your belief that I have something to offer others flatters me.

Love you.

"Am I under arrest?"

"No, you're not under arrest. We're just talking."

"I'm done talking," Maria replied sharply. "You have a nice day, Detective."

Maria stood, looked down at Detective Presley, and sounded,

"My father."

She gave a sarcastic laugh and said,

"You're a batshit crazy lady. You can put that in your notes too, Ms. Nancy Drew."

Maria paused and continued to look down at the detective before she added, "You should focus on those pier people."

The Respondent: A Person of Interest
by Thomas Slatcoff

CHAPTER 1

Gheorghi Nikolov sat at his usual coffee shop, the White Star Coffee Company on Panama City Beach or as the Bay County locals simply said, *the beach*. He sipped his typical cup of coffee, the featured dark roast. Today it was Three Gifts for Christmas to celebrate the upcoming Christian holiday, the birth of Christ. White Star described the blend as *a gold label blend, with the aroma of frankincense and an afternote of myrrh*. White Star produced the gold label blend once a year and presented it for consumer purchase on Black Friday until it sold out. Uncannily, it always sold-out by the Byzantine Eastern Rite observation of St. Nicholas's Feast Day.

Gheorghi was enjoying his favorite pastime, hanging out by himself and people-watching when he felt the sharp pain again. The episodes of pain in the nape of his back continued, as did the limp that developed in his right leg. Both physical ailments began about two years into the now six-year procrastinated divorce proceedings.

Gheorghi, forced to be the Respondent to the proceedings, thought the stress from the protracted litigation caused both ailments. The doctors he consulted were unable to diagnose the cause of the pain, and one suggested a prescription for oxycodone, a painkiller the Drug Enforcement Administration placed as a schedule – II controlled substance because of the high potential for abuse that may lead to severe psychological or physical dependence. Gheorghi refused the conventional generous pill-giving of Florida physicians because he did not like to take prescription drugs. He thought the use of legal or illegal drugs was a sign of a weak mind.

The longer Nerezza, the Petitioner to the proceedings and by way of legal strategy, procrastinated with the litigation, the more intense were the episodes of pain. The only consistency with the pain was that every Friday night at seven o'clock, there was an episode, and the pain intensified until midnight, then gradually subsided throughout the early morning hours of Saturday. During the balance of the week, other incidents were random if any occurred at all.

The most painful episode to date occurred the night in April when Gheorghi returned from the telephonic pre-trial hearing at his lawyer's office in Tallahassee. It started to rain when he left and continued to rain the entire return trip. As he continued westbound on Interstate 10, about twenty miles from Tallahassee, the back pain began and intensified during the two-hour journey. The pain, at times so intense, forced Gheorghi to close his eyes as a non-prescription attempt to make the pain go away. Gheorghi was sure he blacked out a few times, and he did not know how he safely operated his sports car, a British IP 568, during the two-hour return trip.

Somehow, Gheorghi made it back to his daughter's house on Panama City Beach, and when he arrived, the intense pain was still with him. Exhausted and in pain, Gheorghi went right to bed, hoping the pain would go away or at least subside. He fell into a deep sleep that took him into another dream about his whirlpool predicament as the recipient of the dilly-dallier opposing counsel and her shenanigans with the divorce proceedings. A vivid dream that further raised suspicion the Petitioner bewitched the Respondent. Dreams that started in year five of the six-year procrastinated divorce.

Early the next morning, Gheorghi woke to the sound of his smartphone, announcing an email. He picked up the phone and saw the email was from his lawyer. He opened the email and then opened the attachment titled AMENDED NOTICE OF HEARING. He read the court notice and sounded a long sigh.

Gheorghi sat up and slid to the edge of his bed. He shook his head and reread the email and attachment. He checked the date three times. His hands started to tremble, and the phone fell to the floor as he recalled his dream from last night that ended with what now just occurred in real life.

Gheorghi's first thought was, *The final hearing is rescheduled. Great!*

Gheorghi shook his head and continued his thoughts,

More procrastination. I don't need this. And the court rescheduled the final hearing for the exact date of the marriage, thirty-two years to the date. I'll probably be the only one to realize the irony. During the last hearing, the Petitioner didn't remember the date of the marriage. How could she forget the date of her marriage? I don't deserve this agitation. Am I under a spell, or are these prophetic dreams?

Gheorghi shook his head and thought about a friend's suggested resolve to the litigation.

Twenty cents. Hmm, only twenty cents. Maybe Motorman was right about how to end this and how to keep all the assets that I labored to acquire, without the dreams and the accumulated legal fees, all for twenty cents. And there's the looming threat of the court order payment of the fees. The Petitioner's attorneys fees. She brings the action, but I have to pay her attorney's fees and my attorney fees too.

Gheorghi shook his head a third time and thought more,

What did I do to deserve the irony? What did I do? After six years of procrastinated litigation, I'm the subject of irony? Maybe I should act out the dream.

Gheorghi reflected on the dream he had last night, the longest in duration since they started.

The vivid dream last night featured a beautiful woman named Angel from the dirt streets of Taganga, Colombia.

Gheorghi closed his eyes and rubbed them with his hands. As he did, the silhouette of Satan appeared to Gheorghi as in his dream last night, and Gheorghi quickly opened his eyes in surprise.

This is concerning. Is something else at play here? Today, the devil presents to me, just like in my dream last night.

Gheorghi, still seated at the edge of the bed, continued to reflect on the dream from last night.

I drove to my lawyer's office for the telephonic pretrial hearing, and during the conference call, the devil presented to me. I drove back to Panama City Beach in torrential rain, and my car hydroplaned out of control and flipped end over end. Then I was in Colombia. I had a cartridge inscribed PETITIONER. And there was this strikingly beautiful woman named Angel. She was seducing me, I thought. I didn't even know if it was seduction, long removed from that play. Her parents had a large luxury yacht, and Angel and I sailed around the Caribbean. Then I was back in the U.S., and the Petitioner was missing. I thought the Petitioner used voodoo spells on me. Yeah. Voodoo spells that made me feel like <u>*The Respondent: A Person Bewitched*</u>.

Gheorghi expanded a breath and continued his thoughts,

Was the change to the final hearing date procrastination, irony or voodoo? A way for the Petitioner to control me.

Maybe, like in the dream, the Petitioner is missing and is the reason for a continuance. What would happen to the litigation if the Petitioner goes missing? Would I have to continue to pay the court-ordered monthly payments? Deposit them into a bank account her cohabitant could access.

These are the questions I will have to ask my lawyer. Or should I keep her out of this? I have client-attorney privilege, but does it extend to crimes, to murder specifically? And then how would I get the Petitioner declared dead in absentia? How would I get a court order in absentia?

What am I thinking? Murder is nonsense.

On the right side of Gheorghi, the bed moved as though someone sat next to him. Gheorghi jerked to look and saw the devil was seated. Like in the dream, the image was displayed as a mythical two-horned man dressed in a red suit with a black goatee. Absent was the three-pointed rod. This time the devil was seated with his legs crossed right over left and his hands rested on his knee, left atop right. The devil's tail, like a snake, was fully extended and neatly position on the unmade bed.

Gheorghi stared at the image, and it began to distort from the devil to the Petitioner. The morphed image displayed the Petitioner in her youthful beauty.

Gheorghi jumped up from the bed and moved away from the morphed devil. As conditioned, he began to verbally petition for help from an immortal being who could slay the devil and maybe slay the dreams. Gheorghi's petition was the same when he was a law enforcement officer and knew he was going into harm's way. Now a procrastinated civil action in family court recoiled Gheorghi, and he found himself petitioning help from the Archangel Michael.

The vision went away, and Gheorghi just stood there trembling from the unknown details to appear in the final decree. A court order with the potential to cause personal financial ruin.

CHAPTER 2

"Sir. Please calm down," said the clerk from behind the thick bullet-resistant glass of the main visitor window at the Bay County Sheriff's Office (BCSO) Headquarters.

"Calm down! Okay. Okay. I'm sorry. But please understand. Put yourself in my position," mumbled the man at the window.

He paused. He looked away and overtly brought his emotions under control, which included wiping tears from his eyes with a well-used ball of white tissues he pulled from his front pocket. The used tissues left white lint about his eyelashes and eyebrows.

He looked back to the clerk and continued,

"It's been a week now, and no one has called me."

He stopped talking and again dabbed his eyes with the balled-up tissues before he continued.

"What are you people doing? What are you people doing to find her?"

The clerk replied, "Sir, let me help you by getting the duty detective. Would you mind taking a seat in the waiting area? Please."

"Okay."

As the man walked away from the clerk's window, the clerk picked up the telephone receiver, punched three digits on the keypad, waited a moment, and said, "Aaron, can you come out and talk to an inquiring citizen."

"Who is it?"

"It's some guy who's looking for information about his missing friend."

"Missing friend? Is he related to the missing person?"

"Aaron, I don't know. I don't ask questions like you. It's hard to understand what he's saying. His thick accent is difficult to understand, and he's emotional."

"What kind of accent? From where?"

"From the pier. You know, those pier people out on the beach at St. Andrews State Park. What do they call themselves?"

"Oh, no. The pier cult who call themselves the Other World Order — OWO. So much for a slow day. Thanks. I'll be right out."

Aaron slowly stood up from her desk. She was not rushing to the lobby because she knew a trying public contact waited for her since the gentleman was from the OWO. She thought,

Those pier people are hard to understand. Between their thick accents, poor command of the English language, lack of formal education, and emotional personalities, I know it will be slow going. And they have a chip on their shoulder that everyone is better than them. Everyone is financially better off than they are. Not to mention, it is common for them to be drunk or high.

She pushed her chair to her desk and picked up her ballistic notepad case as conditioned.

Aaron stepped through the employee door that opened to a government-fashioned public waiting area painted a high gloss off-white, flooring laid in twelve-inch square linoleum tiles with a green background and contrasting speckle and dark green flimsy plastic chairs with thin chrome legs and arm supports. Aaron surveyed the area as she walked up to the thick bullet-resistant glass and tapped on it. She directed her attention to the clerk, and the clerk pointed to the man seated off by himself.

Aaron walked up to the gentleman and said, "Hello. I'm Detective Presley. I'm the duty detective. How may I help you?"

The man sat as he looked up at Detective Presley. In a quiet tone, he rapidly ran all his words together.

"Pardon me. Please repeat that."

Again, in a low tone, but slower, the man ran all his words together.

"Sir, I'm having a hard time understanding you. Please repeat that, slower this time."

Slower, the man repeated himself a third time.

"Did you find her?

"Find her? Find who?" replied Detective Presley.

As the inquiring citizen continued to look up at Detective Presley, Detective Presley looked down at him and displayed a puzzled look. To the advantage of officer safety, she stayed standing.

The inquiring citizen raised his hands up at his sides, palms up, and shrugged his shoulders to display a nonverbal *what*.

Detective Presley thought,

Here we go. Communicating with the pier people is worse than trying to interact with the Hispanic community or the poor, uneducated southerners from the most rural areas here in the panhandle.

Detective Presley exhaled and continued her thoughts,

I have talked to the impoverished locals all my life. I learned how to listen, understand, and communicate with the snowbirds, the fast-talking Yankees from the north and the Canadians too. I taught myself Spanish to be semi-fluent to talk with the Cuban transplants from Miami and the Hispanic transplants from the various Central America countries who relocated to the Florida Panhandle for the proverbial American Dream. But the people from the OWO, the pier people, they were impossible. They were harder to understand than the Deep South, rural, Louisiana Creoles.

Again, she drew in a breath and exhaled and continued with the citizen inquiry.

"Sir," sounded Detective Presley as she reached out and tapped the inquiring citizen on the shoulder to make sure he was listening to her. "Do you have a case number?"

"What?" replied the citizen.

"A case number," Detective Presley said a little louder.

She thought if she talked louder, he would somehow understand her.

A bit slurred, but more explicit, he said, "Case number. No, I don't have a case number."

Detective Presley continued her inquiry and asked, "Who are we looking for?"

The inquiring citizen just replied, "Sandy."

"Who is Sandy to you? How do you know her?"

"She is my friend."

"What is her last name?"

"Diddler."

"And your name?"

"My name?"

"Yes. What's your name?"

"I am Jack. Jack Prat," said the inquiring citizen as he puffed his chest out and appeared to become gleeful and proud someone asked him his name.

"May I see your driver's license? Please."

"It's not with me. It's back at the house."

"Okay. Let me go back to my desk and see if I can find a case number. I'll be right back."

Detective Presley paused before she walked off. She continued to look down at Mr. Prat and studied him as he looked up at her. His slight smile appeared to visually display his continued high-spirited delight that someone asked him his name. Despite the glee, his face showed the strain of physical ailments. Perhaps physical ailments that manifested into mental illness or neurological disease. Or his state of health was the result of years of drug abuse, maybe alcohol or narcotics, illegal or prescription or both. Frequently, BCSO homicide detectives were dispatched to St. Andrews State Park on the beach to respond to a tourist's discovery of a lifeless body in the park. The hunch of the Homicide Division was fawning members of the OWO moved the overdosed members from their place of death, so law enforcement did not focus on the group.

Detective Presley, without saying anything, finally turned and walked back to the employee door. She touched her employee access badge to the access pad and the electronic lock disengaged. She opened the door and disappeared behind it.

Back at her desk, she flicked her mouse. A log-in screen appeared on her laptop computer, and she entered her log-in name and password. The machine processed the information and gave her access. She clicked on an icon, and another log-in screen appeared. Again, from memory, she entered her username and password, pressed the enter button, and access was granted. Another box appeared. In that box, she typed Sandy Diddler and softly touched the enter button. The hum of the computer signaled the processing of the information.

Shortly, the screen changed and in the center was the lone name Sandy Diddler. Presley moved the cursor over it and right-clicked the mouse.

A text-filled screen appeared. Near the upper left corner was the name match for Sandy Diddler. In the top right corner was the case number MP3090917. The complainant was Jack Prat. The balance of the first page was the general identifying data required to complete a public contact report.

Arron clicked *page two,* which displayed a summary dated September 9 and two short paragraphs. Paragraph one disclosed Jack Prat reported Sandy Diddler went missing on September 9. He informed she went missing on that date, but the responding deputy told him he had to wait forty-eight hours before the BCSO would do anything. He was instructed to call back if she was still missing after the forty-eight hours. Paragraph two was as short and disclosed Mr. Prat believed Diddler was a victim of foul play on the part of her estranged husband, Gheorghi LNU, signifying Last Name Unknown to Prat.

Aaron clicked back to *page one* and scanned the contents that included identifying information and an address for Prat and Diddler. Prat, the complainant, and Sandy, the missing person, had the same address. There was no address listed for Gheorghi.

There was nothing else in the electronic file. There was no investigation conducted on the day of the report nor any follow-up investigation. Aaron thought that was odd. She looked and noted Patrol Deputy S. Rayes (pronounced Rays) responded to the dispatch assigned call; but the report did not have an assigned detective, that block was empty.

Aaron closed the screen and logged out of the report system. She also logged out of her laptop. She rose from her desk, pushed her chair in, and walked back to the waiting area and the inquiring citizen.

Detective Presley announced to Mr. Prat, "Sir, here is my card. The case number is on the back."

Mr. Prat took the detective's card and said, "Thank you."

The detective added, "I have nothing further to report."

The detective paused momentarily and then asked,

"Did you have anything to add? Did anything new happen?"

Strained and frustrated by the inaction of the BCSO, Mr. Prat looked up to Detective Presley and sharply replied, "No, I have nothing to add."

"Okay."

"What has the sheriff's department done since I reported her missing? Has she been found?" asked Prat directly.

"No, sir, she was not located. I'm sorry to report, but there was no investigation conducted since you reported two months ago the person was missing."

"Oh. Hmm. I see. The pier people report a crime, and the law does nothing. That's the way it always is. Just because we are who we are and live the way we live and believe what we believe."

"Sir, I don't know why the lack of investigative efforts. I find that odd myself."

"So, what are you going to do about it?"

"It's not up to me. It's not my case. I'll talk to my commander about this. I have to see what he says."

"Yeah, I bet," said Mr. Prat. "You're all the same. It's only the pier people. Who cares about the pier people?"

"One last question, Mr. Prat. Why did you wait so long to check back with us? It's December."

Mr. Prat either did not hear Detective Presley's question, or he intentionally ignored it because he turned and slowly walked away from her. His walk was deliberate with a limp from the left leg, another sign of his apparent deteriorated health. He exited the building and continued to limp toward the parking lot.

Concerned and curious, Aaron watched as he walked away and entered a white Toyota Tundra pickup truck that appeared well maintained, cosmetically, and parked in a handicap accessible parking spot. For some reason, Aaron was drawn to move into a position to see the registration plate. As Prat drove out of the parking lot, Aaron wrote the registration number on her palm.

Back at her desk, before Aaron wrote her contact report for the file, she ran the registration plate. It came back to a 2009 Toyota Tundra pickup truck, white. Nerezza Nikolov was the lone registered owner.

The vehicle's registered address was within a gated community, the Turtle Shore, on Panama City Beach.

Aaron knew Turtle Shore was an exclusive waterfront community under a Homeowner Association deed restriction. The values for the single residential homes held a wide variance, from a minimum of a quarter million dollars for the interior dwellings to multi-million dollars for the St. Andrew Bay waterfront properties.

In her automated Supplemental Investigative Report (SIR), Aaron included the description and the registered information of the pickup truck. She also noted Jack Prat was the operator.

Aaron completed her short three paragraphs, made them part of the electronic file, and marked the record for commander review. In the BCSO automated reporting system, when a report was so marked, the system automatically sent an email to the noted individual. It sent a daily email reminder until the receiving party opened the file in the automated report system and clicked the notification off. When used, this process created an automated oversight or as the rank and file called it, a DCYA, a *digital cover your ass*.

Aaron had an uneasy feeling about this matter. In the law enforcement vernacular, Jack Prat was hinky, which only served to substantiate a gut feeling. The lack of investigative effort also concerned her, an incredibly thorough detective. A hinky complainant, lack of investigative efforts, and constant rumors of corruption within the command ranks of the sheriff's office made Aaron suspicious of her commander, once again.

The file number also caught her attention. The two letters indicated the type of case – MP for missing person. The next digit was the report number, a three that signified this was the third missing person's report taken on September 9.

To Aaron, that seemed high for missing person cases in one day. The other six digits were the date.

And there was a disparity with addresses. The initial MP report listed the same address for Prat and Diddler. It was to an apartment in an old apartment complex on Shore Drive, Panama City Beach. The registered address for the truck was within a highly affluent residential deed-restricted community, also on Panama City Beach.

Lastly, the registered owner of the pickup truck was Nerezza Nikolov. Who was that? How was that person related to Prat or Diddler? Or was Nerezza associated with Gheorghi LNU? Though, why was Prat driving a truck registered to someone possibly associated with Gheorghi?

Aaron thought,

Had Diddler fallen for the rhetoric of the OWO?

This rhetoric was familiar to Aaron from past investigations of self-declared members of OWO. The acronym used in their logo tattoo that all female members, in what appeared to be a ritual of dominance, had tattooed on their derriere, as disclosed to Presley from the review of intelligence photographs of the deceased members.

CHAPTER 3

Prat was stopped at a steady red light at the intersection of Martin Luther King Jr. and Twenty-Third Street when his government-subsidized Lifeline cellular telephone rang.

Since 1985, the federal government, through the Lifeline program, provided discount phone service for qualifying low-income consumers to ensure all citizens of the United States of America had the opportunities and security that phone service offered. The Lifeline phone provided them the equality and ability to connect to jobs, family, and emergency services. The Lifeline program was available to eligible low-income consumers in every state, territory, commonwealth, and on tribal lands. Funding for the Lifeline program was from the Universal Service Fund. A federal tax collected from hardworking, self-paying, wireless customers and disguised on their cellphone bills as a monthly surcharge.

Prat flicked the speaker button and said, "Hello."

A female voice replied, "Did you get the money?"

"No. I'll tell you again, I'm not on the account. I can't get the money."

"Where is your friend? Get her to get the money out."

"She's not around. I don't know where she is."

"Well, you better get your part of the money up. The shipment is coming in from Colombia, and we need to pay those guys. We can't be late, and we can't fool around with them."

The caller abruptly disconnected the call.

Prat used his federal government subsidized cellular telephone to connect to jobs. Illegal activity, in his mind, was work in keeping with the program regulations for what became known as the *Obama Free Phone*. For him, crime was a job, and a criminal was his occupation.

Prat turned right onto Twenty-Third Street and continued his slow drive back to the beach.

CHAPTER 4

Prat navigated the approximate eight miles from the BCSO in Lynn Haven to an old apartment complex on Shore Drive, off Thomas Drive, on Panama City Beach (PCB). Prat and Diddler cohabited in an old apartment at the Big Lagoon Apartments of Panama City Beach. Before this location, they cohabited at the Gulf Life Condos. Prat cohabited with the still married Diddler since she moved out of her marital home six years ago, and they did it without concern for morality.

Nerezza Nikolov became infatuated with the beliefs and lifestyle of the OWO. She quickly received her cult name, Sandy Diddler. To become a member of the cult, Sandy had pledged, among other things, to divorce her husband, strip him of his assets, change her name to her cult name, and direct deposit 30 percent of the court order division of all monitory holdings to the OWO bank account. The latter was perpetual payment by the cult member for OWO's counsel on tax-free living and legal representation for divorce proceedings.

Nerezza or Sandy abandoned the God-blessed marriage when her husband was away from the Panama City Beach marital home. He was in Orlando, Florida visiting two of his four daughters from the union. With a cellular telephone call, she told her husband of then twenty-seven years she was leaving him. Then, with the push of the red end button, Nerezza or Sandy imploded a family. The conversation was brief. Gheorghi said very little because he was in shock. Nerezza's proclamation left Gheorghi replaying what could have been a chorus to a country song. *Left, on a cell call. Left, on hold.*

While Gheorghi was away from the marital home, Nerezza or Sandy, with the help of her pier lover and cult darling, Jack Pratt – also a member of the OWO from the St. Andrews State Park – pilfered the marital home and took what she wanted.

As required by the OWO cult pledge of allegiance, and with the full weight of antiquated government family laws in her favor, Nerezza filed a PETITION FOR DISSOLUTION OF MARRIAGE. She replaced the affectionate title of wife and became a money-grabbing, floozy Petitioner. She and the one-sided antiquated family laws forced Gheorghi to be the Respondent and to defend himself from what became many false allegations.

Overcome by deep feelings of betrayal, deceit, and helplessness, the Respondent's shock lasted well over two years. The Petitioner's announced decision created a state of mental suspense for the Respondent. Unlike the Petitioner, the Respondent did not pursue companionship from the opposite sex and knew he would not until the civil judge signed the final decree. He had to continue his moral standards and be an example to himself and his children. Indeed, the protracted event created stress for the Respondent, which replaced the shock.

At the Big Lagoon Apartments of Panama City Beach, Prat and Diddler used a housing choice voucher for their rent payment. They received the voucher from the Federal Public Housing Assistance, commonly referred to as Section 8.

The housing choice voucher program was the federal government's primary program for the disabled, the elderly, and low-income families to afford decent, safe, and sanitary housing in the private market. The housing assistance, provided on behalf of the family or individual, allowed accommodation in the form of single-family homes, townhouses, and apartments. The participant was free to choose any house that met the requirements of the program and was not limited to units located in subsidized housing projects referred to as Section 8 housing.

Housing choice vouchers were administered locally by public housing agencies (PHAs). The PHAs received federal funds from the U.S. Department of Housing and Urban Development to administer the voucher program.

A family issued a housing voucher was responsible for finding a suitable housing unit of the family's choice where the owner agreed to rent under the program. Rental units had to meet minimum standards of health and safety, as determined by the PHA.

A housing subsidy was paid directly to the landlord by the PHA on behalf of the participant family. The participant family then settled the difference, if there was any, for the actual rent charged and the amount subsidized. Under certain circumstances, if authorized by the PHA, a family was permitted to use the voucher to purchase a modest home.

The housing subsidy was not the only government social financial public assistance program from which the cohabitants drew free untaxed money. The two cohabitants, one divorced and one still married, connived to avail themselves of all the top five public assistance programs. As members of the OWO, a Bay County public support subculture, they were coached and were now skilled in accessing all five federal government social assistance programs – welfare, food stamps, Medicaid, the Lifeline cellular telephone service, and the housing choice voucher.

And of course, the married cohabitant continued to receive a monthly payment from the Respondent. The monthly payment was not under court order at first; it became court ordered in year four of the procrastinated divorce. At first, it was more than a gesture of goodwill by the Respondent; it was the right thing for the Respondent to do. He provided what the Petitioner demanded, to what they verbally agreed. The Respondent hoped this effort to cooperate with the Petitioner would expedite the conclusion of the litigation. A situation that continued to wear on him physically, mentally, and financially.

The Petitioner did not expedite the legal matter. Instead, the cohabitants enjoyed a tax-free income. An income maintenance model designed by the hierarchy of the OWO. A revenue model to facilitate married women into the OWO lifestyle that compelled them to divorce and rape Respondents of their assets.

Apparently, for many women, the income maintenance model, related counsel to achieve it and legal representation in family court were well worth the 30 percent. That was the fee charged by the hierarchy of the OWO for its services. A perpetual monthly payment paid only by female OWO members and as required, directly deposited into the bank account of the OWO. By the terms of their verbal contract, only the death of the female member stopped the payments.

CHAPTER 5

"Good morning, Commander. How are you today?" said Detective Presley.

"Very well. Please sit. How are you, Detective Presley?" replied the commander.

"I am doing well. I got your message. What is it you want to see me about?"

"Yes. I want to see you about the MP case. I want to assign that case to you."

"Okay. Good."

"Before you start any investigative efforts, I want you to go to the Global Intelligence Division (GID) and see the commander. He will assign you an analyst, and you and the analyst work together on this case. You and the analyst read everything GID has on the OWO. That's your first step. Your second step, have the analyst complete a link diagram. Your third step, you and the analyst bring the link diagram to me, and we can have a meeting."

"Oh. Okay."

"Easy, Detective. You know I rarely supervise a case with step-by-step directions. Please yield to me in this case."

"You're the boss."

"Don't worry; I'm not going to get in your way. I don't do that to my most capable detective. You know that."

"Okay, sir. As you wish."

"How's your caseload? Are you all caught up?"

"Yes, sir. I have ten open investigations, and I'm current with all the SIRs."

"What else did I expect? And drop the sir. You and me. Well, please drop the sir."

"I sense you know more than you're telling me."

The commander ignored Presley's comment and said, "If this MP case takes off, it will become your priority. I'll reassign your other cases."

"Well, then, I better get to it."

"Yes. Please."

Aaron rose from her chair and walked to the door, where she paused with her hand on the doorknob.

The commander noticed she stopped, and he asked, "Is there something else, Detective?"

Aaron did not turn around. She opened the door and replied, "No, nothing else, sir."

Aaron closed the door, and on the other side, she continued to hold the doorknob behind her back. She paused again leaning on the commander's office door and thoughts ran through her mind, which were sentiments of her past with the commander.

She was brought back to focus when she heard the commander shout, "Leave my door open, please."

She turned the knob and pushed the door open as she walked off.

CHAPTER 6

Aaron swiftly walked to her desk and sat down. She was shaking. She needed to take a moment to focus herself back on her job and to suppress her emotions. Every so often, her professional interplay with her commander swelled her romantic feelings from their past extended relationship. She ended her relationship with the commander fifteen years ago, but from time to time, there was pain from the scar left from the deep cut of romance, love, and the conception of a son. Pain from the retention of memories that swelled Aaron's emotions.

Detective Aaron Presley was from Millville, Bay County, Florida. In 1927, Millville and three other neighboring communities were annexed to form the then newly incorporated city limits of Panama City. The residents, locals, and visitors all continued to this day to refer to the area as Millville. Her family lived on the west side in a small, wooden, single level, classic Florida style home.

Interesting, no matter what part of Millville one lived or whether they were black or white, they were all in the shadow of the paper mill and the foul stench from it. For Aaron and her family, when the coastal breeze blew east to west, it carried to them the nasty smell of the chemicals used at the mill. Many times, the scent lingered on the front porch, inside the house, on the household furnishings, on their clothing, and on their skin. Aaron's worst memory was when she awoke from a deep sleep from inhaling the foul stench. It was spooky how the smell crept up without notice.

Aaron lived her whole life in Bay County. She was born in Panama City, grew up in Millville, and lived there until she moved in with her high school sweetheart, Henry Boudar, whom she met the first day of her junior year at Bay High. They were inseparable from the day they met, despite the apparent opposition from family, friends, and unknown onlookers.

Two loving parents, both blue-collar workers in a southern mill town, in the Bible belt, raised Aaron. Her mother was a cafeteria worker at Bay High. Her father was a mill rat. Aaron's father and grandfather both worked at the paper mill. They each labored their lives to provide for the next generation. They exchanged their most valuable asset, time, for marginal means. That was all they gained. They considered themselves fortunate to be able to trade their time for money at the mill since they were black. An unsubstantiated stigma attached to people of color brought them limited employment prospects in the county or neighboring counties.

Bay County did not escape the cicatrix of the south caused by segregation practiced in the towns and throughout the county, as it was throughout the South and to this day, as attested by some people.

Of African descent and six feet in height, Aaron was a tall, striking black woman. Her beauty radiated from her light skin, perfect complexion, and thick, soft, black, flowing shoulder-length hair. Her height came from her long slender legs, but her legs did not put her curvy, slim body out of proportion. Her thin, fit torso carried her defined midsection, modest breasts, and toned shoulders and arms. Her shapely derriere was in balance with it all. In all respects, Aaron's well-proportioned, shapely, and fit figure was more suited to don the latest high-end clothing of the global fashion designers. Or to walk the runways of the worldwide fashion shows in Miami, Los Angeles, Paris, London, Tokyo or Milan, to name a few. But to carry a law enforcement duty belt and the bland agency uniform or the professional gender-neutral detective suits made of blended materials seemed to be out of place. Perhaps in another time or another era, Aaron would have seen an opportunity in modeling. Her time only presented the challenge of skin color. Though light and sometimes confused as a suntan, it suppressed chances. But that too seemed to be out of place and left the unanswered question – why is Aaron in law enforcement?

Henry Boudar, Aaron's high school sweetheart, was of European descent, French ancestry. A white man raised by two white prominent business owners in Panama City, a town in the deep south. Preppy was the one word to describe Henry from all angles, though he attended and graduated from a public school and on many occasions, moved about the county in redneck fashion. To date, Henry, like Aaron, lived his whole life in Bay County. Unlike Aaron, he grew up in Panama City among the white elites and was a member of the good old boys and sustained his preppy looks as he aged. It was his timeless, youthful looks that drew him to a life of debauchery.

Their unmarried relationship produced one child conceived on the night of Henry's senior prom. A son Aaron named Hank Aaron Presley. The pregnancy, birth, and raising their son was the easiest of the challenges they faced.

From the first day they met, their biggest challenge was their interracial relationship in the underground-segregated South, which created the overt opposition from family, friends, and the unknown onlookers. The segregation was pushed underground by the advancement of colored people from the persistent efforts of several civil rights activists through the 1960s and 1970s. The improvements forced the segregationists to work out of the shadows to suppress fellow humans based solely on skin color.

Their second challenge was their religion. Aaron was Protestant. She followed a form of Christian faith and practice that originated with the Protestant Reformation, a movement against what its followers considered to be errors in the Roman Catholic Church. Henry was baptized and followed the doctrines of the Roman Catholic Church, which were not so much a conflict for Aaron or Henry, but it was one of the many prejudices held by Henry's parents. Deep-seated prejudices handed down from ancestors who had owned plantations in the deep south.

The finale to their relationship came from an ultimatum issued by Aaron. Aaron and Henry lived together on and off over ten years. Henry was not committed to Aaron, and he continued to evade giving a reason why. Aaron had enough of Henry's indecision and turning a blind eye to Henry's womanizing. On the eve of their son's eleventh birthday, she gave Henry an ultimatum. Either they married, or she was moving out. The day after her son's birthday, she moved out. She took only her clothes and the clothes, toys, and sporting equipment for her son.

Over time, she rose through the ranks in the BCSO to detective. The first black female detective for the BCSO which did not have a stellar track record of equal employment opportunity mostly due to the Good Old Boy network. Many white candidates, who were passed over for the position, started a rumor that Aaron was selected for the detective position to mitigate litigation against the county brought by the National Association for the Advancement of Colored People and a federal lawsuit considered by the

U.S. Department of Justice, Equal Rights Division. The rumor was her selection gave the current sheriff two minority birds with one stone, a black and a female. She never ascertained if that rumor was true or false.

And of course, because of her striking beauty, there were abundant rumors that she slept her way into the position. Aaron, in private, helplessly bristled at these suggestions and innuendos, which were the most troubling to her because they portrayed her as a slut and someone without morals, and she was neither.

Henry progressed up the ranks in the BCSO faster than Aaron. It was rumored Henry swiftly rose to commander because of his parents' monetary support to the current sheriff during his initial run for the political position of top law enforcement officer in the county. Aaron knew this rumor was true because Henry told her so. A fact Henry disclosed to Aaron during their embrace of post-intimacy.

Aaron quickly regained her focus. She picked up her department-issued cellphone and call GID.

CHAPTER 7

It was three days since Prat visited the BCSO. He stayed at his apartment all three days because he was concerned for his safety and well-being ever since he received the telephone call on his way back from the sheriff's office. A few months earlier he saw firsthand the punishment Colombian enforcers inflicted on someone who did not pay when they agreed to pay and did not pay the entire amount on which agreed.

Prat's thoughts drifted to replay the events of one Saturday evening.

It was a Saturday night at the pier at St. Andrews State Park. A group of people from the OWO prepared to night-fish for sharks. The waters were calm and smooth. The sky was clear and gave way to a gorgeous burnt red sunset that was ending. The tourists were starting to leave since they had their sunset pictures.

Collectively, the group of people from the OWO prepared the bait and attached it to a large hook. They lowered it over the pier's front railing and held it until Joey was directly under it. They dropped it farther until Joey took hold and controlled it by wrapping it around his waist. He secured it to his body, so his hands were free to paddle his surfboard. Laid flat on his board, Joey paddled out to the first sandbar to place the bait in the water.

At the first sandbar, as he sat upright on his board, along came a small motorized boat with three people. It was too far from the pier for anyone to see the details of the occupants. As the boat approached Joey, it slowed and drifted up to him. Two of the three people on the small boat started to throw something overboard into the water and onto Joey.

Back at the pier, the shark fishermen were not able to see what the people threw at Joey. What they saw was Joey floundering. He flung his arms about in a display of panic. His white shirt was darkening, but the color or cause was not distinguished. These actions went on for about five minutes.

When the boat pulled away from Joey, the operator piloted it in a circle that expanded with every rotation around Joey. The same two people continued to throw something overboard from what looked to be five-gallon, white plastic paint buckets.

Joey just sat on his surfboard and appeared to be in shock.

After six rotations, the boat pulled away and sped off in the direction of the St. Andrew Bay pass. It turned left and disappeared into the pass.

Joey did not move; he continued to sit on the board. His feet out of the warm Gulf waters rested straight out on the board, and his hands, he crossed on his chest. His head continued to move in a controlled rotation for what appeared to be an extended visual search of the water.

Prat exclaimed to the group on the pier, "There goes a shark!"

He pointed into the water on the left side of the pier, then took a step to the left and quickly turned around and limped right.

"There it goes. It's an eight-footer at least," sounded Prat.

Prat moved back to the front of the pier and pushed his way to the railing. As he waved his hands, he yelled, "Joey get in here. Get back here."

The group realized what Prat was doing, and they too began to yell for Joey to return to shore.

Joey was not moving. He just stared into the water around him. The board started to rock, and Joey fell off and went under the water as the board buoyed and righted itself.

The group of OWO shark fishermen on the pier fell silent. They stared out to the place they last saw Joey before he went under the water. Two. Three minutes. Nothing.

Prat exclaimed, "Shit! Son of a bitch! This can't be happening."

One of the group members was running down the pier toward the rest of the group, and he carried binoculars. He rushed past Prat and went directly to the front railing. He raised the binoculars to his eyes, adjusted the focus, and searched the Gulf waters around Joey's surfboard.

The group member with the binoculars exclaimed, "Holy shit! Holy shit!"

Someone in the group shouted, "What? What is it? What do you see?"

In a muffled, thick southern accent, the man with the binoculars said, "I see sharks. I see a lot of shark fins."

Silence came over the pier again.

The gentleman with the binoculars continued, "There must be six or eight sharks circling Joey. Wait. There he is. There's Joey. His head just popped up. He's swimming. He's back at the board."

The group chanted, "Come on, Joey. Get on. Get back on. Come on, Joey."

"Okay. Joey's on," said the man with the binoculars.

The group gave a positive cheer of relief.

"Oh, no. Joey fell off again. Holy shit! He just punched a shark. He just punched a shark in the snout. Did you see that?"

Joey worked his way back onto the board and started to paddle with his hands. The entire crowd on the pier continued to watch as Joey frantically paddled the board toward shore. Loudly, the group chanted encouragement for Joey, knowing he did not hear their support.

Someone in the group shouted, "What's going on? What do you see?"

"He's being followed. The sharks are following him. It looks like his shirt is red. Yes, his shirt is red. He's all covered in something red."

"Oh, God!" exclaimed Prat. "Is he bit? Look closely. I'm going down to the beach. Someone come with me, and someone position their truck on the beach. We're going to have to take him to the hospital."

The group moved into action. Prat ran with a limp, and two others followed, then passed Prat, as they ran down the pier, down the steps, through the soft white sugar like sand of St. Andrews State Park beach and to the shoreline.

Another group member ran to the parking lot. He came back with his truck and positioned it on the beach and lowered the tailgate. He prepared to take Joey to the hospital.

Prat shouted up to the pier, "Do you see anything? How does he look?"

The gentleman with the binoculars shouted back, "He stopped again. He's just sitting on the board."

Another person shouted, "What's that? What's coming from over there?"

The person with the binoculars swung around to his left. He leveled the binoculars on the object speeding down the shoreline.

"That's the boat. That same boat is coming back, still three people in it."

The boat motored directly to Joey. When they got to him, two people pull Joey off the board and into the boat. The pilot steered the boat into a turn and sped off in the direction of the beach. It headed directly to Prat and the group of OWO shark fisherman. It came to a sudden stop in shallow water and was steered sideways, parallel to the shoreline. Two of the occupants threw Joey from the boat. He splashed into the water and then popped to the surface in a dead man's float. The boat sped off.

Prat led the group into the shallow warm gulf water, and they struggled and splashed to get to Joey. At Joey, Prat directed people to turn him over. They began to pull him to shore, and as they did, Prat gave him a visual inspection. Prat saw no bites, and all Joey's extremities were attached. Joey was all red, but it did not appear he was bleeding.

When they got Joey back on the beach, the group called to him by his first name while one person gently shook him.

Joey came to, his breaths were shallow, and he coughed. He just lay in the sand for a minute, then coughed again and water drained from his mouth and nose.

Joey strained and said, "I'm okay. I'll be fine."

Excitedly, Prat shouted, "Any bites?"

"No," replied Joey in a slow, strained, quiet voice.

The fisherman with the pickup truck parked on the beach returned to his vehicle and moved it back to the parking lot. He did not want to risk a ticket for driving a motor vehicle on a state beach from the energetic, duty-conscious locally assigned officer of the Department of Law Enforcement, Florida Fish and Wildlife Conservation Commission.

Others in the group started to walk back to the pier steps.

Prat sat down by Joey and said, "What the hell went on out there?"

Joey looked deep into Prat's eyes and said, "That was my warning."

"What do you mean a warning?"

"My only warning. The people on the boat threw fish blood on me. They threw chum in the water all around me, even as they circled away from me. They wanted to lure the sharks to me. Around me. And it worked. There were sharks all around me."

"Why?"

After a pause to catch his breath, Joey said, "I owe some people money."

"How much?"

"Two hundred dollars."

"Two hundred dollars," Pratt said with excitement in his voice. "Only two hundred dollars."

"Yeah. I miscounted the money, and when I paid, I was off by two hundred dollars."

"Did you tell them that?"

"No. I didn't have a chance. I didn't mean to short them. I miscounted."

Joey paused again. He coughed and was still catching his breath, but he continued,

"When they first came up to me out there, they told me my payment was short. That was the first I knew I was short."

"Are you ready to get up? Can you walk to the pier?" asked Prat.

"Yeah. I think so," answered Joey still with a strain in his voice.

Joey started to get up, and Prat extended his hand to help, and they walked in the direction of the pier steps.

Halfway to the steps, Prat stopped and said, "What about your board?"

Joey stopped and glared at Prat before he said, "I don't care about it; I'm never going to get back on it. If it floats into shore, I'll get it. If not, I don't care."

Joey started to walk again. It was apparent the attack disturbed Joey psychologically. They climbed the pier steps, then walked down the weathered wooden pier and joined the rest of the OWO group at the end.

Prat and Joey stood at the right-side rail off from the group. They were silent and stared out at the water and into the darkness of night.

Prat broke their silence and asked, "Were they the Colombians?"

Joey did not break his stare from the water. Eventually, slow and weak, he said, "Yes."

A knock at Prat's apartment door brought him back from the remembrance.

CHAPTER *8*

"Thank you. I'll be out by ten thirty this morning. Yes, sir. I understand. Thank you."

Aaron lowered her sheriff's office issued smartphone and tapped the red end button, and the telephone call disconnected. The time was nine fifteen; Aaron organized her desk, locked it, and checked to ensure her filing cabinet was secured. Everything in order, Aaron stood and slid her chair under her desk. She patted herself down to check her duty gear; everything was in order. Aaron picked up her smartphone and her ballistic notepad case and walked off to the secure parking lot at the southern side of the BCSO headquarters. She entered her assigned take-home car and departed to her meeting with GID.

She drove north on State Route (SR) 77. Eight miles past the intersection of SRs-77 and 20 she turned left onto an unmarked, unpaved, two-lane road cut out of a forest of tall, slender southern pines. She followed the way for three miles and arrived at a clearing in the woods, the private location of the Bay County Emergency Management Center. It was in a rural area for both the security and safety of the facilities and personnel. The BCSO, Florida Highway Patrol, and the four-county city police departments, as well as county and city fire services, and county medical emergency services shared the facilities. All the entities staffed the center with one person on a full-time basis. Contingency plans, classified secret, dictated the policy. The only part of the program declassified and released to the civilian population was a list of agencies that staffed the center, the command structure, and the daily hours of operation for public contact by telephone or electronic mail. The facility had no walk-up service.

Aaron parked her vehicle and walked to the main entrance door fitted with security controls. She pushed the call button, and a voice sounded, "Presley, come on in."

A buzzer sounded and the electronic lock disengaged. Aaron pulled the door open and entered a facility built in 2008, the result of the nationwide ramp-up of security and safety preparedness after the 2001 terrorist attacks.

As Aaron entered, she waved to the attendant at the duty desk. This area was the control station for the facility and was staffed twelve hours a day during nonemergency operations and twenty-four hours a day during emergency operations. The team rotated the control station attendant duty on four-hour intervals. During nonemergency operations, there was an after-hours duty schedule rotation. One person per every seven days starting Friday evenings through Thursday evening, including all day Saturday and Sunday.

Aaron followed the hallway around to GID and entered the large room fitted with many desks, computers, and communication equipment. Large television screens covered the four walls. The BCSO staffed the GID on a full-time basis with sworn law enforcement officers: the commander, two sergeants, and six civilians divided into two teams with a sergeant and three civilians.

The commander of GID rushed to greet Aaron with his hand extended.

"Hello, Presley. How are you?"

"Fine, thank you, sir," replied Aaron. "How are you?"

"Fine. Just fine," responded the commander as the two shook hands. "Follow me. The analyst is waiting for us."

Aaron followed the commander through the large room to a small conference room built off an interior wall. The three protruding walls were glass from floor to ceiling. On the one solid wall was a large flat screen television. The only other furnishing was a large black conference table with low back chairs with chrome trim and artificial leather, creating seating for sixteen.

Inside, the commander introduced Aaron to Harry Harper. Harper and Aaron shook hands and professionally greeted each other.

The three sat and huddled at the end of the large conference table, and the GID commander began,

"The commander of the Criminal Investigations Division (CID) requests assistance from GID. Harry, you are teamed with Aaron until further notice. All your work efforts are to assist with her investigation."

"Yes, sir," replied Harper.

"Aaron, please brief us on your investigation."

"Information is insufficient at this point in a missing person case. A female. It's my hunch she is a member of the OWO on the beach, falling for the cult's rhetoric. In September she was reported missing by a friend. Last weekend, the friend stopped by headquarters and requested an update. The file consists of the initial public contact report and my supplemental. A detective was not assigned to the case initially. This morning, the CID commander assigned it to me along with some initial steps."

Aaron opened her ballistic notepad case, flipped some papers, and pulled two out. She slid them to Harry and continued,

"These are all the reports for the case. They provide all the details, names, personal identifiers, vehicles, and addresses."

Harry picked up the papers and studied them as Aaron continued,

"My commander's instructions are to start with these three steps. One. Read everything GID has on the OWO. Two. Complete a link diagram. Three. Brief the CID commander of the findings."

The GID commander looked at the wall clock and said, "I have to go. Do you all need anything else from me.?"

Aaron and Harry, in unison, replied, "No."

"Okay. I'll see you all later. If you need me, call."

The commander rose from his chair, pushed it back under the table, and walked out of the conference room.

Harry continued, "It will take me a day or two to gather all the information. Shall we schedule to meet back here when I finish?"

"Yes. Thank you."

"I'll call you, and we can schedule a day and time."

"Great. Do you need anything else from me?"

"I don't think so, Aaron. I have all the data here." Harry held up the papers that Aaron had slid across the table and added, "If I have any questions, I'll call you."

"Okay."

They both rose from their chairs, shook hands, and left the conference room. Harry returned to his workspace, and Aaron retraced her path through the building to her car and drove off.

CHAPTER *9*

Unit 185 broadcasted: "Unit 185, 10-41. Beginning duty."

Dispatch broadcasted: "10-4 Unit 185. 10-21 Detective Presley."

Unit 185: "10-4."

Dispatched: "10-12. Standby for a telephone number."

Unit 185: "I have the number. Repeat, I have the number."

Dispatch: "10-4. 0705 hours."

Unit 185, Patrol Deputy Sonny Rayes, had both Detective Aaron Presley's work and personal telephone numbers. Since dispatch requested Rayes to call Presley, he dialed her work phone.

"Detective Presley. How may I help you?" answered Aaron to an early morning call on her work phone as she lay in bed, waiting for her alarm to sound.

"Did you find my cat yet?" Deputy Rayes joked unannounced.

"What?" replied a puzzled Presley.

"Did you find my cat yet?"

"Sir, you may have the wrong number. May I give you the phone number to animal control?"

"No. I was told to call this number."

"Sir, I don't handle those matters. May I ask who gave you my number?"

"Bay County dispatch. They said I should call you."

"Oh."

"Presley, this is Rayes."

"Ah. You got me again, Sonny."

"I'm taken aback. Don't you have my telephone number in your favorites? At least in your contacts, so my handsome face pops up on your screen when I call."

"I don't know why it didn't identify you."

"Because I'm not in your contacts. That's why. Aaron! I see how this works. I'm hurt."

"Don't be hurt. Let me make it up to you. Let me buy you lunch."

"Lunch. Okay. I'm feeling a little better. High noon?"

"Yes. High noon. And you can pick the place."

"Oh, boy! Presley's giving up some control?"

"Come on, Rayes."

"Okay. How about the New Orleans snowball place on Back Beach?"

"Sounds good. See you there. Thank you."

"No. Thank you. If you are going to buy, I'm going to let you. It will be unnatural for a gentleman like myself to let a lady buy him lunch, but I'm going to force myself to let you buy. See you there at noon."

Aaron mashed the red end button and lowered her hand with the phone to the bed. She lay on her king-size bed and wondered about her life.

If I had responded to one of the many advances Sonny made toward me. His relentless advances directed my way since our youth living two blocks from each other in Millville where we grew up together. His constant advances in every class we had together since grade school and all the way through high school. We sat near each other because of the alphabetical seating order. He was always kind to me, and his advice was still on my mind. Don't get involved with him. He's not right for you. I may not be the right person for you, but he is not the right person for you. I say that for your benefit, not mine. Maybe I should have listened to Sonny.

Aaron pulled the white cotton sheet off her black naked body. She eased herself to the edge of the bed and sat in thought for a moment before she rose from her bed, made her way across the bedroom to the bathroom, and turned on the shower to let it warm. She stepped in and picked up the soap and began to make a lather and applied it to her body. This was her start to prepare herself for the day. A smile came to her face as she thought, *Lunch with Sonny.*

Aaron noticed the time, 10:35 a.m. She used the floor-to-ceiling mirror by her bedroom door to check herself. For some unknown reason, she felt compelled to make sure she looked good, that all was in order, and that she looked her best for her lunch with Sonny.

She thought, *What am I doing? It's not like I'm trying to make an impression on him. Am I? Maybe I am. Subliminally, perhaps?*

She continued to check herself. She checked her makeup, and all was in order. She adjusted her 100 percent cotton, white, button-down shirt with the top two buttons undone that created a seductive show of cleavage. She felt about her waist to make sure she had all her duty equipment. She even turned to her left and checked her derriere to make sure her black cotton pants were just right. She felt comfortable and confident, and she smiled to herself.

She left her bedroom and walked through the house to the front door. She picked up the keys to her assigned unmarked cruiser and walked out the door, locked it, and made her way to the cruiser. She walked around it for her security sweep as conditioned. Everything appeared normal. She entered and performed an equipment check. Everything was operational. She drove off and made her way to SR-98 and proceeded west to the beach.

The moderate growth of Bay County made travel across the southern part of the county unpredictable. Aaron arrived early; it was 11:27 a.m. when she parked. She sat in the unmarked cruiser outside the restaurant and used the time to mentally prepare for her lunch with Sonny. She wanted to have lunch with Sonny to talk to him about the OWO. Sonny worked the beach beat for ten years, and he made it a point to know everyone on the beach just as he made it a point to know everything about everything that happened on the beach. She wrote a few central questions on a sheet of yellow-lined tablet paper in her ballistic notepad case.

A knock on the driver's door window brought Aaron out of her thoughts about the missing person investigation and the OWO. She slowly turned her head to the window and saw Sonny. She closed her materials and exited the vehicle. Sonny immediately reached for Aaron pulled her into his chest, and the two embraced. Sonny held the embrace longer than usual for two on-duty law enforcement officers of opposite sex given the current uptick in sexual harassment complaints worldwide that the news media focused on reporting, even though all the alleged victims shared one fact in common, years of delay before reporting. Aaron did not mind, and to her surprise, she enjoyed Sonny's hug.

Sonny released Aaron and said, "Please cover your badge like this."

Sonny used his hand to cover his badge, and Aaron did not ask any questions as she did the same.

Sonny said, "You look hot. You look good."

Sonny paused and looked Aaron up and down, then added, "I wanted us to cover our badges when I said that. As if we were not working; we were not co-workers."

"Come on, Sonny. You don't have to play those silly sexual harassment games with me. We know each other way too long for that pettiness."

"Yeah. I guess you're right. In that case, I'm going to hug you again."

Sonny reached to Aaron and hugged her again. This time Aaron moved into Sonny's hug and hoped he would hold it long, like the first hug. He did, and Aaron flexed back.

Sonny released Aaron and said, "Let's go eat. I'm hungry."

Aaron followed Sonny across the parking lot to the entrance, and Sonny held the door open for her. Feeling special, she looked at Sonny and smiled. Inside the small restaurant, they went directly to the counter and ordered. Then they sat at a table in the corner for as much privacy as the small dining area provided.

They made small talk and caught up from not seeing or talking to each other for the past four months. Their food was brought to them, and they ate as they continued their conversation.

Finally, Aaron said, "Sonny, I want to talk to you about a case I'm working. It's a missing person case, and it involves a member of the OWO here on the beach."

"What? Are you using me? I'm hurt. Yet again, I'm hurt."

"Come on, Sonny."

Sonny laughed as he said, "Okay. Ask your questions."

"Do you know a Sandy Diddler or a Nerezza Nikolov? I believe this to be the same person."

"No."

"How about a Jack Prat?"

"No."

"Or a Gheorghi? Possibly a Gheorghi Nikolov."

"No. Are you sure you're on the right beach?"

They both laughed a little before Aaron continued,

"This Sandy Diddler AKA: Nerezza Nikolov is the subject of a missing person report. She is a friend of Jack Prat who reported her missing, and Diddler and Prat lived together. Gheorghi Nikolov, I believe, is Nerezza Nikolov's estranged husband."

"Oh. Anyone can see where this is going," commented Sonny. "But, no. I don't recognize those names."

"Are you familiar with Turtle Shore here on the beach?" asked Aaron.

"Yes. It's a gated community off Panama City Beach Parkway. By the flyover. It's a private community. Why do you ask?"

"That's the community that a white Toyota Tundra pickup truck registration comes back to. It's registered to Nerezza Nikolov, a single registered owner. But Jack Prat was driving it when I saw it and wrote the registration number down."

"Seems you already have a lot of players," said Sonny. "Have you talked with the usual person of interest, the husband?"

"No, not yet. I'm not even sure who's the husband," replied Aaron.

"Do you want to take a ride by the address? I have the emergency services code for the gate. We can get in."

"You have time to do that, Sonny?"

"Yes. For you, Aaron, I have all the time in the world."

They both laughed again.

Sonny said, "Let's go."

They both rose from the table and bussed it. Sonny asked for a refill of sweetened iced tea, and tea in hand, they walked out of the restaurant and to Sonny's marked patrol car and entered. Sonny drove eastbound on SR-98, Panama City Beach Parkway/Back Beach Road.

At the unstaffed security gate to Turtle Shore, Sonny entered the emergency services entry code number into the security keypad. The gate moved out of the way, and Sonny drove into the community. The entrance was wide. To the left, were two fenced tennis courts. Next to the tennis courts was a building that housed the centrally located community mailboxes. The road quickly narrowed to two lanes that led into the community. The homes varied in architectural style, size, and construction material. All were set on relatively equal size lots.

Sonny turned at the first street to the left and slowly made his way as he said, "It's going to be the second house on the right. There it is."

As Sonny drove by the house, Aaron observed the home to be occupied, but no clues to the occupants. No one appeared to be at the single family, one-story, stucco-sided house.

"Do you want to stop?" asked Sonny.

"No. I'm not ready to talk with whoever lives in the house. I need more background information. Just drive by, please."

Sonny continued to the end of the street, turned the cruiser around to retrace his route and passed by the house again.

At the stop sign, Sonny turned left.

Aaron asked, "Where are you going, Sonny?"

"I want to show you a house here. It's on the water. It's a big house."

Sonny drove on, turned right, and then stopped in front of a large house.

"See this house here," said Sonny. "A few years ago, a murder was committed inside. A lady, a member of the OWO, decapitated her husband. When I responded to neighbor's reports of suspicious sounds, I went into the house. Voodoo signs and symbols were on the living room walls, and the husband's head was burning on a stake in the middle of the room."

"Get out of here. You're just telling me a story like when we were in high school, and we sat on my front porch."

"Oh, no, Aaron. This is not a story. I saw it with my own eyes. There was an eerie breeze in the house, but the doors and windows were closed. There was no way for a breeze to get in."

"Sonny!"

"I suspected and reported to the investigating detective that someone was practicing voodoo. All the classic signs were present."

"What did the detective say."

"Nothing. The detective laughed at me and did not take any notes of what I said."

"Why didn't I read about this in the papers? I was a patrol deputy then. Why didn't this make the roll call briefing?"

"The investigating detective did not let it get into the reports. He held the investigation close to his vest and refused media coverage."

"Who was the detective?"

Sonny slowly turned his head to his right, looked at Aaron and in a slow, low, voice said,

"Boudar. Henry Boudar. Then detective. Now commander."

"Stop it, Sonny. You're just making up a story."

Sonny calmly said, "No, I'm not. I think if you have a legitimate missing person case and the person is connected to the OWO, voodoo practices are in play."

"No way," replied Aaron.

"Okay. I did my job. I told you. I gave you the information. You're the investigating detective, process the information as you see fit."

Sonny turned his patrol car around, drove to the front gate, and left the community. They did not converse during the return trip to Aaron's cruiser. Sonny thought about Aaron and their enchanting front porch talks that were brought to the surface of Sonny's memories of Aaron by her comments. Aaron was deep in thought about a voodoo connection to her missing person case. She trusted what Sonny said and now had to research voodoo practices in Bay County.

Back at the restaurant, Sonny parked beside Aaron's cruiser, placed the column gear selector in park, looked to Aaron, and said, "You know."

He briefly paused.

"I'm here for you. With this investigation, if you need any help with this investigation or whatever you need."

"Thank you, Sonny. You're always supportive. Thank you. I won't hesitate to call you."

Aaron opened her door and slid out of Sonny's cruiser. She bent over and looked back to Sonny but did not say anything. She raised back up, closed the door, and walked around the front of the cruiser. Aaron felt Sonny's stare, but she did not look back at him. She just let him stare at her. She felt special and wanted to enjoy the attention.

Sonny tapped his siren twice and drove off.

Aaron entered her cruiser and sat. *Whatever you need*, echoed in her mind. She thought,

Was Sonny flirting with me? No. Maybe. He hugged me. He didn't have to hug me twice and for as long as he did. He stared at me as I walked to my cruiser too. He made me talk about our days sitting on the front porch together when we were in high school.

CHAPTER 10

Aaron, with a smile on her face from thinking of Sonny, made her way east on Back Beach Road. She approached Thomas Drive and clicked on her right turn signal. She decided to drive by Prat's residence.

At the Big Lagoon Apartments, Aaron turned right and then with a guess, turned left. At the end of the first two-story apartment building on the left-hand side, parked in a handicap parking space, was the white Toyota Tundra. It was backed in. In the bed of the pickup truck was a wheeled pull cart with a white cooler and fishing poles in the attached holders. It was the truck Prat drove off at the BCSO.

Aaron eased by the apartment and observed the apartment door was wide-open. She looked but saw no one about and continued further into the complex to turn around and retrace her path. When she came back around, she saw Prat walking up the sidewalk. Aaron automatically lowered the passenger window, stopped by Prat, and called out.

"Hey, Mr. Prat. Do you have a minute?"

Prat looked carefully at Aaron. He gave no verbal reason, but with a limp, he struggled to run away from her. He ran down the sidewalk to his apartment, entered and slammed the door shut.

Aaron thought, *What the hell is he doing?*

Aaron checked her mirrors, reversed the cruiser, and sped back to Prat's apartment. She pushed the gear selector into park and picked up the mobile two-way radio microphone and broadcasted:

"Unit 197 to dispatch."

Dispatch broadcasted: "Go, 197."

Unit 197: "10-6 Big Lagoon Apartments, number 1901."

Dispatch: "10-4, Unit 197. Out at 1352 hours."

Aaron turned on her four-way emergency lights, turned the unmarked cruiser off, got out, and locked it. She continued to survey the area for threats as she walked to apartment 1901 and stepped to the knob side of the door. She took a tactical approach and positioned herself to cut the pie as she gripped her duty weapon and prepared mentally for a quick draw encounter to a lethal attack. Then she knocked and called out.

"Mr. Prat."

There was no answer, and Aaron repeated,

"Mr. Prat."

Again, no reply.

Aaron, poised for action, tried the doorknob with her left hand. It twisted, so she pushed the door, and it opened half-way. She called out again.

"Mr. Prat. Police. This is the police."

Slowly, Aaron moved into the half-opened door and from a tactical position said,

"Mr. Prat. Detective Presley. Bay County Sheriff's Office."

Mr. Prat said nothing.

Aaron inched around to expose herself a little more.

"I'm the detective you talked to last week," announced Aaron. "Can we talk?"

"Oh," replied Prat. "Yes. Come on in."

"No. You step out of the house."

"Okay."

When Prat stepped out, Aaron gave him a blunt order, "No. Get back in. Get back in."

Aaron, conditioned for officer safety, quickly located and studied Prat's hands to visually check for weapons. His hands hung to their respective sides and were empty.

Aaron continued her blunt orders, "Go get clothes on. What the hell do you think you're doing? Get in the apartment and get clothes on. You can't come out here naked."

Prat stood there and nonchalantly replied, "Oh. Excuse me. I was just about to take a shower when I heard the knock at the door. Yes. Let me go back in and put some clothes on."

Prat turned and started to walk back into the apartment. He abruptly turned back to Aaron and asked,

"Would you like to come in while I get dressed?"

"No. Just get in the apartment and get dressed. What the hell," replied Aaron with a disgusted tone because officer safety tactics dictated constant watch of a contact's hands and Prat's hung to the sides of his naked body.

"Okay," replied Prat, who showed no concern.

Prat went farther into the apartment and returned dressed in short pants, nothing else.

"Now, what do you want from me?"

Aaron was about to speak but was interrupted by Prat.

"Do you mind if I sit on the tailgate of the truck?"

"No. That's fine."

Prat walked to the white pickup and lowered the tailgate. He leaned up against it, slid up, and sat.

"Mr. Prat, why did you run from me?"

"Run from you? Oh. I wasn't running from you. I was running to take my shower to ready myself for a meeting at three o'clock."

"Okay. Have you heard from Nikolov?"

"Heard from who?"

"Nikolov. Nerezza Nikolov."

"No. Who's that?"

"Sandy Diddler. Have you heard from Sandy Diddler?"

"No. Have you found her?"

"No."

"Hmm."

"Do you know anyone else who knows her?"

"No," answered Prat. He then quickly added, "Oh. She has two children who live on the beach. On the west side. In apartments. They both live in the same apartment complex. Different ends."

"Do you know their names?"

"Let me think now."

There was a short pause as Prat thought of their names.

"Yes. Maria and the other one. Ann. Yes, Ann."

"Same last name?"

"No. They're not my children. I'm not their father."

"I mean the same last name as Diddler?" asked Aaron.

"No, it's not Diddler. What is their last name? It's on the tip of my tongue?"

"Nikolov. Is their last name Nikolov?"

"Yes. I think it is."

"Do you know where her husband is?"

"Right here. Why do you ask that?"

"Are you married to Nikolov?"

"Who?"

"Sandy?"

"Oh, no. Sandy is still married. We just live together."

"She's still married, but you two live together. How long have you two lived together?"

"Four years now. Yeah. Four years. No, five. Five years. But Sandy is still married?"

"She's still married, but you two live together and have for five years now?"

"Yes. That seems to trouble you, Detective?"

"Oh, no. Trouble me? No. That's the business of you two. I don't judge. I gather facts. I want to make sure I have the facts correct."

Aaron paused to compose her next question and Prat adjusted himself and continued to sit on the tailgate of the pickup.

"Where's her husband then?"

"You mean the guy she is suing for divorce?"

"Yes, Mr. Prat. Her husband? Apparently, she's still married. That is what you said?"

Aaron was starting to lose her patience with Prat. She could not tell if he was mentally slow or if he was playing her.

"I think he's on the lam."

"By *on the lam*, you mean he's running from the law?"

"Yes."

"For what? Why's he running from the law?"

"I think he's wanted for attempted murder."

"Attempted murder of whom?"

"Sandy."

"Sandy? You mean Nerezza Nikolov?"

"Yes. Sandy."

"Just so I'm clear here, Mr. Prat, Sandy Diddler is also Nerezza Nikolov? They are one and the same person?"

"Yes. I told you that the first time we met."

Aaron ignored Prat's sarcasm and continued,

"When? When did Mr. Nikolov attempt to murder Mrs. Nikolov?"

"A couple of years ago."

"Do you know what happened?"

"No, I wasn't there. We had a big fight the Saturday night before."

"What do you mean a big fight the night before? Did you hit her?"

"Well. I'm going to be honest with you…"

Aaron cut Prat off and lectured him,

"Be honest with me. Yeah, you better tell me the truth. If you lie to me, I will arrest you, Mr. Prat. Do you understand that?"

"…we were seeing each other before she moved out."

"Stop. I asked you a question," said Aaron. "Do you understand if you lie to me, I will arrest you for false statements to a law enforcement officer and obstruction of justice? Do you understand that?"

"Yes," replied Prat.

"Okay. Continue then," Aaron directed.

"Like I was saying. We were having an affair before Sandy moved out of the marital home. Maybe a year or so. But it was before she left her husband. That night was the Saturday before Mother's Day. I wanted to go on the boat with her and her friends, another couple who lived on the beach, for Mother's Day. She let it slip to her husband that she was going on the boat with the other couple. He said he wanted to go too. She didn't talk him out of it. I was furious at her for letting it slip and that she didn't take me."

"I see," said Aaron. "So, what does this have to do with the attempted murder?"

"Well. Let me tell you. The boat sinks. G tries to kill Sandy in the water."

"G. Who is G?" asked Aaron.

"G? G is Sandy's husband. G for Gheorghi," replied Prat.

"Oh. Okay. Go on."

"Yeah. G attempted to kill Sandy in the water. Attempted murder."

"Really."

"I told her he knew about our affair. He retired from law enforcement. People like him had a keen sense of people lying, and he didn't lose his investigative touch. We all laughed when he came to the pier."

"Laughed. Why?" inquired Aaron.

"He just stood around and watched people. It was like we had our own security guard," explained Prat. "Anyway, G tried to kill her. He tried to drown her in a boating accident, so it looked like an accident."

"Come on, that sounds a little far-fetched."

"You know he's rich. I mean rich. A lot of money. At one time, six cars. Two Mercedes-Benz. One of the Mercedes was an expensive performance sports car model. Many of us at the pier thought he was on the take."

"I see."

"Yeah. I drove the sports cars when G was out of town."

"Hmm."

"Hey, what time is it?"

Aaron rolled her eyes at yet another distraction from Prat. She slowly checked her cellphone and slowly said, "Two-thirty."

"I must go. I have a three o'clock appointment."

"Wait a minute, Mr. Prat," said Aaron. "I need to talk to you. I have a lot of questions for you. If you want me to find Sandy, we have to talk."

"Okay. Good. I do want you to find Sandy. And soon. I have this appointment, though. Can I come to your office?"

"Okay. Tomorrow. Eleven o'clock."

"Okay."

"Same place. The BCSO headquarters. Ask for me. I'll come out to the waiting area and get you."

"Okay. I'll see you tomorrow. Eleven o'clock," said Prat.

Aaron sharply replied, "If you're not there, I will come out to the beach and find you. I'll arrest you for obstruction of justice. You understand?"

"I'll be there. I don't need that hassle. I'll see you tomorrow. I promise."

Prat closed the tailgate and walked back into his apartment. Aaron returned to her cruiser.

Presley broadcasted: "Unit 197 to dispatch."

Dispatch broadcasted: "Go, 197."

Presley: "10-8 Big Lagoon Apartments."

Dispatch: "10-4, Unit 197. In at 1433 hours."

Aaron drove off from the apartments. She turned left onto Thomas Drive, continued to and crossed over Back Beach Parkway and turned into a parking lot where she stopped to think about the information gained from Prat and to write notes from the interview. Shortly, out of the corner of her eye, she saw a white pickup truck going down Wildwood Road. It was Prat driving the white Toyota Tundra, and he was alone. Aaron drove off after him.

At a distance, Aaron saw he passed the entrance to Turtle Shore. As she gained on him, he continued Wildwood Road and drove by Harbor Boulevard. At Big Daddy Drive, Prat turned right. Aaron was familiar with the area. It was a community of trailers and small homes, and Big Daddy Drive led back to a marina. The area was congested, and there was no place for her to set up and keep Prat under surveillance. She drifted her unmarked cruiser to a stop.

Aaron retrieved her cellphone and dialed Sonny's number.

Sonny answered, "Hey there. Did you miss me?"

Aaron quickly spoke business, "Sonny. I'm on Big Daddy Drive. Where can I set up to surveil the marina?"

"Aaron, get out of there. Now," said Sonny with concern and excitement in his voice. "Just get out of there. I don't think you take me seriously about the voodoo, but that area is rumored to be a hotbed for voodoo practice in Bay County. Get out of there now."

"What do you mean? Why?"

"Don't ask why. Just get out. Now!"

The white pickup truck came back down Big Daddy Drive as Aaron talked to Sonny. Prat, now with a passenger, looked at Aaron as he drove by. Though Aaron's windows were blacked-out with a dark tint, she knew they locked eyes. Aaron lowered her phone when she observed the passenger's raised hand with its thumb raised, index finger extended, and the other three fingers withdrew. The passenger pointed the hand signal of a gun at Aaron and lowered his thumb, a gesture indicative of shooting someone.

"Aaron are you there?" sounded a frantic Sonny over the phone. "Are you there?"

Aaron raised her phone back to her ear.

"Yes, I'm here. I'm leaving. I'll talk to you later."

Aaron ended the phone call and with a U-turn, drove back to Wildwood Road and turned left. She was surprised the white truck was not in sight. She glanced into her rearview mirror, and Prat was now behind her, following her. Aaron thought,

How is he behind me? How is it possible for him to position himself behind me? Maybe Sonny isn't joking about the voodoo thing.

She continued to drive her cruiser south on Wildwood Road. With a steady green light at the intersection of Panama City Beach Parkway and Wildwood Road, Aaron continued with a right turn. The white pickup truck proceeded through the intersection to Thomas Drive.

At this point, Aaron discontinued any attempt to surveil Prat and thought,

I'll see him tomorrow. I can better use my time now to draft questions to ask him. This just requires me to prepare more questions.

Aaron made a U-turn on Panama City Beach Parkway and drove east to go home and end her shift when a thought came to her.

Why didn't Sonny remember the names? Sonny responded to the dispatched call, and he wrote the contact report. It was not like Sonny not to recall names or facts about his patrol area, the beach.

Aaron drove across the Hathaway Bridge and made a mental note to ask Sonny about the discrepancy that was out of character for him.

CHAPTER 11

Aaron was in her bed when she heard a noise outside her bedroom window. It was dark outside, and her bedroom was aglow with a one-watt nightlight. She did not know what time it was, and she did not want to look at her cellphone and light herself up with the glow of the screen.

At first, Aaron did not move. She listened intently but heard no other noises, so she slowly slid herself to the edge of the king-size bed, slipped the sheet off, and pushed herself to the floor where she fumbled around in the dark, found her pants and T-shirt, and dressed her naked body. She retrieved her duty weapon from under her pillow and pushed her cellphone into her left rear pants pocket. She inched to the bedroom door with a slow belly crawl and listened through the gap between the bottom of the door and the floor but heard nothing. She rose to a crouched position and slowly opened the door. Tactically, she did a few quick peeks and saw nothing. Aaron stood up and gradually gained a better view of her living room by inching herself into the doorway. Again, she saw nothing, so she moved out of the bedroom and into the living room. Aaron, with caution and a two-handed grip on her duty weapon held in a low ready position, made her way through the living room to a front window. At the side of the window, she inched the curtain out of the way and looked out. She saw the tail lights of a white pickup as it moved up the dark street. It was too dark, and the truck was too far away to discern the license plate number.

Aaron turned around, slid down the wall, and sat. She pushed back against the wall and looked over to the cable box. The displayed time was four thirty-seven. She turned back around and raised herself enough to move the curtain again. The truck was gone.

Aaron stared out the window and thought,

I'm not sure if the white Toyota Tundra pickup was the truck Prat drove. The same pickup truck that somehow got behind me and followed me on Wildwood Road from Big Daddy Drive in the late afternoon yesterday.

Aaron shook her head and mumbled to herself,

"There are quite a few white Toyota Tundra trucks in Bay County."

Aaron stood upright at the side of the window and continued to look out to the street and the darkness of night. After a couple of minutes, she turned and walked back to her bedroom. She lay down on her bed and rested her duty weapon on her belly.

CHAPTER 12

Unable to sleep, Aaron decided to go into the office early. She prepared herself for the day, gathered her duty equipment, and left the house through the front door. She walked to her unmarked cruiser, and her conditioned walk-around inspection found four flat tires. A closer examination of the tires showed they were punctured in the sidewalls.

She drew her cellphone and called the night patrol shift commander. BCSO policy required the vandalism of county property to be investigated by the Internal Affairs (IA). Notification to IA had to come from the patrol shift commander.

The Commander instructed Aaron to remain at the location, and someone from IA would be out within thirty minutes. Aaron had to answer all their questions before she could continue to staff her assigned shifts.

Two IA investigators arrived an hour after Aaron reported the incident. Given the time of day, this was a quick response for the aloof IA squad. She did not know the two male IA investigators.

Aaron walked the IA investigators around her cruiser and showed them the vandalized tires. She answered their questions and explained in detail the noise she heard in the early morning hours and the white pickup truck she saw going up the street. She also told IA about the case she was currently investigating, and the white truck associated with that matter. And of course, Aaron outlined in detail, the investigative activities of yesterday on Wildwood Drive and Big Daddy Drive on the beach.

The IA investigators, content for now with Aaron's answers, released her.

Aaron finished with the county tow truck operator and now had to get a ride to her office. She decided to take her personal vehicle. It was the most straightforward resolve and the quickest way to get back on track for the day.

It was now nine o'clock when she arrived at her office, and she had to meet Prat in two hours. She went directly to her desk, took out her ballistic notepad case, and began to draft questions for Prat.

The next time Aaron checked the time, it was twelve-fifteen. She was surprised at how diligently she worked, and with a concentration that took her attention from the time. She knew the clerk at the reception window was to call her when Pratt arrived, but she did not receive a call.

Aaron picked up the receiver to her desk telephone and called the reception desk. The female clerk answered,

"Hello, Aaron."

Concerned she missed Prat, Aaron abruptly asked, "Do I have a visitor in the waiting area?"

"No," replied the clerk.

"I thought I might have missed your call."

"No. No one has asked for you. Hold, please."

The clerk directed her attention to the window and a well-dressed lady.

"May I help you?" asked the clerk.

"Yes. I want to speak to Detective Aaron Presley?" replied the well-dressed lady with a pompous attitude.

"Yes. Please have a seat in the waiting area. I will call Detective Presley and let her know you are here. Your name, please?"

"Tell her Jack Prat's attorney is here," replied the pompous lady, this time abruptly.

"Thank you," acknowledged the clerk to the visitor's back.

Prat's attorney was already walking away from the reception window and made her way to the waiting area and sat.

The clerk returned her attention back to the telephone,

"Aaron, are you there?"

"Yes. Did I hear Prat's attorney is here?"

"Yes."

"I'll be right out."

"Thank you."

Aaron pushed her chair into the desk, picked up her ballistic notepad case, and walked to the employee door that opened to the public waiting area. She stepped through and surveyed the area. Then she walked up to the thick bulletproof glass and tapped on it. The clerk pointed to the well-dressed, middle-aged female seated by herself.

Aaron walked up to the lady and said, "Hello. I am Detective Presley. How may I help you?"

The attorney rose, and without any greetings or small talk, spoke,

"My name is Marti Bormann. I represent Jack Prat."

The lady paused a moment and continued,

"He called me this morning and told me you think he killed his wife. He said you ordered him to meet with you today or be arrested for obstruction of justice. I came here as soon as I finished speaking with my client."

Aaron tried to inject a comment, but Ms. Bormann cut her off to continue,

"I'm here to notify you I represent Mr. Prat and any contact you desire to make with Mr. Prat, you will coordinate with me. Mr. Prat will not be here today, obviously."

This was not a surprise to Aaron, who was experienced with the attorney showing up for their client instead of the person who was to be interviewed. Most often, the attorney was obnoxious, and that is what Aaron, a seasoned law enforcement officer, found this time. She knew there was only one way to handle the obnoxious attorney.

"Okay. Thank you. I will document my file as such. If I need to talk to your client, I'll call you to arrange the meeting," replied Aaron.

Aaron also knew how to agitate a pompous, obnoxious, rude person. She said nothing more, turned, and started to walk away.

Bormann, still trying to show her dominance, asked, "Don't you want my name and contact information?"

Aaron stopped, turned around, and replied, "No. As you say, your name is Marti Bormann. If I need your telephone number, I'll look it up. I don't see why I would need it. If your client is a no-show at this meeting, why would I invite him to another meeting?"

"Well, don't you want to talk to Mr. Prat?"

"No. Why? Does he have information he would like to voluntarily provide?"

"You wanted to talk to Mr. Prat."

"Yes. I did."

"Well then let's schedule a meeting."

"Apparently, he didn't want to talk to me; he didn't show today. He sent you instead."

Detective Presley paused for emphasis, then continued,

"That's okay; I understand. If I change my mind, I'll call you, Ms. Bormann."

Finished, Detective Presley continued to look at Bormann.

Bormann was at a loss for something to say. This was unusual for Bormann's narcissistic personality and as an attorney who was labeled a pain in the ass by all the other lawyers in the county. Nevertheless, Bormann said nothing more. This was just what Presley wanted. Now, Prat and Bormann did not know what Presley wanted to talk about.

Maybe this will keep Prat on edge or possibly cause him to slip up and involuntarily provide information.

Bormann, somewhat composed, asked, "Is my client, is Prat a person of interest in your investigation?"

"Why would he be a person of interest to my investigation of a missing person?" queried Aaron. "He's not her husband. As I'm sure you know, the husband is the first person, the first suspect, when a wife is missing or murdered. Are you telling me your client implicates himself in the killing of Nerezza Nikolov?"

Bormann, in a loss of professional composure, excitedly said, "What? Murder? I didn't say that."

"You didn't have to," replied Aaron to stoke the hostility of Bormann.

"Don't put words in my mouth, Detective. And who the hell is Nerezza Nikolov?"

"I have to excuse myself; I have a meeting to go to. Thank you for stopping by. Again, I will make a note in my file to call you if I want to talk with Mr. Prat, your client. Thank you, Ms. Bormann."

Aaron turned and walked away. She watched Bormann in the reflection of the receptionist's glass windows, and Bormann just stood there, apparently dumbfounded by the abruptness. From Bormann's reaction, Aaron sensed Bormann's client did not tell her everything, or at the least, Prat did not mention the missing person's real name to his lawyer.

The clerk caught Aaron's attention as she walked away from Bormann. Aaron stepped up to the reception window and asked, "What do you need?"

The clerk asked, "Did you see that attorney was wearing gloves. Black leather gloves. Did she say why?"

"I saw the gloves too. No, Bormann didn't say why she was wearing gloves, and I didn't ask any questions. It's odd to see someone wear gloves in Florida."

"Yes, very odd."

"Do you know who that is?" asked Aaron.

"No," replied the clerk.

"Marti Bormann, the most despised attorney in the county."

"Oh, so that's what she looks like. Even I heard of her and her shenanigans with divorce cases. Wearing those gloves is odd. Very odd. Does she wear them in court?"

"I don't know. I'll have to find out."

"If you do, let me know."

"You know, I will. Thanks."

"You're welcome."

Aaron returned to her desk to determine who was calling her as announced by the constant vibrations of her cellphone as she spoke to Bormann.

CHAPTER *13*

When Aaron sat at her desk and was about to look at her missed calls, her desk phone rang, and she answered, "This is Detective Presley."

"Aaron, Harry Harper, here. We need to talk now."

"What did you find, Harry? Did you find her?"

"No, I didn't find her, but I found some information for you to absorb. Can you come out now?"

"Yes. But first, let me check to see if my commander can come. I don't want to repeat everything to him."

"I don't think you want to do that," said Harper with a tone of concern.

"Why not?" answered Aaron, now curious about what Harper had to tell her.

"Trust me. And we need to get off the phones."

"What did you find?" sounded Aaron.

"I'll see you in twenty minutes. We should meet at an off-site. How about the Panama Country Club? I'll meet you at the bar."

"Okay. If you say so. Quite odd."

"Trust me, Aaron. Just trust me on this one."

Harry Harper was unknown to Aaron. She saw him around county facilities before and talked with him at various functions out of professional courtesy. Other than that, this was the first time she worked with Harry. So, as odd as his request was, Aaron went along without questions. If nothing else, this was an example of how Harry worked, thought, and carried himself. All points that were good to know as they worked together.

Aaron arrived at the Panama Country Club and drove the long entrance driveway. She parked in the clubhouse parking lot, walked up to the entrance, and made her way to the bar area. She found Harry seated by himself at a booth in the rear corner. When Harry noticed Aaron, he waved to her.

Aaron walked to the booth, and Harry rose out of respect. They both extended hands for a professional handshake and then sat across from each other after their greeting.

"Harry, why such secrecy?" asked Aaron.

"I have interesting information for you, and I find the information disturbing."

"What is it? What is so disturbing we had to meet here?"

"I took all the information you gave me and used it to search all available databases – law enforcement, intelligence, and commercial.

I started with the missing person, Sandy Diddler. I found nothing to that name. Nothing. Not even a social media account.

Next, I checked the name Nerezza Nikolov. I found the typical information."

The meeting was interrupted by a waitress who announced, "Hello, what may I get for you?"

Harry said, "Aaron, what would you like?"

"Coffee, please," Aaron announced in a rush.

"A shot or two of Baileys with your coffee," asked the waitress.

"No, thank you. Just hot black coffee."

"And you, sir?"

"The same and I will have the Baileys, please."

"Yes, sir."

The waitress turned and walked away, still making notes on her order pad.

"Continue, Harry," instructed Aaron.

"Social media – one account, Facebook.

Credit history – a credit history account going back thirty years, a few blemishes, nothing to raise a red flag.

Property – nothing, just some past ownership here in Bay County and two other states.

Litigation – one entry Bay County Courthouse, Family Court, Divorce, Petitioner in Nikolov vs. Nikolov, Respondent Gheorghi Nikolov, filed six years ago.

Department of Motor Vehicles – valid Florida driver's license, one registered vehicle the white Toyota Tundra pickup truck you supplied.

Education – high school graduate, no college.

Criminal history – one summary offense for possession of marijuana, Miami/Dade County Sheriff's Office Florida and one misdemeanor for possession of marijuana and drug paraphernalia, Frederik Police Department, Maryland, both adjudicated with a fine paid in full, no jail time.

Birth city – she was born in Windber, Pennsylvania, eighty miles east of Pittsburgh."

The waitress returned and said, "Here we are. Hot black coffee for you, Aaron. Hot black coffee with Baileys for you, Harry."

In unison, Aaron and Harry replied, "Thank you."

"Enjoy. I'll check back with you all."

The waitress walked off, and Harry continued.

"Residences – she moved to Miami, Florida for about a year, then the suburbs of Washington D.C. where she lived for twenty years at a couple of different addresses, a short time in Georgia, and then Panama City Beach, the address you supplied in Turtle Shore.

Employment – she was gainfully employed until 2010, then to the present nothing found.

In short, nothing seems out of the ordinary. It was just a standard background check. Right?"

"Right. That's the way it sounds," replied Aaron.

"Let me continue," said Harry.

Aaron interrupted Harry to ask, "How did the waitress know our names? I find that odd. Do you know her?"

"No," said Harry. I thought you knew her."

"I don't know her."

"I don't know," said Harry. "I must continue."

"The first twist. For the past six years, I found no other documented information. Nothing. It's like Nerezza Nikolov dropped off the face of the earth around the time the divorce action was filed. From my experiences, this did not often happen. When it did, it was indicative that the individual was in hiding and didn't want anyone to find them.

The second twist. Someone is helping Mrs. Nikolov. Again, from my experiences, this can only happen with the aid of someone or some people. A person cannot do this alone. A person cannot hide or fall off the databases without help.

And before you say she's living in the woods, she's not. She is not the type to live off the grid. Her past lifestyle proves that to me.

She is holding up someplace, willingly or unwillingly. Or …"

"Or what, Harry?" asked Aaron.

"Or she's dead, Aaron," replied Harry. "Most likely murdered."

Harry paused and then continued.

"With all of the above information, my next step was to check the roles of the county government social-financial public assistance programs. The name Nerezza Nikolov was not associated with any free government money, any social programs. Not a surprise to me.

But, twist number three. The name Sandy Diddler is associated with the top five government public assistance programs – welfare, food stamps, Medicaid, Section 8 housing, and Lifeline cellular telephone service."

"Really," injected Aaron.

"Yes," replied Harry.

"What else?" inquired Aaron.

"I turn my attention to Gheorghi Nikolov because as is typical of a missing person case, law enforcement looks to the spouse first. Mr. Nikolov's background runs parallel with Mrs. Nikolov. They even share the same hometown.

Slight differences are: education – college graduate, employment – law enforcement, retired from the feds."

Aaron interrupted Harry,

"We have someone who knows the system. Someone who could manipulate the system. Someone who knows how to organize a cover-up. The spouse is bubbling to the top suspect spot. And you mentioned an ongoing divorce proceeding. There you have it. The Respondent – a person of interest."

"Please keep an open mind, Aaron. To conduct a thorough investigation, I ran a background on the complainant to the missing person case, based on the fact you said he and the missing person cohabitate. I found no records for

social media
credit history
property
litigation
Department of Motor Vehicles
education
criminal history
birth city
residences
employment.

Jack Prat does not exist per the databases."

"Wait, Prat doesn't have a valid Florida Drivers License (DL)?" asked Aaron.

"From all this information, no DL excites you? Okay, but no, no DL. I was surprised by that, but not as much as you."

"Hmm. I just got leverage over Prat, and his attorney is not going to like that. Are you sure he doesn't have a Florida DL?"

"Yes, I am sure. Why?"

"During my first encounter with Prat, I asked for his DL to identify him. He said it was back at the apartment. When he left, he drove the Toyota truck. So, he was driving a motor vehicle without a valid Florida DL. And he lied to a law enforcement officer when he said it was at the apartment. That's a false statement to a law enforcement officer. And, he obstructed justice. Again, by a false statement to a law enforcement officer."

"That last one might be a stretch," acknowledged Harry.

"Maybe. The judge can drop that charge then. This is my leverage with him. I can bring him in and interrogate him. If his attorney lets me and she probably will for a few questions. I'm sure she wants to learn why I have an interest in her client. I don't think he's forthcoming with his attorney."

"That would be an interesting interview. Please let me know the results."

"I won't have to, you'll be there with me. Remember what your boss instructed, you're working this investigation with me, Harry. You need to be at that interview, which may well turn into an interrogation."

"Who's his attorney?" asked Harry.

"Bormann. Marti Bormann."

"Oh. Really. Interesting. This thing just keeps getting more interesting."

"Why is that interesting?"

"Let me continue. You also mentioned the OWO, the pier cult. Here's what I found out about them.

"The OWO was established in the early 1970s. Or at least that was the earliest I found references to it. It was not registered with the State of Florida, anywhere as anything. For the last ten years, Bormann's name appeared every time a member of the OWO was arrested. She was the Attorney of Record for legal representation and contact with law enforcement, both on the local level and federal."

"Federal. What was that about?"

"A few of the OWO members were investigated by the Drug Enforcement Administration (DEA). A few others investigated by the Office of Inspector General, U.S. Department of Agriculture. (OIG)"

"The DEA was for drugs?" asked Aaron.

"Yes. Legitimate controlled substances. You know, diversion of pharmaceutical drugs," replied Harry.

"Hmm. What was the other one? What was the Department of Agriculture about? What did they investigate?" asked Aaron.

"Animal smuggling and cockfighting," replied Harry.

"Really. Cockfighting. Animal smuggling. OIG. Is that a law enforcement agency?"

"Oh, yes. Well respected in the federal law enforcement community. Get this, the missing person's husband was employed by them. For many years, he was a special agent with the OIG, Office of Investigation. There are some interesting write-ups about him on the internet."

"This is turning into a tangled web."

"Oh, yes, it is. Quite the web. And I'm not done yet."

"What else do you have?"

"Your commander. Henry Boudar. I have surveillance photographs of him and Marti Bormann, the attorney for OWO."

"So?"

"Look at the pictures, Aaron."

Harry slid a manila envelope to Aaron. Aaron picked it up and undid the metal clasp. She took a deep breath then drew out a dozen eight-by-ten color photographs. One by one, Aaron studied them and then she flipped through them again and studied each one a little longer.

As Aaron slowly lowered the photographs to the table, still holding them in her hand, she looked at Harry but said nothing.

Harry broke the silence,

"I received those from a federal source. An associate of mine at the agriculture's IG."

Harry paused so Aaron could absorb what he said, then finished,

"That's all I'm going to say for now. As you can see, the pictures put your commander in a compromising situation, at best."

"I don't know where to begin. What do I do with this?" commented Aaron.

"I don't know, Aaron; I'm only the analyst. It appears you have a situation here."

The waitress returned to the booth and said, "Can I get anyone a refill?"

Aaron replied, "No, just the check, please."

"There's no check," replied the waitress. "I took care of it."

"You," replied a surprised Aaron.

"Yes. Aaron, you don't remember me? I'm Henry's cousin from New Orleans. We met a few times. Well, that was long ago."

Aaron did not reply. She reached for the manila envelope and adjusted it to make sure it covered the photographs.

"Oh. I'm sorry, I don't remember. I'm sorry," replied Aaron.

"Oh, don't worry about it. You're looking good girl."

"Thank you."

The waitress said, "See you all next time. Enjoy your evening." She turned and walked off.

Henry quickly got back to the meeting and asked, "Aaron, you were saying?"

The encounter with Henry's cousin startled Aaron. Hearing Harry, she focused back to their meeting and responded,

"Maybe they are dating each other? Dating? Nothing wrong with that."

"You and I both know he shouldn't be dating her; if that is your interpretation of the photographs. But photographs eight, nine, and ten show him taking an envelope from her. What do you think is in the white, letter size envelope? And it appears the contents of the envelope is making it difficult for Ms. Bormann to hold with her small, black-gloved hand."

"I don't know. What are we going to do with this?"

"We?"

"Yes, we. Remember, you're working this case with me. You're working with me now, Harry."

"Okay."

"I had a question for you," said Aaron.

"Sure, what is it?" replied Harry.

"What do you know about voodoo practices in Bay County?"

"There were rumors about voodoo in the county. All the references I came by were associated with the OWO. But, there was no proof, no documentation."

"Will you research that for the case, please?"

"Sure."

"Are you familiar with a gated community named Turtle Shore on the beach. It's an exclusive waterfront community."

"Only in passing, I'm not familiar with it."

"I heard there was a voodoo ritual murder in a waterfront house in that community," said Aaron. "Have you ever heard anything about it?"

"No, I haven't. I'll research that, too," replied Harry.

"Please. Thank you, Harry."

"That's all I have," noted Harry.

"Me too," said Aaron. "When you have more information, call me; we can meet and talk. Thank you, Harry."

"You're welcome, Aaron."

Both Harry and Aaron rose from their seats and shook hands. Together they walked through the empty bar and to the parking lot and their cars.

CHAPTER *14*

He flicked the speaker button and said, "Hello."

"Did you get the money?" sounded a curt female voice.

"No. I can't get the money."

"Has your friend come back yet? Can't she access the money with online banking and move it to your account?"

"I tell you again, she is not around. I don't know where she is."

"I'll tell you again, you better get your part of the money up, Jack. The shipment is coming in from Colombia soon. We need to pay those guys. We can't be late. We can't fool around with them."

The call was abruptly disconnected by the caller.

Prat pressed the end button to make sure the call ended. He returned his lifeline phone to his pocket and continued to lean on the wooden railing on the St. Andrews State Park Pier. He stared off into the horizon, and the sky colored a bright orangish-red with purple hues. The large yellow sun half hid at the horizon line. The gulf water was still. So still, it looked like ice.

Numerous tourists crowded the pier to watch the gorgeous sunset. The pier people always got upset when there was a crowd because they could not fish. They feared they would snag one of the tourists with their hook when they drew back their lines to cast out.

Joey stood next to Prat and could not help to overhear the conversation.

"Who was that, Jack?" asked Joey.

"No one," replied Jack.

"Well, it had to be someone."

"Yeah."

"Whoever it was, they seemed to upset you."

"Yeah."

"Anything I can do to help you?"

"Can you loan me five thousand dollars? Or do you know where Sandy is?"

"For what?"

"I can't tell you."

"Where is Sandy?" inquired Joey. "You mention her, but she hasn't been around for quite a while. Are you two still a thing?"

"I don't know what we are. Sandy has been gone for a while, and I don't know where she is. She doesn't tell me; she doesn't call me. I report her missing to the BCSO and they do nothing. You know, it's only the pier people."

"Hmm."

"Sandy and I were to invest in this business. She was going to put up her money since I came across the opportunity, but she vanished. That was the other investor on the phone, and she was pressuring me to get the money up."

"Oh. I don't need to know all the details. In fact, I don't want to know the details. Five thousand dollars. That's a lot of money. I don't know. How long would I have to get the money up?"

"Are you serious? Are you considering helping me?"

"If I can. I don't know how fast I can get that kind of money up. That's a lot of money. If you don't mind me asking, how does Sandy have that amount of money? I don't size her up to have that kind of money from the way she carries herself, her clothes, her hair and such. You know."

"Oh, she has money. She has money. Her *ex* is loaded. They're not divorced yet, but when they are, she will have half of everything. She has a good lawyer. I saw to that."

"Oh, yeah."

"Yeah. And when I say loaded, I mean loaded. And Sandy's husband, the dumb shit, let Sandy take care of the household finances. She charges up her credit cards and tells him she doesn't have the money to pay them. Meanwhile, she slides the cash out of their joint accounts into envelopes and stores the envelopes in a safe-deposit box at the bank."

Jack laughed then continued,

"Yeah. Sandy never told me how long she was skimming money from her husband. It had to be since she arrived in Panama City Beach. Maybe longer. Maybe when they were still up north. She boasted and always laughed at the fact she planned his retirement party and let him believe she was paying for it. At the end of the party, her cards didn't work because they were charged to the limit. Her husband had to pay for his own retirement party. How was that?"

"Wow. How do you know that?"

"She told me. Sandy told me."

"Yeah. Maybe Sandy was just boasting?"

"Post-intimacy, my friend. Post-intimacy seldom makes one boast."

Jack raised his head high like the cock of the walk. He was apparently proud of his conquest of another man's wife.

Jack continued, "And when we needed money, she made me drive her to the bank. Ten minutes and she came out with a fist full of cash."

"Really?"

"Oh yeah."

"Hmm. And you trust her?"

"What do I care? Could end tomorrow. Could end next year. Could already be over for all I know. If Sandy has money, I'll stay with Sandy. Why not? I deserve it. I deserve someone else's money. Why should anyone have more than me? I'll stay with a sugar momma any day of the year. Look at the truck I drive. Oh yes, I'll stay with a sugar momma."

"Okay."

"What, you don't agree with me?"

"It doesn't matter, Jack. You do what you want."

"Yeah, I do. So, you think you will be able to help me?"

"What's in it for me? I mean, what is my return on my money?"

"I'll double it for you."

With sarcasm, Joey replied, "Oh, okay. Double it. Yeah, right."

"Yeah, double it," said Jack. "Double it the same day I use it."

"You better not be bullshitting me, Prat."

"I'm not. I'll double it for you."

"If you can double it; I'm interested in that. Let me see what I can do."

"Okay."

CHAPTER 15

Aaron was driving her assigned county vehicle to the office. While stopped at the red light at SRs-98 and 77, she took out her cellphone and flicked through the contacts. She flicked Harry's number, and it rang through the car speakers.

"Harry Harper here."

"Aaron Presley here," replied Aaron in a playful mood. "Good morning, Harry. We need to meet and plot our investigative strategy."

"Yes, we do. What do you have in mind?"

"The Panama Country Club is out. I found out Boudar is a member there and a lot of his family and friends hang out at the club and many work there, like his cousin who waited on us last time."

"Okay."

"I don't think it should be here at the emergency center either."

"Yes. Not there. How about White Star on 77 in Lynn Haven?"

"Sounds good."

"I'll even buy your coffee," offered Aaron.

"Oh my, you're generous today. See you at White Star in twenty minutes," replied Harry.

Aaron continued north on Martin Luther King Jr. Boulevard/SR-77. She turned into the White Star Coffee Company parking lot and backed her cruiser into a parking space. She gathered her materials, exited the vehicle, and locked it. Inside, she purchased her coffee, and one for Harry; then she walked back outside and sat at a table off to the side.

Ten minutes later, she saw Harry pull into the parking lot, and he had a passenger with him. He parked next to Aaron's car, and the two gentlemen exited Harry's vehicle and walked toward Aaron.

Aaron did not know the intense and dangerous-looking passenger, with black hair groomed short, cleanly shaven except for a full black mustache meticulously maintained. He wore an expensive suit of 100 percent wool, accented with a silk tie. All giving the appearance that he just came out of an advertising photo shoot for a haberdashery.

Aaron thought,

He must be a silk-tie, slicked-back hair, federal agent. What is Harry doing with a fed?

Out of respect for a fellow co-worker, Aaron stood. Harry and his passenger walked directly to the table.

Aaron extended her hand to Harry and said, "Good to see you again, Harry."

Harry reciprocated the greeting, and the two shook hands.

Harry turned to his passenger and said, "Sid, this is Aaron Presley, a detective with the BCSO."

Then Harry turned to Aaron and said, "Aaron, this is Sid Archer, Assistant Special Agent-In-Charge (ASAIC), USDA, Office of Inspector General, Investigations, Gainsville Sub-office."

Sid extended his hand to Aaron and said, "Aaron, pleased to meet you. Harry speaks highly of you and your investigative abilities."

"Nice to meet you, Sid," replied Aaron as she blushed from the compliment.

Everyone sat, and Aaron pushed Harry's coffee to him. She looked at Sid and said, "I didn't know Harry was bringing someone with him. May I get you a coffee, Sid?"

"No. I couldn't let you do that. May I go and get a cup before we start?"

"Yes, but I don't mind getting it for you. My treat."

Sid ignored Aaron's attempt to buy his coffee and said, "If you two will please excuse me, I'll get a coffee."

As Sid rose, he joked,

"You two can talk about me while I'm gone."

Sid walked off to retrieve his coffee.

Once Sid was through the door, Aaron said, "Harry, who is this guy? Kind of stuck-up. Not to mention a fed."

"He's not stuck-up. He's a good man and an excellent investigator. He's the federal guy with the Boudar photos. Give him a chance, Aaron."

"Okay. Why did you bring a fed here? Well, I did want to know how he got those pictures of Henry."

"I'll let him tell you why he's here and the details about the pictures."

"Okay."

"I have briefed him on everything we have done."

"Okay. Good."

Sid arrived back at the table.

"Did you two have enough time to talk about me or should I go get cream?"

Harry laughed, and Aaron looked puzzled.

Harry said, "Shall we get started? Sid, I think you should go first."

Sid looked at Harry and said, "Thank you, Harry."

Sid took a cautious sip of his hot coffee, set his cup down, and looked to Aaron.

"Thank you for letting me stay and listening to me. I hope you will agree when I finish.

My agency's undercover operative infiltrated the OWO for six months now. He's not just any undercover. First, he's also an ASAIC, the same level as me. He's out of Washington. OIG executive management in Washington believes this is such a serious matter, they sent the ASAIC of the USDA, OIG Biological Security Program, and a capable, proven undercover operative. I'm his handler."

Aaron uttered, "Biological Security Program." She snickered and continued, "You expect me to believe the USDA, an OIG, has a Biological Security Program. I think the FBI handles all terrorist matters. They are the federal agency to handle bioterrorism."

Sid stood up, turned to Harry, looked down at him, and said, "I told you this was not going to work. I'll see you in the car."

"Sid, sit down," directed Harry. "Stay here. Give it a chance. Come on. We all have to work together on this one."

Then Harry looked at Aaron and said, "Aaron, cool it."

Harry looked from Aaron to Sid and back to Aaron and with his hands raised in the air, mediated,

"Everyone slow down. Take a sip of coffee. Sit back down, Sid. Please."

Sid stood a few feet away from the table, and his body language displayed apprehension. He sipped his coffee, slowly walked back to the table, and towered over both Aaron and Harry.

Again, Harry said, "Please sit down, Sid."

As Sid was sitting back down, Harry requested, "Continue, Sid. Please continue."

"Yes. Please continue," said Aaron. "This should be interesting. OIG – USDA."

"Aaron, please," sounded Harry.

"Okay, I'll continue. I'll give it a try. I know I need the support of local law enforcement and that's why I'm here."

Sid took another sip of his coffee and set the cup down on the table. He began,

"USDA, OIG, Investigations is a bona fide federal law enforcement organization. We are sworn, federal law enforcement officers just like the *Federal Five* – the Marshals Service, Secret Service, FBI, ATF, and DEA. We have federal statutory authority just like the *Federal Five* and like you have state law enforcement authority, Aaron. USDA – OIG even has the power for asset forfeiture. I'll let you research that for your reassurance.

I'm controlling one of our agents in an undercover role to investigate the OWO foremost for the smuggling of animals from Colombia. This trafficking, this criminal activity impacts the national security of the United States. Please don't snicker at the national security of your country. The animal smuggling is a far-reaching matter; an issue that has the attention of the president of the United States of America.

Also, the criminal investigation focuses on government program fraud. Namely, the food stamp program, the rural housing loan program, the school lunch program, welfare, Medicaid, and the Lifeline cellular telephone service program.

Other federal agencies supporting this investigation include OIG Health and Human Services, OIG Social Security, and the *Federal Five* is at my disposal as needed.

OIG – USDA is the lead agency because we have statutory authority over the animal smuggling, the crime that impacts national security and the U.S. food supply.

So, I get a little testy. And yes, I get a bit emotional because of my professional passion. I apologize for that, though I shouldn't have to. Sometimes I forget, even in the law enforcement community at all levels, jurisdiction boundaries are not clear."

Aaron was speechless and just sat there. Sid continued,

"BCSO has jurisdiction over welfare violations. USDA wants the BCSO to handle all the food stamps violations also. Right now, that is all local to Bay County. There's no information that it's crossing state lines. All the agencies want the BCSO to participate."

Aaron cleared her throat and said, "Well. That's a lot. Please accept my apology. Please excuse my ignorance. Understand, I'm here because of a missing person case."

Aaron briefly paused from her embarrassment, then continued,

"Until now, this was one-dimensional for me. One violation that I fully expected to go unsolved and be placed on the listing of our cold case files."

"I understand," said Sid. "But we have a huge obstacle. There's no other way to put this. The candor of the matter is all the agencies believe your commander is dirty.

Corrupt. That he's on the take. He takes bribes or a percent, we are not sure which. The former, the bribes, would place him deeper into the criminal activity and facilitate the criminal activities of the OWO from his law enforcement position. And, he is in a relationship with the OWO's legal counsel, a person who will not escape USDA's OIG dragnet."

That string of comments silenced the threesome.

After a few minutes, Sid broke the silence,

"You had relations with your commander that resulted in the birth of your son."

Aaron was surprised Sid knew that fact, but she said nothing.

Harry injected, "When we met last, and you looked at the surveillance pictures, I sensed hesitation."

Harry paused to go slow with a conversation that was sensitive to Aaron and to let her collect her thoughts before he said the obvious. He then continued,

"Aaron, you could be the one to gather evidence that will put him, your son's father, in prison, for quite a long time."

Sid picked up where Harry left off and added,

"This must be difficult for you, but we need your help. We understand if you decline. Frankly, I don't know what I would do in your position. This I know, no one will think any different of you if you decline to help. We all understand the personal complexity of this request."

Aaron looked up from her coffee cup and announced,

"You want me to get close to Henry. You expect me to play the role of his son's mother who wants to get back with him so we all can be a family again."

Aaron lowered her head back down.

Harry and Sid said nothing. They did not know what to say. For both Harry and Sid, this was the first time in their lengthy law enforcement careers such a personal challenge presented itself.

Aaron continued to stare at the now empty coffee cup and asked,

"Do you think Henry is acting alone or conspiring with others in the BCSO with this mess?"

"We don't know," said Sid.

Aaron raised her head and looked directly at Harry.

"How about you, Harry? What else do you know?" Aaron asked.

"My hunch is others are involved. How many, at what levels, I won't venture a guess. And a guess is all any other comment from me would be at this point," replied Harry.

"Okay. I swore an oath to uphold the laws of the State of Florida."

"You sure you don't want to take some time to think on this?" asked Sid to console Aaron.

Aaron did not acknowledge Sid's offer, she continued, "I'll go undercover. I'll help. Harry, you must stay on the case too."

"I'll be with you the whole way," replied Harry. "You can count on me."

CHAPTER *16*

"I stopped by to give you an update on the missing person case," said Aaron. "Do you have a couple of minutes, Commander?"

"Yes. Please come in and sit," replied Henry.

Aaron worked to suppress her nervousness from her second unannounced reason for stopping by her commander's office. She began with the first.

"The missing person case is going cold. The missing person cohabitates with her male lover, Jack Prat. Prat's lawyer won't let him talk to me."

"Did you talk to the husband? Obviously, he's a person of interest."

"No. I can't locate the husband. I even had Harry from GID search everything he could think of to search. Nothing."

"Did you talk to Marti, Prat's attorney?"

"No."

Now Aaron had to work harder to ensure she suppressed her nonverbal signs of surprise at how Henry knew Prat's attorney was Marti Bormann. Henry just incriminated himself and substantiated Sid's comments.

"Well, you have more work to do," said Henry.

Aaron said nothing as she continued to compose herself from Henry's self-admission of participation with the OWO or at least involvement with Bormann.

"Anything else?" asked Henry

"One other thing," replied Aaron.

"Yes."

"It's not work-related. It's about us."

"Us? There hasn't been any you and me for a long time. Ten, fifteen years."

"Yes, it has been a long time. But you were my first. My only."

"First!" exclaimed Henry. "After all these years, that still sounds sweet. The only? I don't know about that. Surely you and Sonny got together during the past fifteen years?"

"No. No, we didn't."

"Come on. Sonny was always hot for you. He wanted to break us up. I had to put that boy in his place more than once."

"Maybe we should continue this conversation Saturday night. Away from work," suggested Aaron.

"Slow down, Aaron. You just can't appear back in my life after fifteen years."

Henry paused a moment, seemingly, to control his emotions and then continued,

"As gorgeous as you still are, after all these years. Hmm."

Henry paused again, this time for thought before he continued.

"The first few of those years, I tried to get back with you. You wanted nothing to do with me. You made it hard for me with our son."

"Okay. I understand. I'm sorry about you and Hank Aaron."

"You didn't even allow him to have my last name."

"Maybe this was a bad idea. Never mind."

"No. Just let me think about this. Let me get my head around this."

"Okay, Henry. Anything else on the case? Any other law enforcement business?" requested Aaron.

"No," replied Henry.

"I'll talk to you when I have more to update."

"As you always do. Thank you, Aaron."

Aaron rose and swiftly moved out of Henry's office. She became nervous from Henry's admission that he was involved with the OWO. How else would he know Bormann was Prat's attorney? Aaron felt Henry staring at her, but she did not look back at him.

Aaron went directly to her desk to make contemporaneous notes of her first undercover contact and end the consensual recording with Henry Boudar as a suspect in a federal investigation.

As Aaron wrote her notes, she wondered, *What did he mean Sonny was always hot for me?*

CHAPTER 17

"I'm on my way," said Sid. "I just checked out. I was on a protracted conference call with Washington."

"What did they want?"

"I'll tell you when we meet. Let's get off the phones. See you in thirty."

"Okay."

Sid proceeded west on SR-98 to the White Star Coffee Company to meet the OIG undercover at their usual location in Destin, an area much more populated than any place in Bay County. It was an area in northwest Florida where someone could get lost in a crowd, at least for a short time.

Sid arrived before Joseph. He bought two coffees and moved to the corner table at the outside seating area. He positioned himself with his back against the wall for a full view around. The secret undercover debriefing meeting required continual lookout for anyone or anything suspicious.

"About time," said Sid. "Where have you been?"

Joseph resounded the typical Florida response for being late, "I'm right on time, this is Florida."

"Yeah. Yeah. So, you need five thousand dollars. For what?"

"To get closer to a shipment coming in."

"From where?"

"Don't know yet, but I will be a partner with Prat. It will get me closer to him. He's in a bad way and needs the money. He really needs it."

"Okay. It shouldn't be a problem. I'll give it to you before I leave. I have it in the trunk. More paperwork. You don't make this easy."

"Results don't come easy. You know that."

"You're right. Does Prat ever talk about a Sandy Diddler?"

"Yes. Prat and Diddler live together, and Prat brags that Diddler has a lot of money. According to Prat, Diddler is missing, and Prat reported her missing to the BCSO, and according to Prat, the BCSO has done nothing to find her because Diddler is a pier person, a member of the OWO. He doesn't know where she is, and he's mad Diddler isn't around to give him the five thousand as is their agreement. Why do you ask?"

"The BCSO, their detective, Aaron, is assisting with our investigation, and she has a missing person case on Diddler, and Prat is the complainant."

"Hmm."

"Keep your ears open for anything that can help Aaron. It would be a feather in our hat to close that case."

"Okay. I sense she doesn't believe OIG is a bona fide law enforcement agency. Do we have to prove ourselves?"

"Yeah. That's getting old. But she didn't know, just like many others."

"Wait. She?" asked Joseph. "Aaron is a male name. Which is it? Don't tell me a transgender law enforcement officer? What?"

"Aaron is a she. I don't know the story behind the spelling. I'm curious, but I didn't ask. Yet."

"Sid, you ask. You find out. That one is not walking by. She could be a transgender officer. Maybe he switched to get promoted. You know, that affirmative action thing."

"No way. She's not transgender. She's drop-dead gorgeous. A beautiful black woman. She should be a model, not in law enforcement. That's another story I want to hear. That's the question I want to ask."

"So, what did Washington say?" asked Joseph.

"Same old shit. This case needs to be closed. Senior management needs something for the semiannual report to Congress."

"What did you say?"

"I said the case will be over when it's over, and this case stays out of the semiannual report until it's over."

"Ballsy."

"What are they going to do, fire me? I'll retire then."

"You're not leaving until this is done. I don't want anyone else handling me with this. There are some heavy hitters involved. Did you read my last undercover action report?"

"Yes. The damn thing reads like a novel."

"A novel. It sure didn't seem that way when I was out in the water on the board. It was real. Fiction my ass."

"Come on. Are you going to let a few enforcers scare you? Intimidate you. Get out of here. You can't fool me. You enjoy it. You thrive on the excitement. The adrenaline rushes. You love it. Besides, they were actors. Which reminds me, you're going to have to come out for the six-month psych evaluation per policy."

"Let me see when I can squeeze that in. I'll have to check my calendar."

Sid cocked his head to Joseph and exclaimed, "Sharks! You punched a shark in the snout?"

"Yes, I did. I hope PETA doesn't get a hold of that," replied Joseph. "You punch them in the snout, and it confuses them. It hurts them too. They swim away to the bottom."

"A shark."

"No, sharks. When we planned that out, I never thought that many sharks would gather. Hell, we hoped for two or three. We weren't sure any would show up."

"Come on, Joseph. I'll give you the money, and you can sign for it. I have to go."

Joseph Chenski – OIG official undercover fictitious identity – Joey Chen. During secret roles over the past twenty years, when people exclaimed, "You don't look Chinese!" Joey, with a smile and in a gentle tone, sure to be understood by the criminal element, explained, "I changed my name from Chenalleveneshski III. I couldn't get that name on the back of my hockey jersey." Then he smiled again and depending on his mood or the circumstances of the encounter he sometimes added, "Got a problem with that?" as he reached into his mouth and removed his four front teeth bridge to signal he was ready to defend his name and honor.

Joseph never knew why that approach quickened his acceptance with the criminal element. He often wondered if it was his gentle tone to the explanation of his name. The dramatic smile that displayed his four missing teeth. The criminal element's pride in violence, believing that was what caused the missing teeth. Or that the criminal element understood the why of a name change due to their chosen profession and their similar habit of name changes for street survival.

Nonetheless, streetwise Joey garnered the respect of the street-toughened suspects and unwitting law enforcement aides. Even those Joey got close to, and then Joseph arrested after the undercover operations. Most of them declared, but not proven felons, while in locked handcuffs secured a second time to a waist chain, admirably said,

"I like your style, Joey. I like your style. I'll buy you a beer anytime."

They never knew if it was Joey or Joseph who replied,

"Okay, when I come to visit you in prison."

An ending comment intended for both parties to share the last laugh together. Though often, it was taken to heart by the accused felons.

Undercover assignments were not for the meek of heart. Mild-mannered agents, female or male, needed to stay on their desk, hang on, and ride it for all they could get.

Working undercover required a flexible personality. A character true to the definition of personality – the complex of all the attributes – behavioral, temperamental, emotional, and mental – that characterized a unique individual.

A radically unique individual who told stories so believable the undercover did not forget what was said to whom. A person with a streetwise background that facilitated a comfortable and credible persona in a criminal environment. Someone with an understanding of the personalities that gravitated to the criminal subculture. Someone who had the fortitude to stand toe-to-toe with criminals and verbally duel with the tough guy – the willingness not to back down – to pass the first background check for acceptance into the criminal subculture. The self-confidence to sarcastically dialogue with the street-toughened offenders, even when asked, *"Are you a cop?"* The self-confidence that replied, *"Yeah, I'm a cop."* as he raised his head and looked directly into the eyes of the accuser, then indignantly turned his head. A streetwise use of body language that all the scofflaws, urban or rural, knew to mean *fuck you, you piece of shit*. No street thug wanted that comment sent their way which typically resulted in a showdown.

It came naturally to Joseph. Something that raised the skeptical brows of management since his days in his first OIG regional office in Hyattsville, Maryland. Something that at least a few of his co-workers understood and admired. Something six months ago senior management pointed to for the resolve of their dilemma, the infamous inside the beltway curse, a congressional inquiry.

Six months ago, the inspector general received the congressional inquiry with an unusual aspect, it was classified top secret, special compartmented information. It was penned by the Republican senator out of North Florida whose district included Panama City Beach. The senator, also the chairman of the United States Senate Committee on Agriculture, Nutrition, and Forestry reported concerns for the safety and security of the U.S. agriculture sector and demanded an investigation into allegations of animal or plant smuggling along the Emerald Coast of his congressional district.

CHAPTER *18*

It was high noon when Joey stepped out of his truck and walked across the parking lot at St. Andrews State Park. He made his way to the pier and continued to walk to the end to meet Prat to discuss the money as they had arranged. As Joey walked, Prat walked toward him, and they met in the middle.

"We should sit here," instructed Prat.

They both sat on a two-sided, weathered, pressure-treated wood bench. Prat sat on the seat and Joey perched himself on the top of the back.

"So, tell me about the shipment," said Joey.

"Do you have the money?" asked Prat.

"Yeah, Jack. I got the money. Tell me what I'm investing in."

"How much do you have?"

"Enough. I have enough. What are we getting into?"

"I can't tell you."

"I can't give you the money then. That's a lot of money for not knowing anything. Why are you wasting my time?"

Joey got up and started to walk up the pier in the direction from which he approached. Prat jumped up and followed.

"Hold up. Hold up. I thought you didn't want to know?" said Prat with a shaky voice.

Joey turned and replied, "I understand. I'm the new guy. I figure we are friends, but I guess you don't trust me. I'd do the same, I suppose. I'm not going to give up five thousand without details."

"It isn't that; we are friends. I trust you, but they don't trust you."

"Who's they?"

"I can't tell you."

"I'm going."

"Okay, wait."

Joey continued to walk away.

"Wait. It's the OWO."

Joey stopped a second time. He smiled, which he quickly changed to the best look of confusion he could muster before he turned to Prat and said,

"The OWO? What's that? Who's that?"

"It's a long story. We need to go now. We have fifteen minutes to get there, and they won't wait."

"Go where? I don't like this. This is moving too fast for me."

"You'll see when we get there. Come on."

Joey and Prat walked to Prat's truck. Prat drove to the other side of St. Andrews State Park, to the boat launch parking lot and parked.

"Come on. The boat will be at the dock."

Prat, with a limp, led the quick walk across the parking lot. When the dock came into view, they saw a small outboard motorboat tied up.

Prat said, "Good. We didn't miss them. Hurry."

Prat and Joey continued to walk up the walkway to the dock where two Hispanic men were waiting. When they got there, there were no introductions. The one that appeared to be in charge looked to Prat and said in broken English, "You have money?"

"Yeah. Where's the stuff?" questioned Prat.

"On the end of the line."

Prat and Joey looked at the post to which the unidentified individual pointed. A rope hung down, and about six feet out, it went into the water, and farther out was a floating container.

"Why can't you just bring it on the boat? This is bullshit," said Prat.

"Where money?" asked the unknown Hispanic man.

Prat looked at Joey and said, "Give me the money."

Joey handed Prat a white business envelope, and Prat pulled one out from under his shirt. He went to give the two envelopes to the unknown individual but pulled back.

Without looking at Joey, he said, "Start pulling the rope."

"You pull it in," replied Joey.

"Can't. My disability."

Joey pulled on the rope and was surprised how easy the container moved. It had some weight to it and some resistance from the rough chop on the water.

Prat announced, "After we check it to make sure it's all there, I'll give you the money."

Prat then focused on Joey and ordered, "Pull it up on to the dock and open it."

Joey complied but made a mental note to punch Prat in the chest when this was over. Just for the point of it.

Joey fumbled with the latches and noticed some markings in Spanish. The word *Colombia* was repeated about the container. Joey, with all the fasteners undone, opened the container and jumped back. Everyone laughed. The two unknown Hispanic individuals more than Prat.

"I told you he would jump back, didn't I," said Prat.

The Hispanics and Prat continued to laugh.

Joey shouted, "Dead chickens. What the hell is this?"

"Easy, Joey. They aren't dead; they are sleeping. They are sedated and will come to in another three hours."

"You got to be kidding me. I gave you money for chickens? Dead chickens."

Prat ignored Joey and handed the two envelopes of money to the unknown individual. No one said anything. The leader took the concealed cash from Prat and hand signaled to his partner to get on the boat. When they were both situated, the leader piloted the boat away from the dock and toward the bay.

Prat said, "Wait here. I'll go get the truck. I won't make you carry it all the way up to the parking lot."

In Prat's absence, Joey thought, *Who does this guy think he is? He orders me around like I'm his slave. I should kick his ass right here.*

Joey contained himself and opened the case. He plucked feathers out of random chickens from both the top and bottom rows, then closed and latched the container. He placed the feathers in a plastic bag and stowed the plastic bag in a concealed pocket on his pants. The random sampling of feathers was destined for the national bio-hazard laboratory.

Prat backed the truck as close to the container as possible. He got out and walked back to the rear and lowered the tailgate.

"Go ahead, load it in," Prat told Joey.

Joey pushed the container closer. He struggled to lift it up and into the back of the truck as Prat watched. He stepped back so Prat could close the tailgate. When Prat turned around, Joey punched him in the chest. The blow pushed Prat back and up against the tailgate.

"What the hell was that for?" Prat said, regaining his balance and rubbing his chest.

"Stop giving me orders. I don't work for you. I'm here to make money, not work," said Joey. "Disability. You're not disabled."

"Come on, man. Easy. We don't have time to waste. We have to get the container delivered," replied Prat as he continued to rub his chest where Joey hit him.

"Delivered. Come on," said Joey, with his right hand clenched into a fist and raised. "I should hit you again."

"Come on. Cool it. When we deliver it, we get paid. Today. Now."

There was silence as the two stared at each other. Joey slowly lowered his hand.

With a stutter, Prat said, "Let's go."

Prat walked to the driver's door and slid in. Joey walked around the truck to the passenger side and, before he got in, he pulled his cellphone out and quickly punched the screen. He engaged a law enforcement proprietary tracking and alert app to be used later to retrieve turn-by-turn directions. He got in the truck and slammed the door shut.

Prat looked at him and said, "Easy with the door, man. Come on. This is my truck. Have a little respect for a man's truck."

Joey, well versed in southern redneck etiquette, said, "Sorry. You're right. Sorry, I slammed the door."

"Next, you'll be kickin' my dog."

Nothing else was said as Prat drove off from the boat launch to the park exit and continued out the gate. He approached Thomas Drive and stayed in the right-hand collector lane; then, he merged into traffic and continued north.

Joey periodically checked the passenger side mirror. He saw no signs of being followed and relaxed a bit.

"Do you have a dog?" asked Joey.

"No. I just said that," replied Prat. "Sandy was the dog lover. Great Danes. She even bred them. Which was an interesting story."

"Entertain me, please."

"Check this out. Shortly after Sandy left her husband, she took her female Dane to Alabama to breed with a breeder that she met through Facebook. The whole time she left the Dane with her husband, and he had to take care of it and put up with all the mess. When it came time for the whelping, she set up one of the bedrooms in the house as a whelping room."

"Her husband didn't say anything?" inquired Joey. "Why would he let her do that? Why would he take care of her dog?"

"Dogs. Two Great Danes," said Prat as he laughed. "I guess G thought Sandy was going to come back or something. Sandy really used him, and not just for his money. When it was all over, and all the pups were sold, she didn't even go back and clean up the room. G had to clean the mess. She just threw the whelping box in the backyard. She didn't want to waste time or money taking it to the dump."

"Where did Sandy stay when she left her husband?"

"With me. We moved in together into a condo on Thomas Drive, the Gulf Life Condos. The two tall buildings. One is right on the beach."

"How did her husband treat her?"

"Like a princess. He was good to her. He gave her anything she wanted. I never asked her why she left him. She took a liking to me, and I needed company and money. She gave me both. Yes, I pursued her."

"But she is a married woman."

"So. Are you going to judge me?"

"No. I just don't understand it."

"You sound like that detective. She said the same thing."

"What, detective?"

"The one from the sheriff's office. She was asking me a lot of questions. She just needs to find Sandy if she can."

"If she can?" sounded Joey.

Joey tried to bait Prat into a conversation about Sandy, because he was becoming suspicious that Prat knew something about Sandy's disappearance or may have been somehow involved in her disappearance. Prat ignored Joey's comment and laughed to himself again and continued the narration of his romantic escapades with Sandy.

"Hell, early on she had me over the house for meals. Once as a joke to me, she left me at her house with G. She left and went to the pier. I had to stay and talk with G. I couldn't leave because it would have been too obvious that something was going on between Sandy and me. Boy, that was awkward. What was I going to talk to him about? Law enforcement?"

Jack laugh by himself at his joke and then continued,

"When I finally got to the pier that night, everyone laughed at me because Sandy told everyone what she did."

"Wow. Where do you think Sandy's at?"

"I don't know," replied Jack.

"Aren't you concerned about her?" asked Joey.

"Sandy does what Sandy wants to do," said Prat. "Seems to me that is the way she is. And if Sandy can't get what Sandy wants, Sandy schemes some way, somehow, from someone. She may be out getting what she wants from someone right now. Something I can't give her."

"Doesn't that concern you?"

"No. What worries me is how I am going to access Sandy's money. How I'm going to get her money. I wish her husband would send a check. I have ways to cash checks. Son of a bitch drives to a branch bank and deposits the money into their joint account."

"Hmm."

"Now the OWO, that's a different story," said Prat.

"How's that?" asked Joey.

"If she crossed them, she's dead."

"That has to bother you if she's dead."

"No. That doesn't bother me. The OWO bothers me. That's my concern. I don't want to piss them off. They're not a forgiving bunch."

"What is the OWO?"

"Not now. Not now. I may have said too much already. But I like you, Joey. I like your style. Stick with me, I'll make you money. Maybe I'll get you in the OWO."

"Okay."

"I really have a disability. I need your help with the heavy lifting. I need you as my partner."

"Okay. Let's see how this deal goes."

"This deal is done."

During the conversation, Prat drove west on Panama City Beach Parkway/SR-98 and had turned right onto SR-79 North. Now they were approaching the city of Vernon. Shortly, Prat turned his right turn signal on and turned right into the entrance to the United States Post Office where a Washington County Sheriff Department (WCSD) cruiser was positioned. As Prat eased by it, he nodded to the deputy seated inside and the deputy returned a nod then resumed his watch.

Prat continued to ease behind the post office to the employees parking lot where a black Chevrolet Suburban with blacked-out windows was parked. Also parked in the rear parking lot was a second WCSD cruiser with a deputy who stood post outside the cruiser.

Prat positioned his truck and backed it toward the rear of the black Suburban. He put the gear selector in Park, shut the engine off, opened his door, and stepped out. He turned to Joey and directed,

"You stay in the truck. Don't get out until I tap on the side. Then get out, come to the back, and load the box into the rear of the Suburban."

"I want to get out with you."

"Here's not the time to second-guess me, Joey. Trust me, just trust me. Do what I say for the safety of both of us. You don't toy with these people. Just stay in the truck."

"Okay. But you and I have to talk."

Prat shut the door and appeared to pay no attention to Joey. He walked to the rear of the truck and lowered the tailgate.

Joey watched in the driver's side mirror. He heard doors open but could not see who got out. Then a huge man appeared in the side mirror. Joey estimated his weight at three hundred and eighty pounds. He was short. Well groomed. Dressed in a stylish white Cuban lightweight open-necked shirt with two breast pockets and two pockets over the hips, short sleeves and untucked, over black slacks, and tan huarache sandals. He was a white male who appeared to have ancestry from Europe. Prat seemed nervous to talk with this unknown gentleman to whom he was extremely respectful. They spoke for three or four minutes and then moved to the tailgate, out of view from the mirror. Joey heard the case rustled around and then opened. A moment later, the case was closed. About two minutes after that, Prat tapped the side of the truck.

Joey opened his door and walked to the rear. He saw Prat, the huge unknown man, and a third unidentified man who also was well groomed and stylishly dressed in Ralph Lauren designer clothing. The third man presented a physically fit physique like a person who worked out with a purpose and a training strategy. He also appeared to be of European ancestry. Joey was not savvy at discerning the country to which suspects associated themselves, nor their weight and age.

Joey stopped at the passenger side rear tire and said nothing.

As if choreographed, Prat ordered, "Load it up."

Joey jumped to the order. He wanted to put on a good show for the unknown individuals and Prat. Joey needed Prat to be more open with him to ease the extraction of information.

Joey loaded the container of sedated chickens into the rear of the Suburban, then he moved back to the rear passenger tire.

Prat immediately dismissed Joey with the order, "That's all."

That was Joey's unscripted cue to get back in the truck, and Joey did.

For five minutes longer, Prat and the two unknown individuals talked. About what, Joey was not privy. It appeared to be a friendly conversation. Joey hoped to draw out details from Prat on their drive back to Panama City Beach.

Joey watched in the review driver side mirror and finally saw the individuals move back to the Suburban. Prat walked up to the driver's door, entered the truck, closed his door, and sat a moment before he spoke with excitement.

"Great. Everything went without a hitch. Joey, you, man, you were perfect. They liked your style and took to you. We're in."

"Okay. Great. Let's go."

"No. They have to leave first. It's a respect thing. And watch."

Joey turned in his seat and watch the choreographed departure of the unknown individuals. The black Suburban slowly moved off to the front of the post office. The WCSD cruiser from the rear of the post office moved in behind the Suburban and followed. The two vehicles followed the WCSD cruiser at the front. In a formation, the three-vehicle motorcade turned left out of the post office parking lot and drove off north on SR-79.

Joey asked, "What's that all about?"

Prat replied, "I'm not quite sure. But does it matter?"

Prat threw the small duffel bag he carried into the truck to Joey.

"Look inside."

Joey opened the duffle bag and exclaimed, "Holy shit! How much is here?"

"Enough to double your money like I said. Count out your fifteen thousand."

"What?"

"Yeah. You get fifteen thousand. Do you need answers to stupid questions?"

"I guess not."

The fifty-mile drive back to St. Andrews State Park was without conversation.

Prat didn't say anything. What was there to say? The deal was done, and he made a lot of money. Now, a criminal said nothing. A criminal just basked in the gain of tax-free cash, knowing they had money to finance their carefree lifestyle for a little while longer.

Joey, to advance his undercover role, said nothing. Joey didn't say anything because he did not want to seem too nosy. Always a guarded concern for a law enforcement officer in an undercover role. Being too curious was a position that aroused suspicion with the criminal element. It led to the question, "Are you a cop?" This was a time that required a delicate balance in a law enforcement cloak-and-dagger role.

When they arrived at Joey's truck, Prat said, "Thanks, Joey. Talk to you later. I want you in. I have to check with a couple of people. Are you in?"

Standing in the passenger door, with his left hand, Joey raised the money in the air.

"I'm in. I'm in. Thank you. Talk to you later."

Joey shut the passenger door, and Prat drove off.

Joey got into his truck, sat in the driver's seat, and decompressed from the prolonged undercover episode. He performed deep breathing and forced himself to relax as he was taught in training classes at the Federal Law Enforcement Training Center. This was an effort to control the buildup of adrenaline. Five minutes later, he drove off. He now had to complete paperwork. The urgent need, the fifteen thousand dollars on the passenger seat. OIG's policy was crystal clear when an undercover operative received cash – any amount – the money had to be documented and turned over to the undercover agent's handler, immediately.

When Joey arrived at the front gate, Prat was stopped in front of him waiting for the gate to open. A female was in the front passenger seat of Prat's truck. It was dark, and Prat drove off before Joey could discern who was with Prat and who Prat kissed so passionately.

Joey thought,

Who was that? He had to pick her up in the park. Somewhere in the park between the parking lot and the front gate. And they kissed a long passionate kiss. Was that Sandy?

CHAPTER *19*

"Good morning, Joseph. I have read your last undercover action report. I'm calling because I'm going into a meeting in an hour. I need you to go to the BCSO website and look around to see if you recognize anyone on their site," requested Sid.

"Okay," replied Joseph.

"I'll hold."

"I'm in. Let me see."

After a few minutes, Joseph said, "Oh my. This isn't good. I do recognize someone."

"Who?"

"The commander of the Criminal Investigations Division."

"Hmm. The other guy at the transaction, was he on the website anywhere?"

"No. That guy would have stood out. He was the biggest person I've seen walk the earth, just a massive human being. For as big as he was, he seemed to be nimble."

"Okay. Thanks."

"Wait. Wait. What's this all about?"

"I had a hunch that a high-ranking BCSO deputy was involved with this."

"A hunch?" inquired Joseph.

"Yes, a hunch. So I sent a recon team to the state park to take pictures of the people there. They stumbled onto what they thought, what appeared to be some type of payoff or a transaction of sorts."

"Hmm."

"Your undercover work and identification just now confirmed that for me."

"Okay. Good."

"This doesn't change anything. Keep up the good work, Joseph. I'll talk to you soon."

"Talk to you later, Sid."

Sid got out of his car and walked into the White Star Coffee Company. He ordered three coffees, paid and gather them, and walked outside to the outdoor seating area. He sat at a table off to the side and took the seat from which to observe his surroundings. He sipped his coffee, pondered Joseph's confirmation, and waited for Harry and Aaron.

Shortly, Harry and Aaron joined him, and everyone greeted each other. Harry and Aaron thanked Sid for their coffees as Sid got right to it.

"I'll start. OIG's undercover has confirmed Henry Boudar's involvement with this operation. He was at a meet with another guy and took possession of the smuggled chickens."

"Gee, Sid, when you start, you start," said Harry.

No one spoke until Harry looked at Aaron and continued,

"We all had the same hunch, Aaron. Now it was confirmed."

Harry paused a moment then inquired of Aaron.

"Everything okay?"

"I'm fine. I'm okay. I'm still in," replied Aaron.

Harry looked at Sid and asked, "Sid, how did your undercover know it was him?"

"I asked the undercover to go to the BCSO website to see if he recognized anyone. The undercover was quick to pick him out."

"Okay," replied Harry.

Sid continued, "There was a second person with distinctive features. He was a large white male. Three hundred and fifty pounds. Maybe more. Meticulously groomed and a stylish dresser. His attire during the undercover transaction was of Cuban fashion. Tropical fashion."

Aaron looked up from her coffee and glanced from Sid to Harry and said, "Harry, are you thinking what I'm thinking? Of whom I'm thinking?"

"Maybe," replied Harry. "Who do you think it is?"

"I don't know his name, but he's out of New Orleans. He was majorly involved in the past presidential election for the Democratic Party and vocal about the Republican nominee. He really pushed his first amendment right of free speech to the point the Secret Service talked to him two or three times for potential threats against the Republican presidential nominee. It was all over the local and national news."

"Yeah. That's who I thought too. A distinctive style of dress and the weight. You don't forget that man if you meet him. Some people say that is why he maintains the weight."

"Harry, can you research him for a full background work up and get a photo spread for the undercover to look at, possibly identify him," injected Sid.

"Yes," replied Harry. "It will take me some time to get six or eight photographs of different people at that weight. I'll work on it."

"Thank you," said Sid. "Aaron, anything to add?"

"I approached Boudar. I may be able to get close to him. He didn't completely shut me down," replied Aaron.

"Great. Keep trying. Now we know Boudar is involved. Maybe he'll open up to you."

"It won't be from lack of my effort, Sid," insisted Aaron.

"Aaron, may I ask you something personal? You don't have to answer if you don't want to. I'm just curious," said Sid.

"Ask. What is it?"

"Why do you use the male spelling of Aaron?"

"That was the name my parents gave me. It really is my given name listed on my birth certificate. My father was a huge Elvis Aaron Presley fan. Our surname is Presley too. No relation."

"Apparently not," commented Harry.

The three laughed.

"And, my father was a huge Johnny Cash fan. He, of course, liked his music, but he had a soft spot for Johnny. My father knew Johnny's story of how Johnny's father blamed Johnny for the death of his other son, Jack, the result of a sawmill accident. The story is Johnny went fishing instead of staying at the mill to help his brother Jack. During Johnny's career, he came out with the song "A Boy Named Sue." My father really liked the song, which reminded him of his personal life struggles. My mother said that it was my father's worry for his children, how rough the world was. The lyrics went

And he said: "Son, this world is rough
And if a man's gonna make it, he's gotta be tough
And I know I wouldn't be there to help you along.
So I give ya that name, and I said goodbye
I knew you'd have to get tough or die
And it's the name that helped to make you strong.

You probably know the lyrics, sorry."

"No. Go on. Please," replied Sid.

"So, he named me Aaron and used the male spelling. Partly because it was Elvis Presley's middle name, partly because it mimicked the Johnny Cash song and a lot to do with he wanted his daughter to be tough. All my life, I have been asked about my name when people realized the spelling. They cocked their eye to me, and I cocked my eye to them. And then I hear my dear father as he sang the song to me when we sat on the front porch. My nerves always stoked his gentle touch too. Corny, ha?"

"No. Not at all," said Sid. "That's a cool story."

"Yeah. That's a cool story, Aaron. Sounds like you had a loving father," added Harry.

"I'm fond of the story," replied Aaron. "My father was loving. Enough about me, we need to get back to business."

"I don't have anything else," said Sid. "Harry, anything?"

"No. Nothing today, Sid."

"I have one other point," said Aaron. "Another point that indicates Henry is a dirty cop. When I briefed him on the missing person case for Sandy Diddler, he knew Prat's attorney. He asked me if I had talked to Marti, meaning Marti Bormann. That was my first briefing to him about the case."

"How would he know that?" asked Harry.

Aaron continued, "I worked to suppress my nonverbal signs of surprise at how Henry knew Prat's attorney was Marti Bormann. I think I suppressed them well enough that Henry's suspicion was not raised.

"Harry, you start a running log of these points. We may need those to emphasize a corruption case against Boudar," said Sid.

"I will," replied Harry.

"Oh. One last thing," announced Sid. "The undercover plucked a few feathers from the chickens. I sent them to USAMRIID, the United States Army Medical Research Institute of Infectious Diseases, Fort Detrick, Frederick, Maryland. That is the Department of Defense's laboratory equipped to study highly dangerous viruses at Biosafety Level 4 within positive pressure personnel suits. The only U.S. facility for such testing. I'll report the results back when I get them."

"Sid, is this a concern for the county?" asked Harry. "Is there potential for some type of biological outbreak in the county? Both Aaron and I are responsible for the safety and security of Bay County."

"You know what I know," replied Sid.

Sid looked at Harry and then to Aaron and added,

"When I find out more, whatever it is, I will share with you all. You know that. We have to wait for the lab's report. With an OIG smuggling investigation, it's standard protocol to send samples to USAMRIID. It's out of an abundance of caution we send the samples to the lab. We have to wait for the results."

"Okay. I know you will tell us. This is starting to put me on edge. This needs to end. We need to get these people, and we need to shut down the animal smuggling."

"You're right, Harry. Let's go to work."

The three said their goodbyes and went their ways.

CHAPTER *20*

"Penka, someone's at the door," said Petar.

"I'm busy, can you get it?"

"No. I'm busy too."

Penka mumbled under her breath as she walked from the kitchen to the front door. When she opened it, Penka was greeted by a black female, professionally dressed and well-groomed.

"Is Petar home?" asked Aaron.

"Yes," replied Penka. "Who are you?"

Aaron presented her law enforcement credentials.

"My name is Aaron Presley, a detective with the BCSO. I need to talk to Petar. Is he your husband?"

"Yes, he is. Come in. Let me get him for you. You can come into the family room and sit if you like."

"Thank you," replied Aaron.

Penka led Aaron to the family room and showed Aaron to a seat. Penka continued to walk to double wooden doors that she opened and said,

"Real busy, are you? You're just playing on the computer. Someone is here to see you."

Petar, without looking from his laptop computer, asked, "Who is it?"

"Someone from the sheriff's office. A detective."

"Did you tell her I was home?"

"Yes. And the detective can probably hear you, she's in the family room."

"You let her in? How many times do I have to tell you, Penka? Don't let people in the house. Damn southern hospitality."

Petar rose from his plush leather chair and made his way to the family room.

"Hello. Can I help you?"

Aaron presented her badge, then lowered it and asked,

"Are you Petar Nikolov?"

"Yes."

"Are you the brother of Gheorghi Nikolov?"

"Yes, I am. Why?"

"I need to contact him, may I have his telephone number?"

"Why do you need to communicate with him?"

"Routine. I need to talk to him. May I have his telephone number, please?"

"Talk to him about what?"

"That would be between him and me?"

"And now me, since you came to see me."

"Mr. Nikolov, I just need a phone number or address, that's all."

"It's never that simple with the law. What's this about?"

"Do you know where he's at?"

"If you would like to leave your name and telephone number, if he calls me, I'll give him your message."

"So, he's not close by anymore? Where is he?"

"Detective, I'm volunteering to assist you the best I can. If you would like to leave your name and telephone number, if I talk to him, I'll pass your contact information to him."

"Where is he?"

Petar stared at the detective as he spoke,

"I'm done here. Penka, you can show the detective out."

Petar turned and walked away as Detective Presley persisted.

"Mr. Nikolov, if you know the whereabouts of your brother and don't tell me, that's obstruction of justice. I can arrest you."

Petar stopped, turned back to Detective Presley, and again, stared down the detective. This time, he said nothing. He turned back around and returned to the room from which he emerged.

Penka said, "Sorry about that. This way, please."

Penka walked to the front door, and the detective followed. When Penka opened the door, the detective stepped out onto the porch, turned back to Penka, presented her business card and spoke with authority,

"If you or your husband would like to help find your sister-in-law, give me a call or have Gheorghi give me a call."

"Oh. I don't think either of us would help anyone find Rezza," replied Penka.

"Who?" inquired a confused Detective Presley.

"Rezza," replied Penka. "The lady you're looking for."

"Rezza? I thought her name was Nerezza?"

"Yes. Rezza for short. Her nickname."

"How many names does she have?"

"I only know of two. Nerezza or Rezza."

"Why's that?" asked Detective Presley.

"Because it's a nickname," replied Penka.

"No. Why would you two not help me find her?"

"What she did to Gheorghi was not right. He didn't deserve it. He did nothing wrong to her. We are both Southern women, and we know how cruel, mentally, and physically, some men can be. Gheorghi was not that way, not by a long shot. Rezza changed. Something or someone changed her after she moved to Bay County. Maybe she started back on the drugs."

Penka paused a moment to control her emotions, then continued,

"Rezza even used voodoo to make Gheroghi suffer, both mentally and physically. She placed him under a spell."

Penka paused again and then finished,

"I said enough. If you don't have anything good to say about someone, don't say anything. I'm sure your mother raised you the same."

"Yes, that is true. But your sister-in-law is reported missing. Aren't you concerned about her safety? Don't you want to help find her?"

"No. Rezza made her bed and apparently laid in it with another man too."

"What?"

"I have to go, my husband's calling. You have a good day. Good luck finding her."

Penka closed the door.

Aaron walked back to her cruiser and drove off. At SR-390, she turned right and continued to drive as she thought,

Those two are on the list. A brother and sister-in-law with comments like that. Their remarks make them suspect as co-conspirators. They're on the list of suspects.

Aaron turned right onto Twenty-Third Street and continued to the beach as she thought more about the missing person case.

One last lead, the children. I have to locate and talk with the children. The in-laws are evasive. It appears they want to protect the brother, who is still a person of interest and who I can't locate and may be living with his brother. The in-laws have no interest in finding their sister-in-law, says the brother's wife. They are both ambiguous in their answers. And the brother, I don't like his attitude. I may have some leverage with him, but I want to talk with the children first.

CHAPTER 21

Detective Presley turned right and continued west on SR-98, over the Hathaway Bridge, and onto the beach. Her business radio sounded.

"Is that you, Aaron?"

She looked around and noticed a BCSO cruiser flashing its top lights.

She picked up the mic and said, "Is that you, Sonny?"

"Yes, it is. Meet me at the Fancy Watch."

"10-4. I'll follow you."

Sonny motored around and in front of Aaron. In tandem, the marked patrol car in front of the unmarked detective vehicle, the two cruisers continued west on Panama City Beach Parkway.

Fancy Watch was a locally owned franchise of a national chain restaurant that served breakfast and lunch. It was a place that local law enforcement dined because of the quick service they received, and if they were called to service during their meal, the management did not charge them for the meal. The officers were able to get up and respond without delays to pay their bill.

"Hello. Here's some water. Would you like some coffee?"

"None for me," replied Aaron.

"I'll have coffee," replied Sonny.

"I'll be right back with it," replied the waitress as she rushed off.

"Sonny, did you see her name tag? Did you see her name tag?"

"No. Why are you excited?"

"She's a Nikolov. I think she is the daughter of Nerezza Nikolov."

"Who is that?"

"The missing person case."

"You still working that case?"

"Yes. It's the only case I have assigned. For some reason, Henry reassigned all my other cases. He wanted me to work on this one only."

"I thought that would have been listed on the cold case log by now."

"What do you mean?" asked Aaron.

Sonny ignored Aaron's question and continued,

"Good old Boudar. Good old Henry. Why would you only carry one case? The commander only wants you to have one open investigation. Don't you think that's odd?"

"I don't know. And I have to brief Henry on the case once a week. That's why I am excited. This waitress could be the missing person's daughter."

"Here's your coffee, sir," said the waitress as she poured a cup for Sonny.

The waitress set the carafe of coffee on the table, took out her order pad, and said, "Have you all decided?"

Sonny replied first, "Yes. I'll have the olive toast."

"Okay. The greens or potatoes?"

"Potatoes. Please."

"And for you, ma'am?"

"I'll have the killer Cajun omelet. Please," replied Aaron.

"That comes with potatoes. Would you like to substitute anything?"

"No. The potatoes will be fine. Thank you."

"Thank you. If you need anything before your meals are served, please ask."

"Thank you," Aaron and Sonny said in unison.

The waitress hurried off.

Sonny asked, "Does she look like her mother?"

"I don't know," replied Aaron. "I don't have a picture of the missing person."

"How the hell are you working a missing person case without a picture?"

"I'm not getting a whole lot of cooperation with this case. The missing person's cohabitant lawyered up. The in-laws flat-out said they have no interest in helping me find her. I was on my way to the beach to locate the children, my last lead."

"Aaron, did you check the DMV?'

"Yes and no record was found."

"The missing person doesn't have a DL?"

"That's correct, Sonny. Harper found no DL for the missing person."

"That's odd. Real odd."

"This case is odd, and the people involved are strange."

"That's the OWO, the pier people. I suspect the case is going to go cold, just like all the other ones."

"What do you mean like all the other ones, Sonny?"

"Do you think this is the first case of a member of the OWO going missing? Oh, my naive lady. I know of ten people who are missing, and there's probably more. How many, I don't know. That number is controlled by Commander Boudar."

"Here we go. Ma'am, the killer cajun. Sir, the olive toast. Anything else for now?" asked the waitress.

"Nothing right now," replied Sonny.

"Enjoy," sounded the waitress as she rushed off to another table.

Aaron looked over her shoulder then back to Sonny. She leaned across the table and quietly asked,

"What did you say, Sonny?"

"Henry holds the number of missing persons from the OWO to himself. No one in BCSO knows the exact number of missing persons associated with the OWO. Anything to do with the pier people goes to Henry. You don't know that?"

"No."

"Oh. Yeah. Many deputies on the beach are suspicious of Henry."

The waitress checked back and said, "Can I get you all anything? More coffee, sir?"

"No, but you can sit down with us," directed Aaron.

The authority in Aaron's voice escaped the waitress who replied, "Oh, ma'am. Thank you. I would like that, but I'm busy this morning."

"No. Please sit down," Aaron said as she presented her badge. "We need to talk. This is official business."

The waitress, with a puzzled look on her face, acquiesced to the symbol of authority and slowly sat down on the same side as Sonny.

"I see your name is Maria Nikolov," said Aaron.

The waitress involuntarily rubbed her name tag and said, "Yes. Why do you want to talk to me?"

"Are you the daughter of Nerezza Nikolov or Rezza or Sandy Diddler?" asked Aaron.

Maria's face displayed a perplexed look to the question, but she replied, "I am the daughter of Nerezza Nikolov. Yes, she's my mother. She answers to Rezza, a shortened version of her name. Why do you ask?"

"Do you know where she is?"

"At this moment, no. She lives off Thomas Drive. What's this about?"

"Does your mother use the name Sandy Diddler?"

"No," said Maria.

Maria caught her breath as she became concerned about the detective's line of questioning.

"I'm not aware of my mother using any other names. The divorce isn't final."

"Where's your father?"

"I don't know."

"You don't know your father's whereabouts? Come on, Maria, you need to answer my questions, and you need to tell me the truth."

"I have to go, my manager keeps looking at me. I don't want to get in trouble here. I need this job. I just had a baby."

Sonny said, "Maria, let me out. You stay here and talk with Detective Presley. I'll handle your boss. You won't get in trouble."

Maria stood and let Deputy Rayes out, then she sat back down.

"Did something happen to my mother?" asked Maria.

"She was reported missing."

"What? Missing? What do you mean missing?"

179

"Jack Prat reported your mother missing about two weeks ago."

"Did you talk to Prat?" asked Maria.

"Yes. But then Mr. Prat lawyered up. The little bit he said didn't help me, and it was hardly intelligible."

"Yeah. You have to listen carefully when he talks."

"I heard him fine. His words didn't make sense. Does he have any education at all?"

"I don't know. That's my mother's thing. What about my mother? You say she's missing?"

"She was reported missing, and I was the BCSO detective assigned to investigate the case. I came up with nothing."

"You're a detective, but you can't find my mother? What kind of detective are you? How long have you been looking for her?"

Detective Presley did not have time to answer before Maria snapped back,

"You know what, I'll just call my mother. She'll answer my phone call."

Maria retrieved her cellphone from her black apron, tapped the screen a few times, and raised the phone to her ear. She began to wait and listen and gave an eye roll to the detective. Maria took the phone away from her ear, looked at it, and returned it. Maria took the phone away from her ear a second time and again looked at the screen. This time she mumbled, "That's odd. She doesn't answer. I know she's not working."

Maria ended the call, and nervously, she began to fidget with the phone.

"When is the last time you talked to your mother?" asked Detective Presley.

"About three weeks ago."

"You two don't communicate too often?"

"Not that often since she walked out on the family."

"She walked out. She left the marriage?"

"Yes."

"What did your father do to make her leave?"

"Nothing."

"Nothing?" Detective Presley repeated sarcastically. "I find that hard to believe. The man doesn't do anything? That's an unusual man."

"No, that's a gentleman."

Detective Presley paused as she remembered her abusive relationship with Boudar before she tried again to crack the witness.

"Maybe he hit her, and you didn't know? Maybe your mother never told you. Maybe there was some type of verbal abuse of which you were unaware?"

"I told you my father didn't do anything. Nothing. My father didn't do anything to her, and my father sure in the hell didn't hit her or abuse her mentally. Make sure you put that in your notes, Detective Nancy Drew. One day she told us she was leaving. I think she told my father too."

"How many siblings do you have?"

"Three. Three sisters. All younger than me."

"Where is your father?"

"I tell you again, I don't know."

"Hmm."

"Detective, you're on a witch hunt if you think my father has something to do with my mother's disappearance. I know my father doesn't like how long the divorce is taking, and who would like losing half of their income when they're in retirement. Job prospects are going to be slim for him, an aged white male with a bad back. And my mother is asking for payment for other things that would put my father in debt for a long, long time."

Maria stopped abruptly and looked away from the detective. She held her emotions in check before she looked back at the detective and asked,

"Am I under arrest?"

"No, you're not under arrest. We're just talking."

"I'm done talking," Maria replied sharply. "You have a nice day, Detective."

Maria stood, looked down at Detective Presley, and sounded,

"My father."

She gave a sarcastic laugh and said,

"You're a batshit crazy lady. You can put that in your notes too, Ms. Nancy Drew."

Maria paused and continued to look down at the detective before she added, "You should focus on those pier people."

Then she walked away from the table, shaking her head.

Sonny returned to the table, sat, and asked, "How did it go?"

"I'm batshit crazy."

"You are, but how did it go? What did you learn?"

"She was adamant her father had nothing to do with her mother's disappearance."

"Hmm. Is Detective Presley losing her touch? Presley can't get a witness to talk?"

"That's not the case I can assure you. Though I may be looking at this case the wrong way. But, until I have evidence, hard evidence, that someone else is involved with the disappearance of Nerezza Nikolov, AKA Rezza, AKA Sandy Diddler, the Respondent is a person of interest. I need to talk to him."

"Yes, you do," replied Sonny. "And I know when and where you can find him."

"What are you talking about, Sonny?"

"I'm just trying to help a neighborhood friend, a longtime colleague, an old high school crush."

"What did you say, *old high school crush*?"

Sonny ignored Aaron's question and continued,

"I'm just trying to help a colleague, and according to the manager, Maria's baby's baptism is on Sunday. Now, do you think the grandfather is going to stay away from that? Stay away from his first grandson's baptism."

"Where's the baptism?"

"Oh, man. I forgot to ask where."

"What?" replied Aaron.

Sonny broke out into laughter.

Aaron playfully threw her balled-up napkin at Sonny.

Composed from laughing, Sonny said, "Sunday, at the Catholic Church on the beach."

Sonny thought,

I know she heard me when I said old high school crush. That was dumb of me. I'm embarrassed.

Aaron heard Sonny's comment, but she did not ask Sonny about it a second time. Aaron remained consumed with the missing person investigation.

CHAPTER *22*

"I told you never to call me at work," said Henry into his cellphone as he sat at his desk at the sheriff's office headquarters.

Henry paused and listened to the caller for a moment, then cut the caller off when he continued,

"I don't care if you think you have an emergency or not. You are not to call me on my work cellphone. Call me tonight on the other phone."

Henry pressed the end button.

CHAPTER *23*

There was a gentle knock at the front door. Aaron put the knife down, wiped her hands, and walked to the door. She was surprised when she opened it.

"Henry, what are you doing here?"

"I thought I would stop by because of the conversation we had in my office the other day."

"Oh."

Aaron thought, *Now what am I going to do?*

"May I come in?" asked Henry.

"Yes. I'm sorry. Excuse my manners. Please come in," replied Aaron.

"You have a lovely home."

"Thank you. Please sit. May I get you something to drink? Beer? Wine?"

"Beer would be nice."

Aaron walked back to the kitchen, braced herself on the granite countertop, and thought,

I offer him a beer instead of an excuse so I would not invite him in. Maybe our conversation the other day was a little

too much for my undercover role. A little too much for me, personally.

Aaron retrieved a bottle of beer from the refrigerator, opened it, walked back to Henry, and handed him the beer.

"Would you like a glass?" asked Aaron.

"Thank you," replied Henry. "No, I don't need a glass. You know I always drink out of a bottle."

"I guess I forgot."

"I'm disappointed in you, Aaron."

"Please excuse me. I have to use the powder room."

"Yes."

Aaron walked off and down the hallway.

Henry quickly stood and walked over to Aaron's desk. He looked around and moved a few things to get a better look at the papers on top. Then he walked over to her floor-to-ceiling bookcase and studied the titles.

"Would you like to borrow one," asked Aaron.

"No. I don't have much time to read lately."

"Why not?"

"Work keeps me busy."

"Even at night, before you go to bed? I remember that."

"Maybe I lost my interest in reading."

"That's a shame. You were such an avid reader back then."

"Yes, back then I was."

Aaron moved to a small chair opposite the couch and sat. Henry walked back to the couch, sat, and sipped his beer before he said in a monotone interview voice of a law enforcement officer,

"Your comment to get back together is a surprise. That is what you suggested the other day? Did I understand you correctly?" asked Henry.

"I think that's what I meant," replied Aaron.

"You think that's what you meant?"

"I don't know, Henry."

"You don't know?"

Henry sipped his beer before he broke the silence that had taken the room. With a tone of compassion, Henry said,

"Aaron, I'm here to tell you in person. A gentleman would say this in person. It's too late. It's too late for us. There can never be *us* again."

"Oh. Okay. I'm sorry. I don't want to put you in an uncomfortable position."

"You don't, even after all these years. Being comfortable around you is one of the things I really like about you."

Henry paused, sipped his beer, and looked back at Aaron.

"I have been seeing someone for many years, and it has been serious for several years now."

"Okay. I understand. Again, I apologize. Do I know this lady?"

"I don't know; she is well-known in the county's legal circles, so you probably heard of her."

There was a knock at the door that interrupted Henry.

"What!" exclaimed Aaron. "Please excuse me."

Aaron rose, walked to the front door, and opened it. She was surprised again when she saw Sonny standing on her porch.

"Hello, Aaron," said Sonny.

"Hello, Sonny. This isn't a good time. May I call you later?"

Sonny gently pushed his way in.

"I'll wait in the kitchen. Take your time."

Sonny walked through the living room, and condescendingly sounded, "Hello, Henry. How are you?"

"Just fine," replied Henry in a surprised tone.

Sonny continued to the kitchen.

Silence retook the room before Henry rose from the couch and said,

"I also came here for another reason."

"You did? What is it?"

"It's not important now."

"What is it?" urged Aaron.

Aaron's curiosity was agitated by Henry and his seriousness with a lady. She wanted to know the name of the lady because Henry's clue, *she is well-known in the county's legal circles*, did not bring anyone to mind.

"I have to go now. I should have called first."

"Henry, please sit back down and finish," requested Aaron.

"No. I was finished. I just thought – I wanted to tell you in person, and I didn't want to do it at work. It was many years ago for us. But, again, from what I thought I understood, I wanted to be a gentleman about it."

"You said there was something else," inquired Aaron.

"It's not important," replied Henry. "Thank you for the beer. You take care of yourself."

Henry set the beer bottle on the coffee table and walked to the front door. He paused, turned, and gazed at Aaron. He turned back and walked out the door.

Aaron just stood there.

"Aaron. Aaron, " announced Sonny from the kitchen archway.

Aaron slowly looked to Sonny and in a daze replied, "Yes."

"Are you alright?" asked Sonny.

"Yes. I think so," replied Aaron.

"Please excuse my boldness and for barging in on you."

Aaron, in a daze, interrupted Sonny when she said, "What? What's that, Sonny?"

"I saw Henry pull up to your house from my parents' house. I didn't want you to be alone with him. It was just a gut feeling I had," finished Henry.

Still, in a daze, Aaron replied, "Yeah. Okay. Thanks."

"Do you know who was with him?" asked Sonny.

"With him? No," replied Aaron.

"He was with two other people. They all arrived in a black Suburban with blacked-out windows."

"I have no idea what you're talking about. Other people?"

"Please don't take this any other way than I don't think you should be alone tonight. May I make us dinner and I'll hang around for a while, too."

"You don't have to do that."

"I know I don't have to; I want to. I think it would be good for you to let someone help you."

"Okay. Thank you, Sonny."

"You just sit down. What can I get you to drink?"

"Just water, please. It shouldn't be anything more than water with you in the house."

Aaron quickly thought, *Why did I say that? I didn't have to say anything but thank you.*

Sonny did not inquire what Aaron may have meant by the seemingly flirtatious comment. He stayed focused on helping a friend who he knew was in a situation that was starting to overwhelm her; a case Sonny knew would bring Aaron harm.

"Here's your water, Aaron."

"Thank you, Sonny."

Sonny removed the half-empty beer bottle from the coffee table on his way back to the kitchen.

Aaron rose from her chair and walked to her bedroom but did not close the door behind her. She moved to her bed, sat, unbuttoned her blouse, and removed the recording device she put on for her chance meeting with Henry.

Sonny emerged from the kitchen to check on Aaron, and when he did not find her in the living room, he started down the hallway toward her bedroom. Sonny saw Aaron seated on her bed with her blouse unbuttoned. She held the recorder in her hands. He stopped and stared at her breasts.

Aaron spoke to place an end marker to the recording.

"The time is 5:10 p.m., the same date and that is the end of this consensual monitoring undercover recording approved by U.S. Department of Justice, from a chance meeting with Henry Boudar at the home of Aaron Presley, detective, Bay County Sheriff's Department."

Sonny continued to stare at Aaron's breast and was oblivious to what Aaron held in her hands or what she spoke.

Aaron pressed the stop button and held the recorder as she thought.

After a minute or two, feeling like a pervert, Sonny moved away from the door, retreated back the hallway to the living room, and called out.
"Aaron. Aaron."

Aaron was brought back from her thoughts of Henry and many years ago.

CHAPTER 24

"Hey Prat, what's up?"

"Joey. Nice to see you. Let's move over here."

Prat motioned for Joey to follow him. He walked up the pier to the west railing.

"Joey, I talked to the people, and I was given the go-ahead to bring you in. Are you still interested?"

"In what?"

"What, you're going to ask questions? Even after the money you made?"

"Yes. Why wouldn't I?"

"Okay. To bring you into the operation. To continue to do just what we did last time."

"I put the money up-front. We get the chickens and haul them to Vernon?"

"Yeah. That about sums it up. I don't know why you have any questions. It doesn't get any simpler."

"This seems too good to be true."

"Well, don't think so hard about it. Go get your money and be back by four-thirty."

"Today?"

"Yeah. Is that a problem for you?"

"No. I'm ready right now. I don't have to go to the bank."

"You have five thousand dollars on you. Right now? Right here?"

"Yeah. You got a problem with that?"

"No. But I think you're crazy for carrying around that kind of money. Especially to the park, the pier."

"Why? Are you going to take it from me?"

"No. Not me. Others might."

"Who?"

"Other people who hang down here. Other pier people."

"Who?"

"Look, I told you. Do what you want. We have to meet the boat at four-thirty. This time, not here at the park."

"Where?"

"Joey, slow down. You start to ask too many questions I may not want to work with you. Just slow down."

"I'll be back at four-thirty," said Joey.

Joey bandied with Prat in an attempt to keep Prat on edge. An undercover tactic used to ward off the target's suspicion that the operative was a cop or ward off the target's street vernacular label, *Five-O.*

"No. I think you better stay here until four-thirty," replied Prat.

"What?"

"Just stay here until I come back and pick you up."

"I don't know about that."

"It's either my way, or I'll find someone else."

"How much am I going to make?"

"Same as last time."

"I'll be right here until you come back."

"I thought so."

Prat walked away, down the pier, and then in the direction of the parking lot. He disappeared behind the dunes, and Joey observed nothing else.

Joey, to comfort himself while he waited, stretched out on one of the large wooden benches. The sun was warm, and the gulf breeze eased the humidity. He fell asleep.

Shortly, Joey awoke from the noise of the commotion at the end of the pier. He sat up and saw the disorder was a fight. A couple of the people fishing when he lay down were now in a full-on, bare-knuckle, fist-fight.

A young lady, dressed in a skimpy bright orange bikini which left little to the imagination, was walking away from the fight. She shook her head as she talked on her cellphone.

Joey asked the young lady, "Hey, what started that?"

The young lady slowed and said into her phone, "Let me call you back, Leo."

The young lady ended her phone call, and with a slow, deliberate gait, walked over to Joey. Absent shyness, she sat next to him and explained,

"There's two different groups of people fishing. One group is from Georgia. The other group is from Alabama. A person, from the Georgia group, crosses the fishing lines of a couple of individuals from the Alabama group. And that's the result."

"That's it, crossed fishing lines? That's what caused the fight?"

"Yep. That's it."

"Hmm. What group you with?"

"I'm not with any group. I'm here by myself. Those rednecks, no. No, not me. I'm not with any of them."

The young lady stood and began to turn around in front of Joey.

"Look at me, do I look like I'm from Georgia or Alabama?"

She stopped and faced Joey and added, "Take your time and think before you answer."

"Well. Give me a minute." Joey answered quickly, " No."

"Good answer. My name is Rosie. What is yours?"

The young lady extended her hand to Joey.

Joey reciprocated, shook Rosie's hand, and said, "Joey."

"Joey. That's kind of plain for the *Redneck Riviera*."

"The *Redneck Riviera*," exclaimed Joey as he laughed.

"Yeah. You never heard the Panhandle called that?"

"No, I haven't."

"Fits, doesn't it?"

"If you say so."

"Well, I'm not from here. I'm from NOLA. New Orleans, Louisiana. If you don't know this is the *Redneck Riviera*, you probably don't know what NOLA means."

"I do now. How long have you lived in NOLA?"

"All my life. I was born and raised there, and I stayed there."

"What is there to do in NOLA?"

"Everything and anything you want to do."

"Really."

"Really. It's a party city."

"Hey, I met someone from NOLA."

"Oh, yeah. What's her name?"

"She's a he, and I don't know his name. I can describe him to you.

"You forgot his name?"

"I don't remember his name because I don't know his name."

"Are you sure? What's my name?"

"Rosie."

"Just checking to see if you're paying attention to me. I like attention."

"I would never have guessed."

Rosie laughed and then said, "You're funny. I like that. Describe the person to me."

"What? Do you know everyone in NOLA?"

"Maybe I do? Just describe him, it's worth a try."

"Male. I'm not too good at this. White male, about the early fifties. Huge. And I'm not funny here. This man is huge. Four hundred and some pounds easy. Dresses in fashionable clothes, Carribean style."

"What's your business with him?"

"No business. I just saw him. He stuck with me. Like, I wondered who that was? Since you were from NOLA and that was where I saw him, I thought you may know him. He was nimble for his size."

"Hmm. What I can tell you is you shouldn't be asking questions about him. What I hear is people who ask questions about him all become sick and die."

"What do you mean? Die?"

"I mean, you don't want to ask questions about him. Yeah, I know who you mean. No, I don't want to talk about him."

"Come on, Rosie. I'm just curious. Like I said, he stands out."

"I have to go. I don't know if I can say it was nice to meet you, with a question like that."

"It's nice to meet you," and I have to say, "you're cute."

"Are you flirting with me? I estimate you're a little old for me. You look in good shape though. You work out?"

"Yes. A little."

"A little, shit. You're tight. Tight. Let me feel that muscle."

"You're going to embarrass me," Joey said softly.

Rosie reached out and felt Joey's bicep while she said, "That guy is politically connected. He's rich. Filthy rich doesn't even come close to how rich he is."

"What's his profession?" asked Joey.

"I don't know. I don't ask questions about him. I don't want to get sick and die."

"Rosie, are you being a little dramatic here?"

"No."

Joey and Rosie were interrupted by a voice from the end of the pier near the dunes.

"Hey, Joey, we need to go."

Joey turned, saw it was Prat, and waved and shouted, "Be right up."

Joey turned back to Rosie, and immediately, Rosie asked, "Do you know that guy? Do you hang with him?"

"Yes. I shouldn't hang with him, either? Is he going to make me sick and die?"

"He's a pig. He's always hitting on me, and I know he's with Sandy, though I haven't seen her for some time."

Rosie stopped talking and shook her head in disgust.

"I have to go," said Joey. "It was nice to meet you, Rosie. May I have your number? I'd like to call you. Would you be interested in dinner sometime?"

"You're a little older than me," replied Rosie pointing out the age difference a second time. "But, Joey, I think that would be fun. Are you ready?"

"Yes. Give me the number."

"No. Not for my number, for me. Are you ready for someone like me? You know, your age and all."

"Wow!"

"I'm joking with you."

"Come on, Joey," shouted Prat again.

"I have to go," said Joey as he handed Rosie his phone.

"Here's my number," rushed Rosie as she punched it into the setting Joey created for it. "Please, call. I think we could help each other."

Joey took his phone back, thanked Rosie, turned, and walked away. As he walked toward Prat, he wondered

What did she mean help each other? That's an odd comment, an odd reply to a pickup line.

When Joey reached Prat, Prat immediately queried, "Who was that?"

"Rosie."

"Oh, yeah. Rosie. Haven't seen her for a while."

"Do you know her?"

"Just from the pier. I think Rosie's from NOLA. She visits here every so often."

"She's a real looker."

"She's not bad. Not bad."

"Nothing like your Sandy, though."

"Sandy. Yeah, Sandy. Hmm."

"What does that mean?"

"Nothing. Let's go."

CHAPTER 25

Prat and Joey slid into Prat's truck. Prat drove out the front gate of the state park and continued on Thomas Drive to the intersection of Thomas Drive and Panama City Beach Parkway. He drove straight through the intersection and continued on Wildwood Road. At Big Daddy Drive, Prat turned right and advanced all the way back to the marina. He fidgeted with the truck to back it up to the large marina building doors on wheels.

"Wait here," Prat instructed Joey. "When I need you to pick up the box, I'll tap on the side of the truck. Just like last time."

"Okay," complied Joey.

Prat closed his door and walked away from the truck to the man door entrance to the building. He entered and closed the door behind him.

Twenty minutes went by before a black Suburban with blacked-out windows pulled up and was jockeyed into position facing the way it approached. A white male, the same person in Vernon, and whom Joey identified to Sid as a commander with the BCSO, presented from the front passenger seat. He closed his door and looked all around. After he had studied the environment, he eased to the passenger side rear door and opened it. The huge man from Vernon slid out of the Suburban. The white male closed the door, and they walked to the man door entrance and entered the same building as did Prat.

Another fifteen minutes went by, and Prat emerged from the building. He was followed by the two people from the Suburban and a third unknown white male carrying a large black case, the same type of case Joey fished out of the water the last time. The unidentified man loaded the case into the black Suburban.

The people from the black Suburban entered their vehicle, and it was driven off by a third individual unseen and unidentified. Prat returned to his truck, and the man who loaded the case into the Suburban returned to the building.

"Why did you bring me? You didn't even use my money. This was a big waste of time for me," sounded Joey.

"I wouldn't say that," replied Jack. "There's a shipment in two days. We will have to use our money then."

Prat threw a small black bag to Joey and instructed, "Count yourself out ten thousand dollars."

"Ten thousand dollars. Why? I didn't do anything."

"You invested your time, and I gave you my word that I paid people for their time. And your time wasn't wasted; you showed your face again."

"No, I can't take any money for today."

"The individuals in the black Suburban are getting to know you," added Prat.

"I didn't do anything today. You said in a couple of days. You said you need my money in a couple of days."

Joey zipped the black bag closed and set it on the floor by his feet.

"I can wait. I'll make money off that deal. I'm good."

"Yes, you are, Joey. You're good. And with a move like that, you're golden with me. That's cool, man. Cool. I like your style. I need to buy you a beer."

Joey and Prat were silent the rest of the way back to the state park. At the park, Prat took Joey to his truck.

Before Joey got out of Prat's truck, Prat said, "If I don't see you tomorrow, remember to be at the pier for four-thirty on Thursday. I'll need your help."

"See you then," replied Joey.

Joey slid out of Prat's truck, shut his door, and Prat drove off.

Back at his apartment, Joey called Sid and left a request for Sid to check the listing for Rosie's cell number. Then Joey completed his reports and went to bed.

CHAPTER *26*

Detective Presley and Patrol Deputy Rayes walked out of the church.

"Well, I thought for sure he would be at his grandson's baptism," said Sonny.

"It was worth a try," replied Aaron. "I'm not sure I'm even on the right track."

"What do you mean?"

"His daughter is adamant that her father is not involved in her mother's disappearance. People aren't like that when they think or believe someone is guilty. If she is going to cover up for her father, she will talk thinking she can outwit law enforcement. She will try to convince law enforcement her father is not guilty or involved. She says nothing, absolutely nothing. In fact, Maria was cocky with her answers to my questions. If she suspects her father did something to her mother, she would say so. Rare is it that a child will protect one of the parents over the other in a divorce. They want to help the parent they see as the victim. But they don't abandon the other parent. The children can't, and it's human nature for the children to work with both parents. That's what is going on here. I'm starting to doubt Gheorghi Nikolov is involved in this missing person case. And at this point, only a missing person. I have no evidence to move this matter to a murder investigation."

"Where does that leave you?" asked Sonny.

"With no suspect."

Sonny suggested, "What about the cohabitant?"

"He's a possibility. But he has a lawyer. I can't talk to him, and I have no evidence to make him a person of interest," replied Aaron.

"You still have to build a case."

"Yeah. And I have nothing. Nothing, Sonny."

Sonny and Aaron went silent until they reached the car.

Aaron asked, "Sonny, would you like to have lunch with me?"

"Only if you let me buy it."

"Sure, why not," replied Aaron with a disappointed tone.

"You're going to have to be a little more excited than that to have lunch with Sonny. Maybe we shouldn't ..."

Aaron cut Sonny off.

"I'm sorry, Sonny. Yes, I will. Thank you for always being nice to me. Where are we going?"

"That's better. You pick."

"That's too much pressure."

"You can handle it, Aaron."

"Sonny, why are you always nice to me?"

Sonny went silent and thought, *How do I answer?*

Aaron drove out of the church parking lot, turned left, and stopped for the steady red light at Panama City Beach Parkway.

Sonny was still silent, and Aaron did not pressure him for an answer.

The red light changed to green, and Aaron turned right as she said, "I know where we can go."

Aaron continued to drive eastbound on the Panama City Beach Parkway.

CHAPTER 27

"Where are we?"

"We are in the Pre-Attack Surveillance and Planning phase. This step will take the longest primarily because we are still determining the best means to weaponize the virus, and we're still acquiring the virus. The target you selected, with a massive security presence all the time, isn't the easiest target to attack. There is also a security presence extended to all the immediate family."

"Okay. I understand. But you can still do it, right? You can still get to him? His security isn't the best and the brightest. They're just government employees."

"I believe I can get to him for that very reason."

"And you will be able to make it look like he caught a virus somehow?"

"That's a must. We have to make this thing look as natural as possible. I suspect there will be those in and out of government who will spin up conspiracy theories, which is a good thing for us. Those people will put a focus on a terrorist attack. But, it's a virus, and people are susceptible to illness. Particularly, people of his age. And this is known to be a lethal virus. That should make his death look natural and believable."

"Okay. I'm still nervous about that Bay County deputy. Are you positive he's not a double agent?"

"I've personally known him for many years. No, I'm not worried about him. You shouldn't worry about him either."

"If you say so."

"Besides, I have some powerful leverage on him should he decide to betray us."

"Excuse me," interrupted the waiter. "Do you wish to order?"

"Yes," replied an elegantly dressed man, who then looked to his dinner guest and said, "Are you ready?"

"I'm ready too," said the portly, well-groomed man, dressed in a stylish white Cuban guayabera shirt, black slacks, and tan huarache sandals.

"Sir, what will you have tonight?" the waiter asked the portly man.

"Shrimp Creole, please. I'm watching my weight."

"Yeah. You're watching your weight alright," commented the elegantly dressed man.

The waiter, with a slight smile from the comment about the portly man's reason for his order, turned his attention to the other guest and requested,

"Senator, what will you have tonight?"

"Jambalaya, please. And a side of red beans and rice. May I have the red beans and rice first?"

"Yes, sir."

The waiter dutifully walked off.

"Why does Boudar want to use the guys?" inquired the senator.

"I wasn't aware he wanted to, sir," replied the portly man.

"That's what I was told. Do we have a problem somewhere?"

"Not that I'm aware."

"Check on that, okay."

"Yes, sir."

CHAPTER *28*

"Oh. Now you have time to talk to me," scolded Jack.

"I can't have you calling me at the office, on my county phone. You know that," replied Henry.

"Okay, Boudar. What is it I can do for you?" asked Jack.

"How would you like to make some money?" replied Henry.

"I always like to make money. That's why I'm doing that other thing for you."

"Good. I need someone to go away."

"What do you mean, go away?"

"You know what I'm saying; don't you play stupid with me."

"Okay. Who and when? And I'm going to need an address."

"I'll give you all that when the time comes. Today, I need to know you will do it, and you will be able to do it when I call you and tell you who and where. You'll have to stay prepared. I have to plan to take advantage when they drop their guard."

"I can do that. It will cost you more. If I can't get drunk or high, because I am waiting for your call, it will cost you more."

"Okay, I'll take care of you. You know I always do."

"Good. And you do. Thank you, in case I haven't said that to you lately. I appreciate all the work you give me."

"I'll call you," said Boudar, who ended the call before Jack said anything else. That was Boudar's narcissistic personality. It did not bother Jack; he just wanted money.

CHAPTER 29

Gheorghi drove his sports car on Thomas Drive. The windows were down, and the sunroof fully opened. The weather was perfect – optimum temperature, sunny, blue skies, and no clouds. His music was loud, and though he did not know how, "Voodoo Doll" by Fergie played from his music list. The song hypnotized Gheorghi and caused him to lose control of himself. He became someone he did not know as an unknown source directed him.

Gheorghi turned off Thomas Drive and drove to the Big Lagoon Apartments. He eased through the unsecured front entrance and steered left. He moved slowly past the white Toyota Tundra truck backed into the last handicap parking space on the left-hand side. Farther past the truck, Gheorghi turned around and retraced his path back. This time, in front of the white Tundra, he stopped, placed the floor-mounted gear selector in Park and turned the car off with a press of a button.

Gheorghi looked around and saw no one. He reached over and picked up his gun from the passenger seat. He ejected the magazine and examined it. It was loaded with a single bullet. He reset the magazine, held the gun in his left hand, and picked up two fully loaded thirty-round magazines. He placed them in his rear pants pockets as he slid out of the car.

Outside the car, Gheorghi scanned the area again and saw no witnesses. He closed the driver's door and walked around the rear and directly to the apartment door. He kicked the door open and advanced with purpose into the apartment.

As Gheorghi entered the living room area, he raised his gun with two hands and extended it straight out in front of him. Still advancing, Gheorghi aligned the sights, continued to advance into the apartment, and found his target seated at the dining room table eating. He fired the gun, and the bullet hit the middle of the target's forehead. The velocity of the bullet pushed the target away from Gheorghi, out of the chair and onto the floor.

Gheorghi advanced closer as he tactically exchanged the empty magazine with a fully loaded magazine and inspected the target for life. There were no signs, and the lifeless body lay on the floor with a fork still clenched by the right hand with a pierog on the prongs. Gheorghi took a second look at the target whose face slowly morphed to the youthful looks that attracted him when they first met many years ago.

Gheorghi steadily looked around and saw no one else. He stopped his visual search when his eyes locked on the upright empty casing on the table. The dining room light illuminated the inscription *PETITIONER*.

A noise from deeper in the apartment drew Gheorghi to continue his scan, but he saw no one. His attention was taken from his scan a second time by what appeared to be a shrine in the corner of the living room. He stopped and studied several dolls in his likeness, and the longer he considered them, the faster his heartbeat. His hands started to shake, and his legs weakened. The noise sounded again and brought Gheorghi back from his thoughts of a shrine, a voodoo shrine, erected in his likeness by the Petitioner.

Gheorghi quickly turned, and his exit retraced his path into the apartment. At the doorway, he stopped to observe the outside, and with no one in sight, he moved quickly to his car. He slid in, threw his gun on the passenger seat and sped away from the Big Lagoon Apartment complex and out to Thomas Drive to continue his getaway.

As Gheorghi concentrated on his rapid escape, Angel appeared in the passenger seat. She said nothing. Gheorghi looked at her and smiled broadly.

Gheorghi's cellphone rang. Two, three times.

"Are you going to answer that, Gheorghi?" asked Angel.

"Maybe," replied Gheorghi.

"It may be someone important."

"Someone important is sitting next to me."

Gheorghi's ringing cellphone woke him from the dream. He rubbed his eyes and then pulled the phone out to determine the caller. The caller ID linked the telephone number to a previous telemarketer.

CHAPTER *30*

Detective Presley sat at her desk and reviewed her case notes. She wanted to study them one last time before briefing her commander in fifteen minutes, but she was interrupted by the ringing of her cellphone.

Aaron answered confidently, "Detective Presley."

"Aaron, Harry, here. I need to talk to you. Meet me at St. Andrew's Marina in twenty minutes."

"Okay. Is everything alright? Are you alright?" asked a puzzled but concerned Aaron.

"We'll talk at the marina. See you there."

"On my way."

Detective Presley ended the call, stowed the case file for the only case she had assigned to her, locked the filing cabinet, and set off for her commander's office.

"Boudar," sounded Aaron.

"Boudar. Aaron, call me Henry. I thought we were all square?" replied Boudar.

Aaron ignored Boudar's comment, seemingly referring to his visit to her house.

"Boudar, I can't brief you right now, I have to go see Harper. Sounds like he has some good information."

"Now?"

"Yes. I'll brief you tomorrow, and you will have what Harper adds tonight."

"Okay. Where are you meeting him?"

"St. Andrew's Marina. I have to go."

"Go. Go. I'll talk to you tomorrow."

Aaron rushed directly to her unmarked silver cruiser and drove off.

Henry retrieved a cellphone from his backpack and dialed a number.

"Hello, Henry. How are you?" answered Jack to Henry's cellphone call.

"Now. I want you to do it now. You need to be at the St. Andrew's Marina in twenty minutes," instructed Henry.

"Okay. But what do you want me to do?" asked Jack.

"I want you to make someone go away like we talked before," directed Henry.

"Who is it? What does the guy look like?"

"Shit. I never saw the guy. I don't know."

"Come on, Henry. This is starting out sloppy."

"I'll be at the marina too. I'll call you and tell you who it is. The target will be with Detective Presley. I think you know her."

"Yeah, I know her. She's good-looking. What a waste of a body as a sheriff's detective. I can think of better ways to use that body."

Henry ignored the macho overtures and remained focused on the opportunity to eliminate someone who may have information about his criminal escapades.

"I'll call you when I get there," replied Henry. "You won't see me; don't look for me."

Commander Boudar ended the call and immediately stood up from his desk chair. He quickly walked to the parking lot and to his unmarked cruiser, which he entered and drove off.

The commander arrived at the marina and positioned himself to see the entire marina from the point of concealment. He took out his cellphone and hit the redial button.

"No answer. This can't be happening. I need this to be done tonight," said Boudar to himself.

Boudar's cellphone rang.

"Why didn't you answer me?" demanded Boudar.

"I just got here," replied Jack.

"Where?"

"I'm driving by the shrimp boat with the vendor's sign on it."

"I see you. Who's that with you?"

"My shooter."

"What! I thought you were going to do this. You brought someone else with you?"

"Henry, you want it done or not?"

"Yeah. I don't have any options. See that silver car, the unmarked silver cruiser?"

"Yes."

"It's the guy in the passenger seat."

Jack asked, "You want me to wait until he leaves? Until they separate?"

"No. Just don't shoot the female," replied Henry.

"Hmm."

Jack put his hand on his phone and turned to his passenger.

"See that silver car up front?"

"The unmarked cruiser?" replied the passenger.

"Yes. Think you can get the passenger and not the driver?"

"Yeah. No problem."

Prat took his hand off his cellphone, raised it, and spoke.

"No problem here. Just waiting for your go."

"Go. Go."

Jack looked at his passenger.

"Do it. I'll reposition the car for a quick getaway."

The passenger did not respond verbally. With a show of
confidence, he opened the front passenger door and slid out
of the car holding a Ruger Mini-14, with a collapsible
stock, in a low ready position, and made his way to the rear
of the cruiser. When he was ten yards away, he raised the
Mini-14 to waist level and began to fire fully automatic.
The rounds hit the target – all the target – the passenger
side and the driver side. The cruiser's rear window blew
out. The back of the car was riddled with bullet holes from
one side to the other. The two rear tires went flat, and
multiple rounds went through the windshield.

When the firing stopped, the shooter changed magazines
and placed the spent magazine in his pants pocket. Then the
shooter commenced firing and continued to riddle the

cruiser with more rounds, this time with a shorter volley. When the killer stopped shooting, he turned and quickly walked back to Jack and entered the car. Nothing was said as Jack sped the vehicle away.

Detective Presley took deep breaths. She had her duty weapon in hand, but because of the fierce firing, she could not return fire. Presley looked over to Harper who was slumped over in his seat and held in place by his seat belt. She reached up to his neck and checked for a pulse. There was none. She reached for her two-way hand-held radio, which was hot to the touch. She looked closer and saw it took two rounds and was inoperable.

Detective Presley took more deep breaths. She checked the driver side exterior mirror and saw no one advancing on her. She checked the passenger side exterior mirror and saw no one. She felt herself for blood and wounds. Detecting none, she thought,

How did I escape taking rounds?

Then Presley remembered,

My ballistic vest was slung over my seat, and my ballistic notepad cover was held by the pocket on the back of the driver's seat. Both deflected the rounds and protected me even though I wasn't wearing the vest or holding the pad.

Presley took deeper breaths as she checked the rear-view mirror and the driver's side mirror again. She saw no threats and eased the driver's door open. She tactically quick-peeked to the rear. Nothing, no one. She changed the height and quick-peeked a second time. Again, nothing, no one. She rolled out of the driver's seat, remained in a crouched position, and hugged the driver's side of the cruiser as she slowly made her way to the rear with her 9-mm Glock model 19 fully extended in front of her with a two-handed grip. She faintly heard a siren as she came to the corner of the car where she caught the flashing of emergency lights out of the corner of her eye. She remained undistracted and continued to clear the rear area of the cruiser, the area the threat was last known to be. She saw nothing. No one was there.

A responding officer shouted, "Stay there. Stay there, Presley."

Presley looked toward the sound of the voice and saw it was Boudar to whom she tactically hand signaled she was stationary and would not move.

Boudar advanced toward Presley with his 9-mm Glock 19 in a high ready position. He appeared to be clearing the area as an officer safety tactic. He neared the cruiser, moved to the front, then around to the passenger side, and at the passenger side rear corner, sounded,

"Clear. Clear."

Boudar continued around the rear of the vehicle toward Presley.

Presley started to stand with her gun at the high ready.

Boudar ordered, "Gun down. Gun down. It's over Aaron. It's over, no one else is here."

Presley slowly lowered her duty weapon and thought,

How did he get here so fast? What is he doing here? Is he the shooter? Is he after me? I would be dead if it weren't for my ballistic vest and pad. Is Harry dead at the hand of a law enforcement officer?

Presley slowly positioned her weapon to a low ready, but her thoughts kept her alert to respond if Boudar became a threat. She was uncomfortable that no other deputies were responding.

Presley asked, "Did you call it in?"

"No," replied Boudar. "I thought you did, and I was busy coming to your aid."

"I couldn't call it in, my radio was hit."

"It's over, Aaron. Holster your weapon. I'll go and call it in."

Boudar holstered his weapon and snapped it in as he moved to his cruiser. Presley continued to hold her duty weapon in a low ready position with two hands and watched Boudar. She shuffle-stepped to maintain a tactical stance to engage him if that became necessary. Presley was concerned for her safety because she knew Boudar was a subject of a national security investigation, and she was a confidential informant to that federal investigation, tasked with getting information from Boudar. All this she knew, but her concern was what Boudar knew.

While Boudar was at his cruiser reporting the shooting, other deputies started to arrive. It had to be the result of citizens reporting the sound of gunfire from the St. Andrew's Marina. Presley relaxed a little with the arrival of the deputies. She holstered and secured her duty weapon since it was highly unlikely Boudar would do anything in front of witnesses even if he orchestrated the ambush and killing of Harry Harper.

Now, foremost on Presley's mind, what did Harry have to tell her? What new information had he developed? And why did he want to meet at the marina and not his office?

CHAPTER 31

The sheriff's office policy required post-shooting administrative leave and Detective Presley's was short, only three business days. Internal Affairs quickly investigated the shooting along with the Bay County Medical Examiner and Coroner's office. The reports from both entities concluded Presley did not fire her 9-mm duty weapon, Harry Harper was murdered with multiple .223 caliber bullets, and there was no evidence Presley conspired in the killing of the BCSO intelligence analyst.

Back at work and at her desk, Presley was busy reviewing the case notes for her one assigned case. She studied the records in preparation to brief her commander. It would be a short briefing since nothing new was developed since she last informed Boudar.

Presley's thoughts wondered,

I still need to find out what Harper wanted to tell me. What he had discovered that we had to meet at an offsite. I need to get into his desk. I hope I'm not too late and it wasn't already cleaned out. Or worse, sanitized by perhaps Boudar or one of his inside cronies.

With the file organized and placed back into its folder, Presley stood and walked off to her commander's office for the briefing.

Aaron lightly knocked on Boudar's opened office door.

Boudar raised his attention from his computer monitor and said, "Yes, Aaron. Come in, please. What can I do for you?"

"I wanted to update you on the missing person case."

"Yes, how is it going?"

"I have nothing new to report."

"Oh. Do we have a cold case here?"

"I suppose."

"Okay, thank you. Anything else?"

"No."

"Okay."

Aaron did not know what to say or do. She stood there in thought,

What all did Boudar know? Why did he respond to the shooting? I didn't put out a distress call, and Internal Affairs said the responding deputies were summoned by citizens' complaints of gunfire. Why did Boudar reassign all my cases? Did Boudar or someone else clean out Harper's desk?

"Anything else?" sounded Boudar.

Boudar's question brought Aaron back from her deep thoughts, and she answered, "No, sir. I need to regroup and plan a path forward."

"Great. Please keep me updated."

"I will, sir."

Aaron turned and left her commander's office and walked outside to her cruiser. Her immediate thought was to go to the Emergency Management Center to search Harper's office. She needed the information Harry was going to provide her five days ago. She started her cruiser and drove north on 77 then quickly reversed herself and stopped on the side of the road to collect her thoughts,

I need to slow down, or I'm going to make mistakes. I need to think this through and come up with a plan. Maybe I should reach out to Sid. Sid has an interest in this, and as Harry's friend, or at least a professional association, I should include Sid. Okay, that's the beginning of the plan, I will call Sid to determine his interest.

CHAPTER 32

"Jack, what the hell happened to you? Who kicked the shit out of you? You look bad," said Joey.

"It's nothing," replied Jack.

"Nothing. Oh, no, it was something," said Joey.

"It's nothing," insisted Jack.

"Did you owe someone money? Why didn't you come to me?" persisted Joey.

"It's nothing."

"No, it's something, and I want to know. I need to know if you expect me to continue to work with you."

"Guys out of New Orleans."

"Guys out of New Orleans. Who? Why?"

"Enforcers for the cell I'm associated with."

"Cell! What cell? What do you mean?"

"Can I trust you, Joey?"

"Sure. Yes, you can trust me. I'm here to help you, and I need to know."

"It's a terrorist cell. A homegrown terrorist cell who call themselves the Other World Order. They have cells throughout the United States, and their objective is to overthrow the United States of America."

"What? No way."

"Oh, yes. You can believe me or not. There's a cell here in Panama City Beach, and we are working in conjunction with the New Orleans cell. The New Orleans cell is planning something big. Really big. It has something to do with the chickens of all things, but I don't know the details."

"You're joking, right?"

"No. I'm not joking. Joey, this is serious stuff, and you're involved too."

"So, the enforcers were here asking questions about me?" asked Joey.

"No, not about you, someone else," replied Jack.

"Who?"

"You don't need to know."

"I think I do. You said I'm involved."

"You're just involved with hauling the chickens. That's all."

"I'm going to have to know more."

"No, you don't need to know more. What you need to know is the day after tomorrow, another shipment is coming in, and we must take care of it. That's all you need to know."

"What time?"

"I don't know yet. I'll call you the day of the delivery to let you know. Stay by your phone all day."

Joey's cellphone rang, and he looked at the number. He did not recognize it, so he did not answer it. It stopped ringing and immediately began to ring again. He looked at the screen, and it was the same number, and still, he did not respond.

"Aren't you going to answer your phone," inquired Jack.

"I don't recognize the number. I don't answer calls from numbers I don't know," replied Joey. "Area code 504. Where's that?"

"New Orleans. Who do you know there?"

"No one. That's why I didn't answer it."

At that moment, Joey's phone sounded again.

"Answer it, Joey. See who it is."

"Not interested," sounded Joey in a disgusted manner to show concern for his involvement with a crime to maintain his undercover role.

"Here comes Rosie, show her the number. Maybe she'll recognize it."

"Rosie? Who's Rosie?"

Joey turned to look in the direction Jack was looking.

"That's Rosie. You don't remember her? I wouldn't want to be you. Watch what you say to her."

"What are you talking about?"

"Hey, Jack," said Rosie.

"Hey, Rosie. How are you?" replied Jack.

Rosie turned to Joey, looked hard at him and then said,

"You can't answer your telephone? You're too good for me?"

"I didn't recognize the number," replied Joey.

"Okay. Whatever. I wanted to ask you something, but I got my answer. You probably didn't even remember my name; Jack had to tell you."

"Whatever," replied Joey.

Rosie continued to walk to the end of the pier.

"Jack, what's with her?" asked Joey.

"I don't know," replied Jack. "But you better watch your back."

"Why?"

"I'd just watch your back. I don't trust Rosie. I think she's a rat."

"A rat? Really. For whom?"

"Don't know. It's just a funny feeling I have about Rosie. I don't trust her. How does she have your number?" asked Jack.

"I don't know. That's a good question," answered Joey.

"Yeah. Hmm."

"I'm going," sounded Joey.

"Make sure you stay by your phone," directed Jack. "I'll be calling you."

"Maybe."

"Maybe! Bullshit. You stay by your phone, Joey. You better answer, and you better have the money."

"Maybe."

Jack turned and walked to the end of the pier.

"Hey, Rosie. What do you know?"
"A lot more than you, Jack."

"Hey, that's funny."

"And I know I'm not doing anything with you. Don't even ask, Jack."

"Come on, Rosie, why are you mean to me?"

"We're not going there, Jack."

Rosie walked away from Jack, down the pier and behind the dunes to the parking lot. As she neared her car, Joey pulled up in his truck and lowered his passenger window.

"Where are you going, Rosie?" asked Joey.

"You should have answered your phone, and you would know," replied Rosie with an attitude in her voice and walk.

"Let me buy you a drink?"

"I don't drink."

"Right."

Rosie stopped and slowly turned around and glared at Joey before she said, "Now you're calling me a liar?"

"No."

"Then what? Why do you want to buy me a drink?"
"Just to apologize."

"Why?"

"Because I'm a gentleman. Would you like to hang out?"

Rosie looked deep into Joey's eyes, sighed deeply, and seductively smiled.

"I guess," said Rosie playfully. "Come on, I'll drive."

"No, let me drive," replied Joey.

"I don't know you; I'll drive myself, thank you."

"Okay. I'll follow you. You pick the place then since you don't know me. I want you to be comfortable."

"Good. You follow me if you can keep up."

Rosie slid into her car and sped off, and Joey struggled to keep up.

Jack stood in the parking lot and thought,

What was that all about? Joey and Rosie?

Jack rushed to his car, entered, and sped after them.

CHAPTER *33*

Petar was commuting from work when his telephone sounded through his truck speakers. He mashed the display answer button and sounded,

"Hello."

"Hey, what are you doing?"

"I'm on my way home."

"So, you worked today."

"Yeah."

"You don't know who this is, do you?"

"Well."

"Well, nothing. This is Gheorghi."

"Yeah, I know."

"No, you don't. Why isn't my name displayed?"

"Well."

"You don't have me programmed into your phone. Hmm."

"Where're you at, Gheorghi?"

"Pittsburgh. I was thinking about coming down soon."

"I don't know if you want to do that."

"Why not?"

"I had a visitor the other day."

"Was it Rezza?"

"Why did you say that?"

"I didn't say that. That was a question. Here, let me say it in a way you can understand. Petar, was the visitor Nerezza? There, how was that?"

"It wasn't her. It was a detective."

"A detective?"

"Yeah. From the sheriff's office. She wanted to talk to you about Rezza."

"What about her? Why do I keep getting bothered about her?"

"Rezza is missing. The detective was investigating a missing person case," said Petar.

"Good. I don't give a shit if Rezza's dead," replied Gheorghi.

"I suggest you don't talk like that."

"What did the detective ask you?"

"She wanted to know where you were and how to get a hold of you."

"What did you tell her? Did you rat me out?"

"No, I didn't rat you out. I didn't tell her anything. She had an attitude."

"Hmm. So, if the detective didn't have an attitude, you would have ratted me out?"

"Well, she's a beautiful black lady. The most attractive black lady I've seen."

"So, you thought about ratting me out because she was attractive? Oh, brother."

"I must ask," said Petar. "Did you do that thing Motorman talked about? You know?"

"The twenty-cent thing?" answered Gheorghi.

"Well, yeah."

"No."

Penka asked, "What's the twenty-cent thing about?"

"You know Motorman, the retired police officer with the vintage Japanese motorcycle club," replied Gheorghi. "When we were at the Retro Affair Vintage Motorcycle Show in Orlando, he joked, 'Twenty cents. That's all it takes to end it. If you want to end the litigation, it shouldn't cost you more than twenty cents.' And he held up a 9 millimeter round then handed it to me. That's when I saw it was engraved, PETITIONER. It's just professional humor. Cop humor. Boy, did we laugh."

"Was he joking?" Petar asked rhetorically. "Motorman's crazy enough to do it."

"Maybe," replied Gheorghi. "You know I don't have anything to do with the money-grabbing, floozy Petitioner."

"Yeah."

"That's why I didn't go to my grandson's baptism because she was there."

"Yeah, I wouldn't have done that."

"You're not me. I don't want to talk about the Petitioner, okay."

"Are you going to call the detective?"

"No. Why would I?"

Hey, I have another call coming in. I have to take it; it's the president of the club. I'll call you later."

"Okay, talk to you later."

CHAPTER *34*

Aaron answered her work phone, "Detective Presley. How may I help you?"

"Aaron, this is Sonny. How are you today?"

"Hey, Sonny. I'm fine, thank you. How are you?"

"Great. I was wondering if you would like to get together tonight?"

"Oh, Sonny. I hope you didn't take last Sunday the wrong way."

"What do you mean 'the wrong way'?"

"Sonny, slow down. We had sex. That's all. I hope I didn't mislead you."

"Well, maybe I'm confused. It was more than sex for me."

"Sonny."

Sonny cut Aaron off and said,

"Aaron, I think you should be honest with yourself. You know you have feelings for me, and I have feelings for you."

Aaron tried to interrupt, but Sonny continued,

"We had these feelings for a long time, but we never acted on them for one reason or the other. It was more than sex, and you know that."

Aaron said nothing.

Sonny persisted and asked again, "Would you like to do something tonight?"

There was a brief silence before Aaron spoke,

"Yes, I would. What would you like to do, Sonny?"

"Why don't you come over to my place? I'll make us dinner. We can open some wine and sit and talk."

"That sounds nice, Sonny. Okay. What time?"

"Any time after 6:30. Will that work for you?"

"Yes. I have one more meeting then I'm done for the day. I'll see you tonight," said Aaron.

"Good. See you tonight," replied Sonny.

Aaron and Sonny ended their phone call. Aaron knew Sonny was right, and that was why she did not say anything or resist the opportunity. Aaron thought,

I've had feelings for him since we were in high school. I didn't treat him right then, but now it is time to act on my emotions. Sonny is right."

Aaron steered her cruiser into the parking lot of the White Star Coffee Company and backed it into a parking space. She sat and surveyed the area for threats or anything unusual or out of the ordinary. Since Harry was murdered, Aaron's officer safety awareness has been on high alert.

Aaron detected nothing for concern and slid out of the cruiser and walked into the coffee shop. She went to the counter, ordered, paid, and took her coffee outside on the patio where she waited for Sid as they had arranged to meet.

A car at a high rate of speed rolled into the parking lot and doubled parked. The driver's door opened, and Aaron reached for her duty weapon. She saw the person was Sid and slid her gun back into its holster and snapped it in.

Sid said, "Aaron, come on, we need to go."

"What? What's going on, Sid?" replied Aaron.

"Come on. Get in. We need to go."

Aaron rose from the chair, snatched her coffee, ran around the rear of the car, and entered the front passenger seat.

"What's going on, Sid?"

"We need to go to Harry's office and gather all the information he had on the case."

"How are we going to do that?"

Sid handed Aaron a piece of paper. Aaron unfolded it and read it before she spoke,

"This is a search warrant? It's a FISA warrant. What is going on here, Sid? We talked about this, now you have one."

"I obtained a FISA warrant for Harry's office, Aaron."

"I see that," replied Aaron.

"I thought this would be the best way not to draw attention to our case but still gather the information."

"What is a FISA warrant?"

"It's a Foreign Intelligence Surveillance Act warrant. It allows us to be anonymous. We don't have to disclose the subject of our investigation for quite some time."

"I thought FISA warrants could only be used for gathering foreign intelligence?"

"That is true."

"I thought we were working a domestic case?"

"No. This case is a matter of national security. Please understand, the international aspects are the norm for a national security matter. This is a big case, Aaron."

"So, Henry is involved in a national security matter?"

"Oh, yes. And if my hunch is correct, Henry is deeply involved."

Sid turned his head to Aaron and said,

"My suspicion, Harry was murdered, and Henry had Harry killed for what he knew."

Sid turned his attention back to the roadway as he continued to speak,

"I just hope we aren't too late, and his office has not been cleaned. We need to have the information."

"Cleaned?" questioned Aaron.

"Yes, cleaned out. Sanitized. Someone beat us to the information Harry wanted to share with you."

"Hmm. Won't my presence affect my undercover role with Henry?"

"No. We're done with that."

"What do you mean done? Where does that leave me?"

"Aaron, you weren't getting anywhere with Henry. Henry ended that avenue of investigation when he came over to your house. He was a few steps ahead of us, or he was, in fact, a gentleman with you? Either way, he didn't want to get close to you because of a relationship. Where did that leave you? How were you going to continue to gather information from him?"

"I understand what you're saying. I just want to do more. If Henry is involved in Harry's murder, then I want to get Henry for that, replied Aaron. "Harry was a really nice person, and he didn't deserve to die like that."

"You are helping. You're going with me to execute the search warrant," said Sid.

"Yeah. Okay."

Aaron took her cellphone and from her recently called number list, dialed Sonny's number. Sonny's phone rang, but there was no answer and no prompt to leave a voice message.

Aaron pressed the end button and secured the phone in its holster as she continued to direct Sid to the Bay County Emergency Management Center.

When they arrived, Sid eased the car to a stop and parked it near the building. They both slid out, and tactically walked to the front door. Aaron tapped her code on the keypad and the electronic lock disengaged. They entered the building, approached the security post, but no one was there to greet them.

Aaron whispered, "That's odd. Someone should be posted here. The operating procedure states someone is to be posted here 24/7, every day of the year."

"This place is eerie," commented Sid in a low voice.

"It sure is when no one is here."

"Can you get us in?"

"Yes. Follow me."

Aaron moved to the door and again tapped her security code into the pad. The door's electronic locked disengaged and Aaron pushed the door open. Sid followed, and they walked deeper into the building. There were no lights on, but Aaron knew her way from using the facility in the past.

Sid followed Aaron deeper into the building and to Harry's office. They entered, and Aaron turned on the light.

"Stop right there," announced Sid.

Aaron turned to Sid and saw he had his gun drawn and pointed in her direction.

Aaron replied, "What?" as she reached for her duty weapon and thought in rapid succession,

Is this a setup? Is Sid on the take too? Is he working with Boudar? Is he going to shoot me?

Sid commanded, "Don't move, Aaron. There's a body in the corner over there."

Aaron looked in the direction Sid looked and saw a body on the floor, slumped over in a sitting position.

"No!" exclaimed Aaron. "That can't be."

"What? Who is it?" asked Sid. "Do you know who that is?"

"It's Jo. Josephine. Cover me. I'm going closer."

"Careful, she has a gun in her hand."

"Gun clear," declared Aaron and she slid the gun back toward Sid.

"This can't be. No way."

"What do you see?"

"My first analysis of the scene is that she committed suicide. But that's not her. She wouldn't commit suicide. She was a strong person. I need to call this in."

"No. No, Aaron. You can't call this in," ordered Sid. "What are you going to tell them when they ask what we are doing here?"

"The truth," said Aaron.

"That's just it, you can't. I can't. That's how a FISA warrant works. It's secret."

"What are we going to do?"

"Search the office and get out of here. The murder can't compromise the federal investigation," said Sid.

"No. I can't do that to a fellow officer," replied Aaron.

"You have to. Look, go be the lookout while I search. Now, Aaron."

Reluctantly, Aaron shuffle-stepped to the office door and remained there with the vision of Josephine in her mind.

Sid searched the office and found nothing. He sat down at the computer, and when he moved the mouse, the machine lit up.

"That's odd," sounded Sid.

"What's odd?" inquired Aaron.

Sid did not answer. He continued to work on the computer. After a few minutes, Sid spoke,

"Nothing. Son of a bitch. Nothing. Someone was here. Someone was just here. We must have scared them off; they left the computer on."

Sid quickly turned his attention to search the desk and file cabinets and sounded,

"Nothing in the desk drawers or file cabinets. All of it was cleaned out, no papers, nothing. The computer was the same. No files at all."

"Are you sure?" asked Aaron.

"Yes, I'm sure. Quite sure," replied Sid in a disappointed tone.

Aaron quickly said, "Think of three places."

"What?" replied Sid.

"Quick, think of three places you would hide a thumb drive in your office when the information put you in harm's way."

A short silence was broken by Aaron when she said,

"Under the chair. Under a drawer. In the restroom under the garbage can. Those are my picks," said Aaron.

"Hmm. Those are all good picks. Let me see. I say under the drawers. Under the rug in one of the corners. And third, outside the window."

"Pick another one, the windows don't open. This building is set up to withstand airborne attacks."

"Okay. The office of Harry's boss."

"That's cliché."

"Yeah. But that's how I size Harry up."

"Okay, now let's check the six locations. Let's start with the bottom of the drawers since we both picked that one. And check the backs too."

Aaron and Sid began to pull the drawers out. They checked the bottoms, sides, and backs and found nothing. As Aaron checked the bottom of the chairs, Sid checked the corners of the rug. Nothing was found.

"Let's go to the restroom," said Aaron. "And let's stick together, so there's a witness if we find anything."

Aaron led Sid to the men's restroom, and they flowed into the room. Aaron moved to the garbage can and took the lid off. She gave it a thorough inspection and found nothing.

Sid pulled the bag out and inspected the outside of it. Nothing. He set the bag down and turned the can upside down, and something fell out, hit the floor and made noise as it slid along.

Aaron looked about and saw an object off to the side. She moved to it and picked it up.

"Wow. It's a thumb drive. I can't believe this."

"You must have done this before?"

"Yes, Sid. Henry taught me the trick."

"Let's go. We need to get out of here," ordered Sid.

"Sid, we have to take care of Jo," replied Aaron.

"No, we have to go. Speed is important here."

"I can't leave her here like that."

"What are you going to do with her? You. We. We can't be associated with her. It must be like we weren't here. We can't call this in."

Sid moved to the door, opened it, and stepped out. Aaron followed. As soon as Aaron stepped through the door, Sid fell to the floor. As Aaron bent down to assist Sid, she was struck on the head and blacked out.

CHAPTER 35

"There you are," said Jack.

"Just like you ordered," replied Joey. "I'm here for our work this afternoon."

"Where's Rosie?" asked Jack.

"I don't know. How would I know?"

"You left with her the other day."

"So. What does that matter to you?

Jack said nothing.

"Jack. Jack. Jack. You're interested in Rosie. But what about Sandy?"

"What are you talking about?"

"I'm talking about you, Jack. You have your eye on Rosie, but you don't know what to do with Sandy. You know Sandy has money, but you're not sure about Rosie. If Rosie has money, you'll dump Sandy," said Joey.

Jack said nothing.

Joey continued, "Oh, my. What are you going to do, Jack?"

"You don't know what you're talking about," replied Jack in a raised voice.

"Oh, yes, I do. You like Rosie."

The two went silent. Joey finally broke the silence and said,

"Why don't you kill Sandy. You can take her money and pursue Rosie? There's your answer. Kill Sandy."

"Maybe I already did," said Jack as his voice cracked.

There was silence again as Joey looked at Jack, and Jack looked away. Joey thought,

Shit. What if Jack answers yes, then what do I do? Arrest him? Detain him and call Detective Presley? Who would I have to get me closer to the OWO or the final receiver of the smuggled chickens? My investigation would end. I may have pushed it a little too far with that undercover roleplay. But his voice expressed emotion for the first time since I have been working with him, and it was related to Sandy."

Joey finally sounded, "Jack, I'm just kidding."

Jack looked at Joey and said, "It's a good idea. I wouldn't have to put up with an ex's drama that way, and I would have her money. Why didn't I think to kill her?"

Jack looked deep into Joey's eyes and held Joey. Joey braced himself for a confession to murder. Jack released Joey and with a snigger said, "Do you think I'm stupid, Joey?"

"I'm joking with you, Jack," replied Joey.

"I already thought of that option."

"You didn't kill Sandy, did you?"

Again, Jack did not answer Joey's direct question. Jack didn't even say no or deny killing Sandy and the lack of refutation of killing concerned Joey.

Jack focused his thoughts back to the criminal act for which he asked Joey to help.

"Let's go, they'll be there any minute," said Jack.

"Where are we going?" asked Joey.

"You'll see when we get there," replied Jack.

Joey walked with Jack to the parking lot. They got into Jack's truck, and Jack drove to the other side of the state park, to the boat launch parking lot. Jack maneuvered his truck and backed it down to the walkway. It was positioned the same as the last time they picked up boxes of chickens from the Colombians.

Jack said, "Wait here, I'll go see if everything is ready. Give me the money."

"No. It doesn't work that way," replied Joey. "I'll come with you."

Jack did not insist Joey wait behind so they both slid out of the truck, closed their doors, and walked to the rear of the vehicle. There they saw the two Colombians from before carrying a container and walking up the sidewalk.

Jack turned and lowered the tailgate. When the two Colombians arrived at the truck, they set the container down on the bed and pushed it back. They shook hands with Jack but did not acknowledge Joey.

Jack took his money out of his waistband and looked at Joey as he extended his empty hand. Joey retrieved his cash from his rear pocket and handed it to Jack. Jack placed the two white envelopes together.

"Check the container, Joey," ordered Jack.

Joey said nothing, and to maintain his undercover role, he dutifully opened the container and checked the contents. He secured the container, looked to Jack, and said, "Everything's here."

Jacked looked to the Colombians, extended the money envelopes, and said, "Here you are. Thanks."

One of the Colombians took the envelopes from Jack and said, "Gracias."

The two Colombians turned and walked back to their skiff.

Jack said, "Let's go. We have a tight schedule."

"Where're we going?" inquired Joey.

"You'll see when we get there."

Jack and Joey climbed into the Toyota Tundra, and Jack drove off through the park to the front entrance. Through the front gate, Jack continued to Thomas Drive and merged into the traffic. He continued north on Thomas Drive to Panama City Beach Parkway where he blended into the flow of the eastbound traffic and continued over the Hathaway Bridge and turned left onto Twenty-third Street. Jack drove a short distance and turned left onto Collegiate Drive, droved a short distance, and parked near a shoreline park.

"They should be here soon," Jack informed Joey.

"When do I get to meet Sandy?" Joey asked.

"Why do you want to meet her?"

Joey sensed he may be pushing Jack too hard for information about Sandy. He knew he had to back off or risk suspicion from Jack.

"I don't know. Just making conversation while we wait."

"Yeah. I doubt you get to meet Sandy."

"Why not?"

"I don't know where she's at."

"Oh."

Joey knew he risked Jack's suspicion, which may be counterproductive to the undercover operation, but he had to push a little harder. Joey knew he had to try to solve Aaron's missing person case. So, Joey continued,

"When's the last time you saw her?"

"What?" sounded Jack in a suspicious tone.

"When's the last time you saw Sandy?"

"You sound like a cop, Joey."

"Yeah. I'm a cop. Here, let me show you my badge. You're an ass, Prat."

"Why do you have such an interest in Sandy?"

"Just conversation, man. Forget it."

"I'll tell you what, you take Sandy, and I'll take Rosie," said Jack.

"I don't have a hold on Rosie," sounded Joey. "She's nothing to me. Go for her."

"It doesn't seem that way. Where did you two go the other day?"

"What day?"

"Was there more than one time? How many times did you two *hookup*?"

"What are you talking about?"

"Here they are," said Jack. "We'll finish this later."

"There's nothing to finish," replied Joey. "You're a piece of shit."

Jack gave Joey a hard street style stare before he directed his attention to his left where a lone black Suburban slid to a stop and was positioned in line with the truck. The Suburban's front passenger window went down, and Henry Boudar was seated there. Jack lowered his window.

Henry said, "You have to take the load to New Orleans. No one was available to come and pick it up."

"No. That's not our arrangement, Henry. I told you I don't go to New Orleans," replied Jack.

"How about your partner?"

"No, he doesn't go to New Orleans either."

Joey took the opportunity to mess with Jack. He ignored what Jack just said and volunteered to take the load to New Orleans.

"I'll go," said Joey. "I can take it to New Orleans."

"Good," said Henry. "And he can bring your container back with him. The boss wants it out of the warehouse."

"Maybe I better go with him then."

"I don't care who goes, just get the shipment to NOLA," sounded Henry. "You all need to go now."

"Okay, we'll go. I know where everything is; I better go too."

"Good. See you all later."

"Hey, wait. Where's my money?"

"I almost forgot," said Henry. "Here you go."

Henry threw a small black bag to Jack. Jack caught it by the strap, pulled it into the truck, and threw it into Joey's lap.

"Okay. See you later. We need to go," said Jack.

Henry said nothing in return. He just raised his window as the black Suburban drove off.

Jack held the button to raise his window as he looked at Joey and said, "Look. Let's get things straight. I'm in charge. When I say something, you just agree. If you can't follow my lead, then get out of here."

"I'm just trying to be helpful. This is real money."

"Yeah. And now I must use some of my money on travel expenses. I don't like to travel. I don't like to go anywhere. I just want to stay on the pier."

"Okay. Sorry. I'll cover all the expenses. You can deduct it from my cut."

"You're damn right I'll deduct it from your cut. Yeah."

Jack slammed the console shifter into Drive and sped away, squealing his tires. He maneuvered the truck to the Panama City Beach Parkway and turned right to start the extended drive west.

"Don't think you're going to sleep," Jack announced. "I'm going to stop for gas up here, and when you finish pumping and paying with your own money, you're going to drive. Get it, Joey Boy?"

"Okay, Jack. No big deal. I'll drive the whole way. No big deal, *crybaby*."

CHAPTER *36*

Henry sat and stared at Aaron. The room was small and cluttered with all the emergency medical equipment essential to sustaining life. Aaron was tethered to four machines, and each sounded a different tone on a regular cycle.

Becoming restless, Henry got up from his chair, stretched, and walked to the window and gazed out.

Aaron opened her eyes and immediately saw Henry but did not say anything. She was startled by the sound of the medical machines and being attached to wires that led back to them. She looked about, and it was quite apparent she was in a hospital. It felt like her head was compressed, possibly by a tight bandage, but Aaron did not raise her hands to investigate; she did not want Henry to know she was awake.

She wondered, *What am I doing in a hospital, and why is Henry here?*

At that moment, a nurse came into the room and observed Aaron was awake.

"Good to see you're finally awake," announced the nurse.

The nurse moved to Aaron's machines and surveyed them.

Henry's attention was drawn back to the room by the nurse's announcement. He turned from the window and watched as the nurse tended to Aaron.

The nurse finished her check of the machines and continued, "The doctor was concerned you may have a concussion. How are you, Aaron?"

"What do you mean?" asked Aaron.

Henry interrupted before the nurse said more.

"I got this. The doctor and I discussed this, and the doctor agreed I was to talk with Aaron first since this was a sensitive law enforcement matter."

"Okay. Would you like me to stay?" asked the nurse.

"No. I'm good," replied Henry. "I'll take care of this."

Before Aaron could say anything, the nurse left the room. Though Aaron was concerned about why she was in the hospital and why Henry was there, she said nothing.

"Aaron, do you know who I am?"

"Yes, Henry. I know who you are," said Aaron with a sigh. "Why would you ask me that question?"

"Do you know what day it is?"

"Yes, it's Wednesday."

"No, it's Thursday. You have been sleeping for almost forty-eight hours. That's why the nurse was happy to see you awake. The doctor was concerned you may fall into a coma."

"Why? Why am I in the hospital?"

"Where were you on Tuesday evening?" asked Henry.

Aaron thought for a moment and could not remember. To gain more time to think about where she was, she replied with a question,

"Why are you asking me questions?"

"I'm concerned about my subordinate's health and safety," answered Henry.

"My health and safety?" asked Aaron.

"Yes. Your loss of memory was the second thing the doctor was concerned about."

"Why would I lose my memory?"

"If you're asking me that question, then you don't remember."

"I remember," said Aaron with the tone of a macho law enforcement officer.

"Where were you Tuesday night last? Two days ago. Think about it."

Aaron said nothing, so Henry broke the silence.

"For now, until I talk to the doctor or he talks with you, you continue to rest."

"Rest! How the hell am I to rest after a conversation like this?"

"It's good you remembered me. The doctor said that it would be a good sign. He said you took a tough blow to the head. Do you feel the bandage on your head?"

"Yes. What happened to me?"

"You don't remember?"

Again, Aaron said nothing and thought,

I know he's Henry. I don't know why I'm in the hospital, but I do feel the bandage on my head. What does Henry know? How much does Henry know? I remember he is under a federal investigation and I'm helping the feds. Does he know that and that is why he's here asking me questions?

The nurse came back into the room, and she was holding a syringe.

Henry looked to the nurse and said, "Good timing. I'm finished for now. Please give her the shot as we discussed with the doctor."

"Yes, sir."

The nurse moved toward Aaron. Aaron tried to push back but quickly discovered she was secured to the bed by straps. The surprise and then the shock of being shackled to the bed rendered Aaron speechless. The nurse reached out and injected Aaron with the syringe, and Aaron slowly passed out.

"Thank you," whispered Henry.

"You're welcome," replied the nurse in a whisper as she withdrew the needle, stepped back from the bed, and turned and walked out of the room.

Aaron, unconscious, was left alone with Henry.

CHAPTER 37

Fifteen miles outside of New Orleans, Jack woke up and ordered Joey to pull over.

"What?" replied Joey.

"Pull over, I'll drive from here."

"I'll finish the drive, Jack. Just tell me the directions. Where are we going?"

"We aren't going anywhere. I'm dropping you on Bourbon Street. I'll pick you up when I'm done."

"It's okay. I'll go with you. It's my fault we are here."

"Just pull over, Joey."

Joey signaled right, took his foot off the accelerator to slow the truck and eased to the side of I-10. He brought Prat's truck to a stop, slid the console shifter into Park and with his hand still clenched on the shifter, looked at Jack.

"Are you sure, Jack?"

"Yes."

Jack slid out of the passenger seat and walked around the back of the truck. Joey pushed out of the driver's seat and walked around the front. When they were both seated, and their seat belts clicked, Jack drove off. He got off I-10 at

Cleveland Avenue and worked his way to Canal Street, crossed over Rampart Street and continued to Bourbon Street and eased to a stop.

Jack instructed, "You can get out here, and this is where I will pick you up."

"Okay," said Joey as he got out of the truck and shut the door.

Jack drove off, and Joey started to walk along Bourbon Street. He walked two blocks and noticed the huge man from Vernon, again in elegant clothing, walking alone two blocks ahead of him. Joey started to follow the man. The man ambled, and Joey quickly closed the distance between them to one block. Joey was at St. Ann Street when the man turned right onto Dumaine Street. Joey promptly walked to the corner of Bourbon and Dumaine Streets and turned right and saw the huge man enter a building midway down the 700 block of Dumaine. Joey crossed over Dumaine and eased down the opposite side of the street. Halfway down, he discerned the man entered a private residence or the Historic Voodoo Museum; he was not sure of the exact door.

Joey moved back toward Bourbon Street and stood near a corner grill to continue to watch the street. As he positioned himself, he noticed Jack emerge from an alleyway near where the man left the street. Joey rushed inside the corner grill, hoping to continue his watch from a table inside, but all the tables along the windows to Dumaine Street were seated.

Joey was startled by a pushy hostess who asked, "Sir, would you like a table for one?"

"Yes, please."

The hostess seated Joey in the far corner overlooking Bourbon Street where Joey thought,

I can't see anything from here. I'm hungry, though. I better eat. I don't know if crybaby will take time to eat or if he will just turn around and go back to PCB.

Joey began to study the menu when he was interrupted by a man who bellowed out, "Sandy, how are you? I haven't seen you for a while. Where have you been?"

The man appeared to be the owner of the grill by the way he carried himself and directed the workers to clear the table by the windows facing Dumaine Street for Sandy.

The lady replied, "In the Caribbean with Marti again. How are you?"

"Just fine. Thank you for asking. Will Jack be joining you? I saw him across the street."

"I don't know. Please leave a menu in case Jack comes over."

"Sandy, does Marti still wear those black gloves?"

"Yes, all the time. Marti had her gloves on the whole time we were in the Caribbean."

"So unusual."

"Odd is how I describe it."

"Okay. Enjoy. If you need anything, please ask. I don't want you to get mad at me and use that New Orleans voodoo on me."

"I won't do that."

"That's not what I hear."

"I'd use the Haitian voodoo."

The owner and the lady laughed. From their interplay, they apparently knew each other and were friends.

Joey was too far away to hear the conversation between the owner and the lady who answered to the name Sandy. Joey thought,

Could that be the infamous Sandy Diddler? I need to get a picture of her to show Aaron.

As Joey raised his cellphone to take a picture, it rang. He looked, and the screen displayed Jack Prat. Joey answered,

"Hey, Jack."

"Where are you?" sounded Jack with urgency.

"I walked along Bourbon Street."

"Why didn't you just wait where I dropped you?"

"Because I wanted to walk, and you didn't tell me to stay there."

"Where you at? I'll pick you up."

"On Bourbon. You can't drive on Bourbon."

"I know. I'll pick you up on another street. Where you at?"

Joey remained calm, though he detected a tone of suspicion in Jack's voice. He thought,

Should I just say Dumaine Street? Maybe he saw me here, and that's why he sounds suspicious.

Joey paused for thought.

Jack shouted into the phone, "You don't know where you're at? I'm holding up traffic."

Joey shouted back, "I'm at St. Ann."

"Walk back to Royal. I'm coming up to Royal now."

"Okay."

Joey rose and threw a twenty-dollar bill on the table. He quickly walked out of the grill, down Bourbon Street, turned left onto St. Ann, and ran to Royal. He made it just as Jack pulled up.

Joey got into the truck, and Jack drove off as Joey shut the door.

"Slow down, Jack. Easy shithead."

"Don't tell me what to do. Remember, I'm the boss here. I told you to wait for me on Canal."

"No, you didn't."

Jack started to laugh.

"I know," said Jack. "I just wanted to see you run."

"You're an ass, Jack. A real jackass."

"Tell me something I don't know. Are you hungry?"

"Yes."

"Good. I'm going to make my way back to Dumaine to park the truck. I know a good grill on the corner of Dumaine and Bourbon. I have to go around and come down Dauphine. This French Quarter is not truck friendly."

Joey thought,

Was Jack going to meet Sandy, who was in the restaurant when I was there? Was that the Sandy he lived with? Was that the missing Sandy searched for by the BCSO detective? And I didn't get a picture of her.

Jack interrupted Joey's thoughts when he spoke,

"I have a surprise for you at the grill."

"What kind of surprise?"

"You'll see when we get there."

"I don't like surprises."

"Too bad. This is New Orleans. There's all kind of surprises, all night long. You'll just have to like it. And don't embarrass me at the restaurant."

Jack maneuvered the full-size pickup through the narrow streets of the French Quarter and made his way to off-street parking near the grill Joey was at earlier. They got out of the truck, Jack locked it, and they walked off to the restaurant.

"Jack, have you eaten here before?" inquired Joey.

"Yeah. This is one of my usual places when I'm in New Orleans. It's close to a couple of other places I hang out at."

"What places are those?"

Jack did not answer. He walked across the street to the grill and entered. Joey followed.

The person Joey saw earlier and thought was the owner greeted Jack in the same robust manner he greeted the lady he called Sandy. The apparent owner walked Joey to a table set for four, and no one else was at the table. Joey scanned the restaurant as he followed Jack and the owner, but he did not see the lady from before. Joey sat across from Jack.

The owner said, "Joey, will Sandy be joining you tonight?"

"I don't think so," replied Joey. "Why would you ask?"

"She was in earlier and only had a drink. She said she was going to have dinner later."

"I don't think it was Sandy," replied Jack. "Are you sure it was Sandy?"

"Yes, Joey. I know Sandy. I'm sure."

"It couldn't have been her."

"What do you mean it couldn't have been her? She said she just got back from the Caribbean."

"I don't think so. It's not Sandy," replied Jack with authority.

"Jack, it was Sandy," protested the owner. "I know Sandy, and it was her."

Jack turned white. He said nothing as he recklessly rose from his seat and ran out of the restaurant, onto Bourbon Street and then in the direction of his truck.

The owner looked at Joey and in a dramatic tone, said, "What's wrong with him?"

"I don't know," replied Joey.

"Are you going after him?"

"I don't know. Jack will be back. He's so dramatic."

"Really, you're not going after him. He looked scared, and he turned white."

The owner walked away from the table, and Joey continued to study the menu. He did not know what to do. Curiosity got the best of Joey, and he got up and walked in the direction in which Jack rushed off. When he got to where the truck was parked, it was gone.

Joey thought, *Now what do I do?*

He retrieved his cellphone and worked through the screens to Jack's number. He touched it, and the phone started to ring. Four, five, six rings and nothing. Jack did not answer.

Joey talked aloud to himself, "Now what am I going to do?"

"You could buy a lady a drink," sounded a voice.

Though it was a familiar voice that sounded, it startled Joey that someone heard him. When Joey turned around; he saw Rosie standing there.

"What?" mumbled Joey.

"Don't be nervous, handsome. I said you could buy a lady a drink," said Rosie.

"What are you doing here?"

"I told you I was from New Orleans, or did you forget that too?"

"No. No, I didn't forget."

"Is little boy Joey nervous?"

"No, I'm not nervous."

"Then why are we still standing here?"

Rosie reached out and with her small hand, took hold of Joey's hand. She tugged his reciprocated firm grip to prod the reluctant Joey to come along as she led him back toward Bourbon Street.

"You know what," said Rosie.

"What?" replied Joey.

"This lady is hungry. I know a good grill here. Let's go eat."

As if under a spell, Joey muffled, "Okay."

Rosie was still holding Joey's hand as she led him along and across Bourbon Street. Now, Joey visually appeared to be in a stupor or perhaps under some type of spell. He gave no resistance, nor did he ask any questions, both not the norm for Joey.

Rosie led Joey into the same grill he had been in with Jack. The owner watched as Rosie walked Joey to the table where he sat with Jack. Joey controlled Rosie's chair as she sat, and then he sat next to her.

The owner came to the table and said, "Rosie, good evening. Good to see you again. And sir, did you find Jack?"

Joey looked at the owner but said nothing.

Rosie answered, "He's a little shy around women."

"I see," responded the owner.

"May I have my usual and Joey will have the same."

"Yes, Rosie, two of those potions, as you call them, coming up."

The owner moved closer to Rosie and leaned down to her ear.

"You didn't put him under a spell, did you?"

Rosie raised her arm and placed it on the owner's shoulder to hold him close to her.

"No. Not this one. I want little boy Joey to remember tonight. To remember me."

The owner did not pull away and said,

"Rosie, shame on you. You're a bad, bad Vodouisant."

Rosie released the owner, and he stood erect. They both laughed, and Joey laughed too, though he did not know what he was laughing about. The owner looked at Joey and raised his hand in the air as his wrist went limp.

"You're a lucky man, little boy Joey. You're going to have a good night. If I weren't gay, I'd be jealous."

The gay grill owner raised his hand and laid it flat on his cheek and sounded, "Mmm. Mmm."

The now self-proclaimed gay owner whose name was still unknown to Joey, walked away laughing to himself.

Rosie looked at Joey, and their eyes locked.

Joey said, "What was he talking about?"

"Nothing, Joey. He's just a big jokester. It's part of the business. The French Quarter and the Bourbon Street ambiance."

"Oh. Okay," said Joey. "So, what's good here? What is your best dish here?"

Joey and Rosie had dinner, drinks, and conversation. Before Joey knew it, it was eleven thirty. Rosie kept Joey mesmerized, and he did not think of Jack until now.

"I wonder where Jack is?" said Joey.

"He probably went back to PCB," replied Rosie.

"No way. And left me here?"

"Yeah. Old Jack doesn't care about anyone but himself. Why did he leave?"

"The gay owner told Jack he saw Sandy here in the restaurant earlier."

"Really! I haven't seen her for a couple of months now; I wondered where she was. Odd. When I asked Jack about her, he only said 'I don't know.' Then he tries to hit on me."

"Jack has an eye for you, Rosie," said Joey.

"Too bad, he's going to be disappointed," replied Rosie. "And if he keeps hitting on me, I'm going to kick the shit out of him, again."

Joey laughed as did Rosie before she composed herself and said,

"I mean it. A lot of effort isn't needed to kick Jack's ass."

Joey continued to laugh, and Rosie joined back in as the owner stepped back to their table.

"What has you laughing so hard, Rosie?"

"Jack. Who else?"

"I understand that. I trust everything is to your liking tonight?"

"Good as always," replied Rosie.

"How about you little boy, everything good for you, my first-time customer?"

"Perfect. Just perfect. Thank you."

"No. Thank you. I hope to see you again."

Before Joey could answer, Rosie replied, "You'll see him again. He'll be back with me."

Joey blushed. The owner went into his gay character again and placed one hand on each of his hips and cocked his hips to the right.

"I'm so jealous, Rosie. If he were gay, I'd give you a run for your money, girl."

The gay owner looked deep into Joey's eyes, dramatically cocked his head a little to the right, squinted his eyes, and asked, "Are you gay? You certainly are stunning."

Joey quickly raised his hand and moved it left to right and declared, "No. No. Sorry, I'm not gay. I like women."

Rosie pronounced, "You like me."

Joey blushed again.

"Rosie!" exclaimed the gay owner. "I'll leave you to your work."

The owner looked to Joey and slowly said, "Enjoy her, Joey."

The owner walked away.

Joey looked at Rosie and said, "What does he mean, he'll leave you to your work?"

"I don't know. That guy is just a crazy gay guy. You know how they are."

"No, I don't know how they are. I'm clueless about that whole gay community thing."

"Good to know. Now, back to us. Where are you staying tonight?"

"I didn't think about that. I thought Jack would be back."

"I don't think Jack is coming back."

"Probably not."

"You can stay with me if you want."

"That's generous of you, but we hardly know each other."

"Then let's get to know each other tonight. Let's explore each other."

Rosie moved closer to Joey and placed her hand on his thigh and began to rub it. Joey quickly pulled his leg away.

"Oh dear, don't tell me little boy Joey is shy?" said Rosie. "I'll slow down. But you really should stay with me. You don't want to be somebody's prey tonight. You know, the new person in a strange town. And New Orleans is a strange place. An exceedingly strange place. Trust me, that's not just a marketing ploy used by the New Orleans Chamber of Commerce. This place is strange and spooky."

"Okay, I'll accept your hospitality."

"Good, let's go."

Joey stood and controlled Rosie's chair as she stood. He pushed her chair to the table and then his. Joey motioned for Rosie to go first and he followed her as she led him out of the grill and onto Bourbon Street.

On Bourbon Street, Rosie, without looking, reached back and took Joey's hand to guide him through the crowd. When Rosie's hand touched Joey's, a weird feeling came over him, as if with the mere holding of hands, Rosie placed Joey under a spell. He felt susceptible, weak, vulnerable, and out of control.

CHAPTER *38*

"This pain. I wish it would go away," mumbled Gheorghi who was sitting in his chair watching TV. It was Friday night, and Gheorghi knew that not by a calendar reference, but by the pain that always came around seven o'clock on Friday night. Randomly on other nights too, but every Friday night.

Gheorghi thought, *Maybe I should have taken the prescription for the drugs. Maybe I should have accepted the Florida physician's medical hospitality.*

Gheorghi used the remote to go to the guide to see all the Friday night programming. He clicked through the menu and settled for the repeats of an old sitcom.

He began to wonder about the detective that was asking questions about him, which lulled him into thought,

I don't need any more drama from the procrastinated litigation. And of course, the law is going to come after me first because they still see me as the husband after all these years though she is cohabiting with someone. No. I'm the suspect. Or as they use the politically correct term of the time, a person of interest. How annoying. I'm curious to whom all the detective speaks about this matter? I wonder where the Petitioner is. I should go find her and piss everyone off. Literally, drag her ass into court. This thing needs to end already.

Gheorghi pulled his phone from his pocket and worked through the screens. He pressed a telephone number and put the phone on speaker.

"Yeah. What's going on?" a voice sounded.

"I'm calling for the name and contact info for that detective."

"Why do you want that?" asked Petar.

"I'm thinking about finding Rezza and dragging her ass into court, so this thing ends."

"I don't think you should do that."

"What if she doesn't appear in court for the final hearing?" said Gheorghi.

"Just let the court handle it."

"Then, the procrastination continues. I just want it to end. I want to be out of this whirlpool of uncertainty already."

"How are you going to find her?"

"I'll start to ask questions."

"You don't think that will make the detective more suspicious of you?"

"The detective probably isn't working the case any longer. The case has probably gone cold."

"You think?"

"Yeah. What's the detective's information?"

"Let me hang up and get it. I'll text it to you."

"Good. Thanks. If I need any help, I'll call you."

Gheorghi looked at his phone and saw Petar had hung up. He did not know if Petar heard his last comment.

Gheorghi rested his phone on his lap, leaned back in the chair, and closed his eyes. He tried to relax and push the pain away as he waited for the text.

CHAPTER *39*

"Good morning, Aaron. How do you feel today?" asked the morning shift nurse.

"I'm feeling good. I'm ready to get out of here," replied Aaron.

"The doctor should be in shortly. Let's see what he says."

The room door opened, and both the nurse and Aaron looked thinking it would be the doctor.

"Good morning, Aaron. How are you?" said Sonny.

"Good. I'm feeling much better."

"I'll let you two to your visit," said the nurse. "I'll be back when the doctor comes to check on you."

"Thank you," replied Aaron.

Sonny held the door open for the nurse as she left the room. She turned his way and smiled a thank-you.

"So, Sonny, what brings you here?"

"I heard you may get released today. I thought I would drive you home."

"Thank you for your concern. A ride home – I guess I do need a ride. But the doctor and nurse aren't talking like I will be released."

"Oh, they aren't? Hmm."

"How did you know I was in the hospital?" asked Aaron.

"You weren't at your house when I came to pick you up," replied Sonny.

"Pick me up?"

"Yes, we had a date. You don't remember?"

"Sorry, Sonny, I don't remember," apologized Aaron.

"Has IA talked to you yet?" asked Sonny.

"IA? Why would Internal Affairs want to talk to me?"

"Has anyone talked to you about what happened? About what you were involved in?"

"No. Henry was here, but he didn't say anything to me."

"Why was he here?"

"He said he was checking up on his subordinate. He was concerned for one of his employees."

"I don't know about that. I don't trust Henry."

"Why don't you trust him?"

"I'm looking into him. When I have facts, I'll talk to you about it."

"Sonny, don't do anything stupid. Just leave it."

Their conversation paused until Aaron continued,

"Sonny, why does IA want to talk to me? Finish about that."

"Do you know why you are in the hospital?" inquired Sonny.

"I have this bandage on my head. Well, no," replied Aaron.

"You don't remember anything about why you would have a bandage on your head?"

"No. Tell me."

"I'll tell you what I know."

Sonny was interrupted by the opening of the room door. They both looked at the door and saw a doctor entering, followed by the nurse from before.

"Good morning, Aaron. I hear you are feeling well today?" said the doctor.

"Yes, I am. I'm ready to go home," replied Aaron.

"Let me," said the doctor as he reviewed the medical chart and then studied it a second time. He put the records back and moved to Aaron and examined her eyes and the bandage.

"Are you feeling any pain about your head?" asked the doctor.

"No. None," replied Aaron.

"I see another shot of medicine is scheduled for you. When we give you that you will have to stay another night."

"I don't want the shot, and I don't want to stay another night."

"I'm afraid I have to give you the shot and keep you overnight. Nurse, please go for the syringe."

The nurse dutifully left the room without comment.

Sonny said, "Sir, she doesn't want the medicine. She said she is fine and wants to go home."

"And who are you?" replied the doctor in a sarcastic tone.

Sonny lifted his law enforcement credentials from his rear pocket and presented them to the doctor.

"I'm a patrol deputy with the sheriff's office."

"Oh. Well, I have my orders."

"You have your orders? From whom? You're the damn doctor – don't you make the orders?"

"That's what I mean," stuttered the doctor.

"Aaron, do you want to go?" asked Sonny.

"Yes," replied Aaron.

"Doctor, you can leave the room, so Aaron can get dressed. I'll be taking her home."

"I didn't release her," the doctor stuttered again.

"You don't have to; she will be signing herself out."

"I have to go and make a call to see if this is okay."

"Who are you going to call? You're the doctor. Go. It doesn't matter. You can't keep a patient in the hospital against their will."

The doctor turned to walk out of the room. As he did, the nurse came into the room with the syringe. The doctor moved to the nurse and whispered something to her, and she turned around and followed the doctor.

Sonny said, "Come on, Aaron, get dressed."

"I can't undo these straps," sounded Aaron.

"What straps?" asked Sonny as he began to scan about Aaron's bed and then observed straps around her wrists that

293

secured her hands to the bed railing. He continued, "Why are you strapped to the bed?"

Sonny moved to Aaron's bed and inspected the straps. First, he undid the one from her right hand and then leaned over Aaron and undid the one from her other hand.

Sonny directed, "Hurry up, Aaron. Get dressed. We need to get out of here."

Aaron disconnected herself from the medical machines, rose from the bed, and walked to the closet to get her clothes. There was no time for modesty, she let the flimsy hospital gown drop to the floor, put on her clothes, and turned to Sonny. She was greeted by a smile from Sonny, who watched her dress.

Aaron exclaimed, "My gun. My duty weapon isn't here."

"No time to worry about that now, let's go," replied Sonny.

Sonny took Aaron by the arm, moved her to the door, slowly opened it, and checked the hallway. He maintained his hold on her arm and controlled her into the hall. They walked to the stairs and Sonny opened the door, and they entered. They continued down the stairs to the ground level and exited the hospital to the parking lot.

They walked to Sonny's cruiser parked in a designated police parking space. Sonny unlocked the doors, opened the front passenger door for Aaron, who entered, and he closed the door for her. Sonny walked around the front of the cruiser and entered. He locked the doors, started the car, and drove off. They said nothing to each other during the self-discharge that fancied an escape.

CHAPTER *40*

"Why isn't Sid answering his phone?" mumbled Joey. "It's three days past my check-in time. This is most unusual for Sid."

"Who are you calling, little boy Joey?" asked Rosie. "I'm right here."

Joey heard Rosie's question and enjoyed her flirtation; however, he had a more pressing issue to handle, how was he going to get back to PCB? A pressing question for Joey, but he focused back to Rosie because he could not help himself.

"Good morning, Rosie. Did you sleep well?"

"As well as I could all alone in my big bed. I had too much room to myself; I tossed and turned."

Again, Joey avoided a reply to Rosie's flirtation, but he stared at her braless breasts that prominently displayed under a short, thin material white T-shirt as she fiddled with the percolator coffee maker to get the coffee brewing. Finished, she turned to Joey and saw him quickly redirect his eyes to the floor.

"Thank you for your hospitality and a place to sleep," said Joey.

"It was nothing," replied Rosie. "You only slept on the floor in the living room. Why didn't you sleep on the couch?"

"The floor was fine."

"Would you like coffee?"

"Yes, please."

"How are you getting back to PCB?"

"I don't know. Let me call Jack."

"Good luck with that."

Joey pulled up Jack's contact information and pushed the call button. The phone rang eight times with no answer.

"No answer," sounded Rosie, who stood in the kitchen and seemed to be uninhibited if she realized how revealed she was.

"No answer," replied Joey. "That didn't surprise you?"

"I didn't think he would answer your call. A user. There were many times I thought about pulling out a doll to enforce a curse on him."

"What?"

Rosie walked from the kitchen to the living room. She handed Joey a cup of coffee, then sat next to him on the couch. The flimsy T-shirt rode up and exposed her thighs and white panties.

Joey did not move. He was becoming comfortable with her and interested. He struggled to remove his eyes from her braless breast, exposed thighs and panties, and back to her eyes.

He finally said, "Thank you."

"You're welcome," replied Rosie with a seductive smile.

"What were you saying about a doll?" asked Joey.

"A voodoo doll. Put a pin right between his eyes," replied Rosie.

"That stuff doesn't work."

"How do you know it doesn't? I see many examples in this town and PCB, the pier, among other places."

"Get out. That's just folklore."

"Believe what you want. I see it in action."

"Where?"

"St. Andrews State Park pier, for one place."

"When? How?"

"Did you ever meet Jack's wife, Sandy?"

"No. Is that Jack's wife or girlfriend? I thought she was still married to someone else?"

"That's Jack's wife for the purpose of the OWO."

"What's the OWO?"

"The Other World Order, a subculture encamped on PCB. In short, they scam public assistance programs and lure rich women to the cult for their money or their husband's money, as the latter is mostly the cases. Rumor has it as a homegrown terrorist cell."

"Really? Hmm."

"Anyway, this Sandy, one day on the pier, she pulls out this voodoo doll and goes through her voodoo thing with a doll she calls G."

"No way."

"Oh, yes. I asked Sandy who G was, and she said G was her husband, but they didn't live together, hadn't for about four years then."

"Really. Are Jack and Sandy married? Legally married? Like bigamy?"

"No. They are only married in the eyes of the OWO. It's a cult thing."

"Hmm. When was the last time you saw Sandy?"

"Why do you want to know?" asked Rosie.

"I think Jack murdered her, to be direct with you," replied Joey.

"He didn't do that. He needs her for her money. That's how the OWO works. That's why they lure rich women to the cult."

"So, it's all about the money."

"The relationship between Jack and Sandy?"

"Yes."

"Pretty much so. I have no reason to think otherwise."

"How do you know all this, Rosie?"

"From being around. Both Sandy and Jack use people, but it doesn't matter. How are you getting back to PCB, that's what matters? You have work to do."

"How do you know? Why do you say I have work to do? Maybe I'm rich and have no financial worries."

"You wish, but I know you."

Joey said nothing. His mind raced with conjecture about why Rosie talked in innuendos. He wondered questions,

How much does Rosie know about me? How does she know what she implies she knows? How does Rosie know what

she says about Jack and Sandy and their relationship? And
she alleges a homegrown terrorist cell, in Bay County
Florida, Panama City Beach. Or was the stress of the
undercover assignment starting to work on me? And now I
have difficulty contacting Sid, my handler.

"Joey. Joey," sounded Rosie, which brought Joey back to
focus on her.

"Yes. What?"

"What were you thinking about?"

"Nothing."

"That's what everyone says. It's bullshit, you were thinking
of something. How are you getting back to PCB?"

CHAPTER *41*

Gheorghi looked and then looked again.

He said to himself, "That's her. Why can't the detective find her? She's right there on the pier."

Gheorghi walked back to his sports car. He opened the trunk and rummaged through the contents then opened a sub-compartment. He pulled his gun out, released the magazine, check to ensure it had the one round, and slammed the magazine back. He worked the slide and chambered the one round marked for the task. Then he tucked the gun into his waistband and pulled his shirt over it. He searched more and retrieved two other magazines filled with thirty rounds each. He shut the trunk lid and walked off as he slid the fully loaded magazines into his left rear pants pocket.

As Gheorghi walked back to the pier, he contemplated,

I must do this. This needs to end, today. Enough of her procrastination. Her control. And should I take him out too? Why not, he doesn't deserve to live either. He's a homewrecker. They want to be together; they can go together.

Gheorghi was focused on the task, and as he walked, he bumped into people leaving the pier. He offered no apology, which was out of character for Gheorghi.

On the pier, he scanned to determine how he would carry out the task. He saw the pier was empty but for two people, his target and her lover. Both were still seated on a bench midway down the pier. The target's lover sat next to her, all close and frisky. The target was fidgeting with something, but Gheorghi was too far away to discern what it was. Whatever it was, it made them both laugh. Then a pain struck Gheorghi's right leg. He buckled but quickly regained his balance. He felt his waistband to assure himself the gun, loaded with the lone bullet for the task, was still in place. He advanced down the pier with a limp, and he dragged his right leg.

Gheorghi was ten yards away from his target, and neither she nor her lover gave any sign they saw Gheorghi coming. Gheorghi, now closer to the two, saw what the target held in her hand and the object that created amusement for the two of them. It was a doll. The target moved her hand toward the doll in a jabbing fashion, and they both laughed. Gheorghi buckled again. This time it took him some effort to stand upright. When he did, he continued to walk with a limp, and he continued to drag his right leg.

Fifteen feet away from the targets and they still showed no signs they knew Gheorghi was there. Gheorghi felt his waistband for the gun. He lifted his shirt, gripped it, and flexed his hand to adjust his grip before he drew it from concealment.

Six feet away from the targets and they still showed no signs they knew Gheorghi was there. Gheorghi continued to hold his gun against his right leg as he dragged the leg along. The female target continued to fidget with the doll.

At two feet away, the sun stretched Gheorghi's shadow in front of the cohabitants. They looked up to see who was near them, and when they saw it was Gheorghi, they pushed back on the bench, and the Petitioner squeezed the doll tight.

Gheorghi felt a tightness to his chest and experienced shortness of breath. Stopped, he raised his gun and fired the lone bullet. The bullet hit its mark, the center of the Petitioner's forehead. She rocked backward as her skull and brain matter expanded out the rear of her head and onto the pier decking and railing. Some landed in the water below like chum. She came to rest, sitting straight up with her eyes wide open, and her jaw slightly lowered. Glheorghi observed as the Petitioner released her grip on the doll, it became easier for him to breath.

Gheorghi adjusted his gun left to the acrid smell of urine and feces. He looked over the sights at the male cohabitant and saw the lover's eyes were also wide open. He sat straight up, motionless. Gheorghi observed no rise and fall of the lover's chest, so he lowered his gun. As he did, he saw the lover's wet groin. Gheorghi shuffle-stepped to him and reached out with his non-dominant hand to check the lover's carotid artery for a pulse. There was none. He adjusted his index and middle finger on the lover's neck and still found no pulse. The lover was dead, presumably from shock and a subsequent heart attack, given the loss of control of his bodily functions.

Gheorghi raised his focus from the lovers and scanned the pier in a 360-degree pan. He saw no one else. He ejected the empty magazine, caught it in his hand, and slipped it into his pocket. From his rear pocket, he retrieved a fully loaded magazine and slammed it into his gun. He slingshot the receiver forward, and the weapon was charged with another round.

With a fully loaded and charged weapon, Gheorghi looked one last time at his completed task. The lone nickel-coated casing, from the lone bullet that accomplished the task, lay on the wooden deck. The inscribed *Petitioner* displayed as the sun reflected from the second *T.* The aged Petitioner morphed to the beauty of her youth, and from the lone bullet hole in the middle of her forehead, blood oozed and slowly trailed down the now youthful looking face.

He moved his eyes to the Petitioner and noticed she still clutched the small doll. He tactically shuffle-stepped closer reached his left hand out and pulled the doll from her lifeless hand. He shuffle-stepped back and examined the voodoo doll. He saw it had a pin in the right leg and another in the lower back. Gheorghi pulled the pin out, and immediately, the pain in his right leg went away. He pulled the pin out of the doll's lower back, and quickly, his lower back pain went away. He threw it down, took aim, and fired six rounds, and they all hit and tore the voodoo doll apart.

Gheorghi raised his focus from the doll to the dead lovers and then to all parts of the pier. He saw no one and turned and walked away. His movements were no longer restricted. He no longer dragged the right leg nor was there pain and stiffness in his lower back. He started to run and found he could. He ran faster and faster back to his car, entered, and sat to catch his breath.

Out of the corner of his eye, he noticed someone seated in the passenger seat. Spooked, he jerked his head right and saw Angel, who in an angry tone, said, "Gheorghi. Why did you do that? You didn't have to do that. Why didn't you call me? I told you I would be there for you if you let me. Gheorghi, I just wanted to help you. Why didn't you let me help you?"

Startled awake by his vibrating cellphone, Gheorghi, though groggy, sat straight up in the chair. He looked around to determine where he was and slowly discerned he was in his living room. He fumbled the phone to see the message, a text from Petar. It was the contact information for the detective.

Startled by the dream, Gheorghi thought,

Maybe Petar is right. I shouldn't look for her. And another dream with Angel? This one violent too. What does that mean?

CHAPTER *42*

Rosie's cellphone sounded, and she slowly rose from the couch with no concern for the exposure from the flimsy T-shirt. She ambled to the kitchen table and answered it. Joey sipped his coffee and stared at Rosie to study her every curve.

"Hello," Rosie said into the phone and then listened.

Joey directed his attention back to how he was going to get back to PCB.

Rosie ended her call with, "Will do."

She placed the phone on the table and walked back to Joey. She stood by a chair and looked at him.

"I have to go," said Rosie.

"Okay. Thank you again for your hospitality. I'll gather my things and be on my way," replied Joey.

"No. You have to go with me. The car will be here in an hour."

Rosie threw a leather case to Joey, and he caught it.

"What's this?" asked Joey.

"Please look," replied Rosie. "Open it."

Joey set his coffee cup on a side table, and he used both hands to open the leather case. It contained law enforcement credentials that Joey read and then studied.

Rosie said, "I know who you are, Joey, and I know what you're doing."

Joey raised his eyes, looked over the leather case at Rosie, and slowly spoke,

"What are you talking about?"

"Joey, as you can see, I too am a federal agent. Like the credentials display, I am a special agent with the FBI. I too am in an undercover capacity."

Joey said nothing.

Rosie continued, "I have to get ready for the pickup. Excuse me."

Joey watched Rosie as she walked into the kitchen. The early morning sunlight coming through the side window made the flimsy white T-shirt more transparent. She placed her coffee cup in the sink and unplugged the coffee maker. Joey continued to watch Rosie walk through the living room and into her bedroom. She shut the door behind her, and Joey stared at the closed door before he slowly looked back at the law enforcement credentials and studied them more.

Joey thought to himself, *What is going on here?*

Joey set the credentials on the side table and began to gather his things. Finished, he sat on the chair.

Rosie emerged from her bedroom, and she was dressed in blue jeans, a denser white T-shirt under an opened button-down light blue shirt, and white athletic shoes. Her breasts were smaller now from what Joey thought was a sports bra. Joey saw the bulge from a gun on Rosie's right hip as she walked to the side table and picked up her credentials. She opened them and inspected them before she pushed them into her left rear pocket. Then she seated herself on the sofa opposite Joey.

The silence was becoming uncomfortable, and Rosie finally spoke,

"The driver will take us to the secret location where the task force Special Agent-in-Charge will brief you on the National Joint Terrorism Task Force investigation. I can't say any more until you finish your in brief."

"What if I don't want to go?" said Joey.

"That's not an option."

"Really!"

Rosie looked at Joey with a harden law enforcement officer's face. She didn't have to say anything; Joey knew the look and had used the look many times himself, a nonverbal statement meaning – *you're going to fuck with me, okay.*

Apparently, Rosie too had street wise experiences to facilitate her undercover role. Rosie displayed her street knowledge and garnered more of Joey's undisclosed romantic interested in her. Joey worked hard to suppress his romantic interest for two reasons. The first, and most important, Joey did not know Rosie's relationship status. Joey was not a homewrecker. He did not pursue married women or women in a relationship. The second reason, he did not want to risk a blemish on his impeccable career record from a sexual harassment complaint. If Rosie did not have a romantic interest to reciprocate, she could interpret Joey's unwanted advancements as sexual harassment, for which a mere allegation was a career-ending event.

Rosie and Joey sat in silence until Rosie's phone sounded receipt of a text. She read it to herself and quickly typed a reply.

Rosie looked at Joey and said, "Let's go."

Joey, without questions, rose with Rosie and together they walked down to the waiting car.

At the secret location, Rosie led Joey directly to the SAIC's office. Rosie, out of courtesy, knocked before she entered. Joey followed.

"Sir, this is Joseph Chenski, ASAIC, Investigations, OIG, USDA. Official undercover fictitious identity – Joey Chen," announced Rosie.

The SAIC looked away from his computer monitor and said, "Thank you, Rosie. Please close the door on your way out."

"Yes, sir."

Rosie turned and walked out of the office and closed the door behind her.

"Joseph, please sit," said the SAIC as he looked back to his computer monitor.

Joseph said nothing and sat.

The SAIC pushed the computer monitor to the side and focused on Joseph.

"Joseph, thank you for coming. My name is Leonardo Coppola. I'm the Special Agent-in-Charge here. I understand you're stuck in New Orleans and need a ride back to PCB."

Joseph, with the coolness of a seasoned law enforcement officer, replied, "Yes. But this seems to be overkill. I can take a cab."

They both laughed.

"I asked Rosie to bring you here because it's time for the OIG USDA and the National JTTF to partner together to expedite the mutual investigation of animal smugglers and more. We both know there's more."

"National JTTF, I thought that sat in Washington D.C.?"

"It does. We developed a case that requires at least a satellite office in the New Orleans area until we complete the investigation."

"Oh."

"Okay, let me brief you on the investigation," said SAIC Coppola.

"I'm very interested to hear what you have to say," replied Joseph.

"First, your IG wanted to be here, which I thought was not necessary and was able to negotiate that your agency handler was the one needed here. I was not able to contact Sid, and that was not good. How about you?"

"It has been five days since I had contact with Sid."

"I have task force people working on locating him, but I have concern for their success."

"He'll contact me. He can take care of himself. There's a reason we can't find him or contact him."

"Hmm," sounded Coppola.

Joseph added, "I'm required by policy to contact OIG headquarters if I cannot contact my handler. That I must do on the seventh day from my required contact date."

"You have a couple more days. Let's see what the task force can do in the next two days."

"Okay."

"The National JTTF case is based on intelligence analysis which disclosed a domestic terrorist group's chatter on a plot to assassinate a high-profile government official in Washington D.C. The official has not been identified yet, by name or title. The chatter comes from New Orleans and Panama City Beach."

"The first one to come to mind is the president of the United States," replied Joey. "Doesn't that make this a Secret Service issue? You want the OIG Agriculture involved? Why?"

"Joey, that's what we thought in Washington, and we met with the Secret Service senior leadership, but they blew off the possibility indicating their protective shield of the president was impregnable," said Coppola.

"Interesting. That's not pompous."

"We even wanted the Secret Service to lead and manage this satellite office here, but they declined."

"And again, you want the OIG Agriculture involved? Why?" queried Joey a second time.

"The terrorist chatter talked about the smuggling of chickens. We learned of your undercover operation from the FBI liaison officer at USAMRIID. He thought it was unusual that chicken feathers were sent for testing. More peculiar the chicken feathers were handled only in a Biosafety Level 4 laboratory, a laboratory with the highest level of biosafety precautions, and appropriate for work with agents that could easily be aerosol-transmitted within the laboratory and cause severe to fatal disease in humans for which there are no available vaccines or treatments.

Further inquiry by our liaison officer disclosed Joseph Chenski submitted the sample for analysis. That is why we wanted OIG USDA involved, Joseph, or should I say, Joey Chen."

"Okay."

"I do like your fictitious undercover name," said SAIC Coppola. "Joey Chen has a nice ring to it."

"I trust you have cleared this with OIG management," asked Joey.

"Yes, I have cleared it."

"What can I do to help you?"

"Joseph, keep doing what you're doing but include us in all your reporting. And work together with Rosie, which should enhance both of your undercover roles."

"I can do all that. No problem."

"I know, your reputation proceeds you. You do good work. I'm excited to have your help with this national security investigation."

"Sounds good to me. When can I read all the National JTTF files to get up to speed with your investigative efforts?"

"Now. Rosie will assist you since she is the author of most of them."

"Thank you, sir."

"You're welcome. I'll call Rosie back."

Coppola picked up his cellphone and tapped out a text message. When he received a reply, he set the phone down.

"Please call me Leo."

"Yes, Leo. Thank you."

A knock came to the door.

"Come in, Rosie," said Coppola.

"Are you ready, Joseph?" asked Rosie.

Joseph looked at Rosie and said, "Yes, I am." He looked back to Coppola and said, "Thank you again, Leo."

Joseph rose and prepared to leave. Nothing more was said. Joseph walked out of the office, and Rosie followed him.

In the hallway, Rosie instructed, "This way."

Joseph followed Rosie to a windowless office with a round table, four chairs, and stacks of file folders.

"This is everything. I'll leave you to it. You have my number, text me when you're finished or if you need something."

"Thank you."

"What would you like to drink?"

"Water. Just some water, please."

"I'll get it for you. Get started on your file review so we can get back to PCB and play."

Rosie walked out of the room, and Joey sat and pulled a stack of folders to him. He selected one, opened it, and began the laborious but necessary task.

CHAPTER 43

"Where are we going, Sonny?" asked Aaron.

"To your house."

"You think that's wise?"

"I don't know what to think."

"Well, I think someone was trying to kill me in the hospital."

"That's what I thought too," replied Sonny, who then rapid fired questions, "How did you end up in the hospital? What happened to you? Where were you?"

"I don't remember, and that scares me, Sonny."

"Okay. Just relax the best you can. One thing at a time. Let's get you home."

"White Star!" exclaimed Aaron.

"What?" asked Sonny in a surprised tone.

"That lady in that car is drinking from a White Star coffee cup."

"What does that have to do with anything?"

"I remember. I was at the White Star in Lynn Haven."

"Oh. What else, what else do you remember?"

"That's about all."

"Would you mind if I turned around and took you to the White Star in Lynn Haven."

"No. I think that's a good idea."

"I'm not trying to play psychiatrist; I'm just trying to figure out the events."

Aaron did not reply. She continued to stare out the side window and showed signs of straining to remember her near past.

Sonny wheeled the patrol car to the left-hand lane, then to a left turn lane. Oncoming traffic clear, he shuffled the steering wheel to the left to flip around to travel back the way they just came. He brought the cruiser to a stop in the right-hand turn lane. A stopped car in front of him was not turning right on red, so Sonny tapped the siren, and it chirped twice. The stopped vehicle drifted into the right-hand turn, and Sonny maneuvered around the car and continued north on SR-77.

"Yes. I was definitely at White Star," sounded Aaron.

"What for?" asked Sonny.

"I usually meet someone there. It's a place I use to meet people for the job."

"So, you met someone. Who?"

"I can't remember. I just can't remember, Sonny."

"Okay. Relax. It will come to you. Relax. We're almost there."

There was silence in the cruiser until Sonny spoke again.

"We are two blocks from White Star. What do you usually do when you get there? Do you stay in the car until the person you're meeting arrives? Do you buy a coffee and sit inside or outside? When we get there, I want you to do what you always do."

"I'm thinking."

Sonny signaled and moved into the left-hand lane. He indicated a second time and maneuvered into the center turn lane, drifted to a stop, and waited for oncoming traffic to clear.

"Do you remember anything more, Aaron?" asked Sonny as he crossed the southbound lanes of SR-77 and eased into the White Star parking lot.

"Yes. Find a parking space and back in. I always back in."

Sonny found an open space near the side door and backed the cruiser into it.

"Then what?" asked Sonny.

Aaron slowly replied, "I scan the area. I do a security check ever since I was attacked at the marina."

"Okay. Let's do a security check."

Both Sonny and Aaron scanned the parking lot for anything unusual or out of the ordinary. They saw nothing of concern.

"Then, I go inside. Yes. I go inside and buy coffee," added Aaron.

"Do you sit inside or outside?" probed Sonny.

"Outside. Always outside when the weather permits."

"So, you were here at White Star. You parked, checked the area, went inside and bought coffee, and went outside and sat. Were you waiting for someone?"

"Well, yes. I would have been waiting for someone. This is my meeting place. Yes, I was waiting for someone."

"Relax, Aaron," encouraged Sonny. "Think about what you were working on. You told me you only had one case assigned to you, and it was a missing person case."

"I don't know why Boudar only has me working one case."

"Yeah, I can't figure that out either. But, you're here, you're working on that case? Maybe you're meeting an informant who had information on the case? Another officer from another department with information, perhaps?"

"An officer. Yes. I sat outside, and this sedan came into the parking lot. It came in fast, and the driver braked hard to stop by the patio area."

"Good. Good. Then what?" encouraged Sonny.

"I went for my gun."

"Good. What next?"

"The driver's window lowered, and it was a man. A white man. Well groomed. He said something."

"Take your time," Sonny encouraged again.

"He said, get in. Yes. He said to get in."

Aaron went quiet and withdrew into her seat. She looked like something scared her.

"Aaron, what is it? What are you remembering? Say it. Tell me."

Aaron started to weep. Tears rolled down her face, and her hands shook.

"Aaron, tell me. Say it."

"It was Sid."

"Sid. Who's Sid?"

"Sid, the federal agent."

"A federal agent. Aaron, are you sure? A federal agent. Why are you meeting a federal agent?"

"Sonny, I remember it all now. I remember everything."

Aaron fidgeted in her seat as she looked around the parking lot.

"My unmarked cruiser. It's silver. I parked it in this lot, but I got in with Sid. My car should still be here, but I don't see it."

"Aaron, please start from the beginning so I can follow and help you."

At that instant, Sonny rocked forward, and when his seatbelt engaged, the force swung him back into his seat. As he recoiled back, his forehead exploded, and blood, soft tissue, and bone splattered on the dash and windshield of the cruiser. Sonny's head fell forward, and there was no more movement of his body.

Aaron looked away and screamed. She screamed a second time before her street survival training automatically engaged.

For reasons unknown to Aaron, at that instant, she remembered the planned date with Sonny. She looked at Sonny, reached out, and placed her hand on his shoulder.

She knew he would not hear her, but she spoke in a soft, tender voice anyway.

"Sonny, I'm sorry I wasn't at the house. I was here at White Star for a meeting that I thought would end in time for me to be back for our evening. Back in enough time to get ready for you. I just had to work. I'm sorry, Sonny. I'm sorry for never."

Aaron stopped talking to Sonny. She fought to hold back her emotion and feelings for Sonny as she withdrew her hand from his shoulder and moved it to her seat belt. Aaron fumbled but released it. As she took a low position with bent knees, she heard a second round go by her. It hit the windshield and created a gaping hole. She reached out and mashed the on button for the siren, and it began to sound. Aaron hoped it would draw someone's attention, and they would help her. Shortly, the siren stopped, and Aaron heard pieces of the speaker box falling on the hood of the cruiser from a third shot that hit its mark. Aaron knew the gunfire came from the rear and quickly planned to get out of the cruiser and move to the front of it to use the engine as cover. She unlatched the passenger door, threw it open, and held it open with her foot. A fourth shot hit the passenger door and shattered the door window. She pulled her foot back into the cruiser, expecting more incoming rounds. But silence took over the ambush.

Aaron inched up to look over the top of the seat. She saw nothing. Traffic on SR-77 was in motion, and there were no signs it was interrupted by a stopped vehicle, the obvious means to conceal a shooter. She quickly looked left and right and saw nothing. She turned to check the front of the cruiser and observed nothing.

Aaron reached to her right side to draw her duty weapon and remembered she didn't have it because it was not among her personal things at the hospital. Aaron reached to Sonny and checked his still warm body for any off-duty weapons. She found two and pulled them both off his lifeless body. One was his 9-mm duty weapon and the other a backup Chief Special five-shot .38 caliber.

Aaron adjusted her grips on Sonny's guns, the semi-automatic duty weapon in her dominant hand, and the double action five-shot revolver in her other hand. She kicked the passenger door open, held it open with her foot, and slid out of the cruiser. She moved to the front, took cover behind the engine, and searched straight ahead for any threats. Nothing. She scanned from left to right, 180 degrees and checked to the rear. Nothing.

Aaron took a deep breath and raised herself up. She turned to the White Star building and ran past it. She ran left and continued to run down the alley with a gun in each hand.

CHAPTER *44*

Joseph finished reviewing the files. He texted Rosie and began to settle in to wait for her reply when the office door immediately opened.

"All done?" asked Rosie.

"Yes," responded Joseph.

"Any questions for me?"

"No, not now. I want to absorb the information and think about it."

"Okay. Let's go then."

"Go where?" asked Joseph.

"We need to get back to PCB," said Rosie.

"How are we going to do that?"

"I have a car."

Rosie turned and walked out of the room. Joseph collected his things and followed. As they walked, Rosie checked her phone.

"The SAIC wants to see us before we head back. We must meet him in the briefing room. Come on."

Joseph did not say anything, he just followed Rosie to the briefing room and then inside. Rosie picked a seat, and Joseph sat in the chair next to her. SAIC Coppola and two others were already seated.

SAIC Coppola began, "I'm glad I caught you two before you started back to PCB. Intelligence has information they thought you should have before arriving back there."

SAIC Coppola looked from one to the other of the two analysts and said, "Please begin."

The first analyst said, "Joseph, we know you are working with the BCSO and their detective, Aaron Presley, and their intelligence analyst, Harry Harper. We also know Harry Harper was murdered in a shoot-out at the St. Andrews Marina, but Presley escaped injuries. That was two weeks ago. We have confirmed a second shoot-out in which Presley escaped injuries, but the person she was with was murdered."

The second analyst explained, "It is my job to monitor the violent criminal activity in the area that an undercover operative is working. When possible and practical, I gather any surveillance video to analyze for the agent's safety. I then brief the undercover operative on any potential hazards to their safety."

Joseph replied, "Hmm."

After a brief pause, the second analyst continued, "Please watch this footage of a second shoot-out. It is from a surveillance camera at the White Star Coffee Company in Lynn Haven."

The group directed their attention to the monitor as the footage began to play.

The second analyst narrated the events as they displayed on the monitor.

"Presley and Patrol Deputy Sonny Rayes are together. Rayes is the driver. See, they're pulling into the parking lot. They park and stay in the car. Watch closely now. Did you see the windshield explode? That is shot number two. Shot number three hits the cruiser's loudspeaker in the roof light bar. We believe the first shot hit Deputy Rayes. If you look closely, there appears to be blood on the windshield on the driver's side. And a fourth and final shot hit the passenger side window as Presley exits the cruiser. But continue to watch."

They watched Presley, in a second attempt, make her way out of the car, to the front and then as she ran toward the coffee shop and then to the alley before she disappeared from the footage.

In unison, Rosie and Joseph said, "Okay. So?"

"So," said the first analyst. "That is the second shootout in two weeks in which Presley was involved and survived with no injuries, not even a scratch."

"Okay," mumbled Rosie.

"Rosie," said both analysts in unison. "Do you know the odds of surviving two shoot-outs in two weeks?"

The first analyst continued, "We don't either, and we don't have time to calculate such statistics now. What we do know and is well documented from research at the FBI Training Division in Quantico is if the shooter wanted to kill Presley, she would be dead. The shooter allows Presley to live in both shoot-outs."

"Do you know it's the same shooter in both shoot-outs?" asked Joseph.

"No, we don't know that. We're not saying that. Again, we are saying whoever the shooter or shooters, they let Presley live. Do you want to see the footage again? She is running away. The shooter is behind her and has a kill shot, but the shooter doesn't take it. The shooter doesn't take the kill shot after hitting the siren speaker on top the cruiser and by reasonable assumption Deputy Rayes. A shot that I could make, but the shooter lets her live. Why?"

The room went silent until SAIC Coppola contributed,

"You all are going to have to be careful. Joseph, you must assume they know you are working with Presley, your meeting with her at that very coffee shop. Rosie, you are associated with Joseph from here in New Orleans. I think the crazy gay grill owner is involved in all we are investigating. And you two were out and about together in PCB. And the worst of it, Jack Prat knows you two are linked."

The first analyst interrupted, "I must add to remind us that Sid is missing. Joseph, your own agency associate, your undercover handler, is missing. He too was in meetings with Presley at the same coffee shop."

The second analyst continued, "The four of you in meetings at that coffee shop. Now Harry Harper is dead, Deputy Rayes is dead, and Sid is missing, but Presley is alive after two shootouts."

"Is there any information Presley is a dirty cop like Boudar?" questioned Rosie.

"No, Rosie. We have no information to confirm or deny that. You both need to keep your guard up," said SAIC Coppola. "I'm glad you two are working together now. You will be able to watch each other's back. You two need to stay close to each other."

"Do we know why Presley and Rayes were at the coffee shop?"

"No, Joseph. We don't," answered SAIC Coppola.

"I need to get with Presley," said Joseph. "I need to talk to her or maybe interrogate her. I need answers."

"Be careful. Just be careful," replied SAIC Coppola, who continued, "Please take Rosie with you for officer safety. That isn't an agency power play. I don't play those silly games. We are working as a team here, and officer safety is paramount. If it becomes too dangerous, I'll pull both of you off the case. Understand?"

"Yes, sir," sounded Rosie.

"Yes," Joseph added.

Joseph pulled his cellphone from his pocket and studied the screen.

SAIC Coppola asked, "Do you have to take the call, Joseph?"

"It's a text."

"Okay, reply. I understand."

"It's from Presley."

An eerie silence took the room, and Joseph began to tap out a reply. Finished, he looked from one person to the next and then spoke,

"I need to go. I need to go right now. Presley needs my help, and she sounds desperate, scared, and alone."

SAIC Coppola picked up his cellphone, dialed a number and placed the phone to his ear. Then he said to the group,

"Rosie, you and Joseph get out to the landing zone and take the bureau helicopter into Tyndall Airforce Base. Take the SUV out of the hangar and use it."

SAIC Coppola looked to Joseph and continued,

"You look concerned, and that's the fastest I can get you there. This is an officer safety issue. You two get there and get her out. Rosie, if you need support, call me; you both hear me. If you need any support, call me. I'm getting concerned about the lawlessness in that county. That place needs to be cleaned up too; it seems as corrupt as New Orleans."

CHAPTER 45

"No. No. You don't have to do this. I'll give you everything. I don't want anything. Don't shoot me."

"Oh. Now you say you don't want anything. After five years. You say that because I'm going to shoot you. You say you don't want anything. Hmm."

"Come on, man. You don't need to kill us," added Jack.

"You, Jack, you shut up. You're just a piece of shit. A homewrecking piece of shit. You want her, you pursue a married woman. Well, now you have the problems of a married woman. Okay, Jackety-Jack Ass."

Gheorghi cocked his leg and kicked sand into Jack's face. Then, in control and comfortable, he pointed the gun at Jack and then back to Sandy.

"You think there is money in the account? We used it. You know that, Rezza. Or should I say, Sandy."

Gheorghi paused a moment.

"Then you say your lawyer this, your lawyer that. You blame everything on your lawyer, but it's you. You are the one that thinks there is all this money somewhere. You think I'm hiding money from you. Squandering it. You know every move I make with the money. Your signature is on the papers as is mine. Did those drugs take your memory away? You say you don't use the drugs, but you do."

"What drugs?" sounded Sandy.

"The drugs you take. Look at yourself. You look like a crack head. You look disgusting."

Gheorghi paused to hold back more of his emotions, but he was not successful. He continued,

"And in court, you didn't even remember the date we married. How pathetic."

"I don't use drugs," sounded Rezza.

"What else would you say? Nothing is your fault. After all, your attorney writes in court documents that I *dissipated the funds*. You let your attorney make me out to be some type of scofflaw. Me. A scofflaw."

"I didn't do that. That was the attorney's idea. Part of her strategy to …"

Gheorghi cut Nerezza off to continue his commentary.

"That's right, part of your attorney's strategy to get money from me. Money that's not there. Money that will put me in debt for years. You even want me to pay your attorney's fees. You think it's right for me to pay for both attorneys? Where am I going to get that kind of money? Where is an aged white male, in his late fifties, with a bad back and limp going to get a job? You don't even leave me enough to live on. I don't even have enough to rent a place to live. But you, you and Jack, have everything. An apartment. A truck that is paid for. You two have everything living together."

"Okay. Okay. I'll talk to my attorney. I'll get this straightened out. I'll take care of it."

"You won't do shit. You just play people for what you can get out of them. Hell, you're playing Jack."

Gheorghi, with confidence, moved the gun with him as he turned to Jack.

"You don't see that, Jackety-Jack Ass?"

Gheorghi's attention and his gun quickly went back to Sandy when she spoke,

"I'm not playing anyone. Just don't shoot me."

"But it's okay if I shoot Jack? Why don't you plead for him?"

Still looking at Sandy, Gheorghi continued,

"Did you hear that, Jack? Your Sandy only asks that I not shoot her. She isn't worried about you."

Gheorghi stopped talking. In slow motion, he raised his gun with a two-handed grip, pushed it out at chest height, and raised it to eye level. He located the sights and aligned the rear with the front positioning them with equal distance on each side and the top level with each other. Blurred were the rear sights and Sandy's forehead, but the front sight was in focus. With the proper sight alignment, Gheorghi placed a steady squeeze on the trigger, and the surprise shot hit its mark, the center of Sandy's forehead. Instantly, her face started to morph from age to youth. Sandy recoiled backward and then fell back and came to rest in the sand. Her face finished morphing to the youthful look of when they married. She lay lifeless with her eyes wide-open as blood escaped from the bullet hole and ran down her forehead.

The slide locked back when the magazine loaded with the lone bullet went dry. Gheorghi ejected the empty magazine and reloaded a thirty-round magazine. He depressed the slide release, and with the sound of metal on metal, the slide slid forward and charged the weapon. Again, in slow motion, Gheorghi raised his gun with a two-hand grip, sighted in on Jack and commenced a volley of rounds that left Jack horizontal, eyes wide-open and lifeless in the sand next to the Petitioner. He pointed the gun in the direction of the Petitioner and fired the gun until it ran dry. All the rounds hit their mark, center mass.

Gheorghi scanned the area and saw no witnesses. He then directed his attention to something shiny in the sand. He moved to it and knelt beside it. Gheorghi's inspection disclosed the bright object was the casing inscribed *Petitioner*.

Gheorghi raised his head and squinted his eyes as they adjusted to the bright sunlight. His entire body was flexed as he held his head up to see what caused the noise that

woke him from an afternoon nap on the beach and yet
another dream of the cohabitants. With his eyes adjusting,
he opened them a little wider to discern the object making
the sound in the sky. He saw a helicopter flying low over
the water and near the shoreline. Gheorghi looked hard but
saw no markings on the aircraft.

Gheorghi thought, *No markings, that's unusual. Must be
some type of military helicopter. Probably on an exercise
mission out of Tyndall or the naval base.*

Gheorghi lay back down to continue to sun himself as he
rolled the inscribed 9-mm round between his fingers to
relax. The more Gheorghi rubbed his thumb over the
inscription *Petitioner*, the more he relaxed.

CHAPTER *46*

The unmarked FBI helicopter flew low over the Gulf of Mexico and along the Emerald Coast of Northwest Florida. The occupants – the pilot, copilot, Rosie, and Joseph were en route to extract Detective Presley from Bay County.

To break the stress of the event, Joseph asked Rosie, "What's your real name?"

Rosie was looking out the window to the horizon of the Gulf of Mexico. She continued her gaze as she repeated the question.

"What's my real name?"

"Yes, your real name. I assume Rosie is your fictitious undercover name."

"Ruža."

"Ruža," repeated Joseph.

Rosie looked at Joseph but said nothing. Joseph continued,

"Czech meaning Rose when translated into English."

"Yes," said Rosie. "Very good. Are you fluent in Czech or just given names?"

"Plynně," replied Joseph.

"I'm not. I never took the time to learn. I regret that. And I use Rosie for my undercover name because it was a childhood nickname. Superstitious or a luck thing, depending on how you look at it."

"Hmm. From your father?"

"Oh, no. My father named me Ruža, and he called me Ruža. My two brothers, they teased me with the name Rosie because they thought I was Father's favorite."

"Were you?"

"I don't know."

"You were. You were daddy's little girl."

Rosie smiled broadly and turned her focus back out the window to the Gulf of Mexico. Joseph thought she was silent and in thought, preparing for a two-person tactical operation and said nothing more. He hoped he calmed her a bit as the personal bandy calmed him.

Still looking out the window, Rosie said,

"What's our plan?"

"To get her out."

Rosie slowly rotated her head and looked at Joseph.

"Get her out. That's the plan? That's the details of your plan?"

Rosie paused, but Joseph did not say anything realizing how pathetic that sounded.

"Does OIG have a nearby safe house for you that we could use?" asked Rosie.

"A safe house? No. We're not one of the top five federal law enforcement agencies. We're not the FBI. OIG's budget doesn't have money for that level of undercover support."

"Then where are we going to take Presley? We can't use her house. We can't take her to a sheriff's office facility. Nor any county law enforcement facilities. At this point, all county law enforcement is suspect, all county emergency services for that matter."

"We'll take her back to the hangar at Tyndall."

Rosie, with a bit of sarcasm, replied, "Oh. That's good. Quick thinking, Joey Chen. Nice recovery."

Rosie displayed a half-smile to Joseph and then continued, "Where is Presley now? Where are we going to pick her up?"

The helicopter's flight path took them over St. Andrew Bay. Joseph looked out his window and saw the St. Andrew's Marina, the place of the first ambush Presley survived, and the place Harry Harper was murdered. This conjured thought in Joseph's mind as he stared out the window and watched the ground and the objects move under him.

"Joey. Joey, did you hear me?"

"What did you say, Rosie?"

Rosie repeated herself.

"Where is Presley now? Where are we going to pick her up at?"

Joseph slid his cellphone out of his pocket. He tapped on the screen and looked at it. Immediately, his phone sounded. He stared at the screen and said,

"She's near the old airport. Tell the pilot to take us there. We don't have time to get the car."

Rosie instructed the pilot, and the helicopter banked left and continued to the new location.

"She's hiding on a boat, in a parking lot to a closed boat service company along 390. I know the place. We can set down in the field adjacent to the parking lot."

Rosie relayed the information to the pilot, and Joseph texted Presley with the extraction plan and that she needed to reposition herself to the field for a touch-and-go pick up.

The helicopter started to descend at the same time the pilot communicated he was maneuvering for the pickup. Joseph looked out the window and saw Presley below moving about from one point of concealment to another to get as close to where she estimated the pick up would be.

Rosie undid her seat belts, reached below her seat, opened the cover to a storage compartment, and pulled out an FN P90. She visually checked the readiness of the weapon, pulled back the slide, and charged it.

Joseph undid his seat belts, drew his duty weapon, and inspected its readiness for defense.

The helicopter landed, and Rosie, with the P90 in a low ready position, moved out first. When she was balanced on the ground, she raised her weapon to her shoulder and was prepared to provide cover fire for Joseph and Presley. Joseph followed with his Glock Model 19 9-mm.

Rosie scanned the area for threats as she looked down the sights of the P90. When Presley went by Rosie, Rosie shuffle-stepped to the rear to follow as she continued to scan the area for threats. Joseph took hold of Presley's upper arm and escorted her to the helicopter door and assisted her entry, then entered himself. Rosie made one last scan, lowered her gun, turned, and climbed in. Joseph reached to the door and closed it while Rosie settled in for takeoff.

The pilot operated the machine into a smooth rise. He hovered for a moment and turned the helicopter 180 degrees and accelerated east toward Tyndall Airforce Base.

Arrival at the base was quick, smooth, and without obstructions. When the helicopter settled, the three passengers got out and went into the hangar.

Joseph's telephone rang. He looked and saw it was Jack Prat.

"Who is it?" asked Rosie.

"Prat," replied Joseph.

"Are you going to answer?"

"I have to."

Joseph pressed the answer button and announced,

"You piece of shit, Jack."

"Now, now, Joey. Where are you?" responded Jack.

"Where am I? I'm where you left me. How am I getting back to PCB?"

"Joey, you're not where I left you, I'm there, and I don't see you."

"Kiss my ass, Jack. I have to go."

"Go. Where are you going to? You don't want to make money? I need your help with another shipment coming tomorrow."

"I'll think about it and get back to you. You don't need my money anymore."

"Why is there an echo? Where are you, Joey?"

"Echo. There's going to be an echo in your head the next time I see you. I'll talk to you later."

Joseph hung up.

"What was that about?" asked Rosie.

"Jack. It was from Jack. He was planning to receive another shipment tomorrow, and he wanted me to help him."

"What are you going to do?" inquired Presley.

"I have to go. We need to document another shipment coming in. Federal prosecutors like three transactions when and if they have to try a case at trial. I also need more samples of feathers," replied Joseph.

The three looked at each other in silence, and Aaron stopped and stared at Rosie. Joseph broke the silence.

"Aaron, this is Rosie. Rosie, Aaron Presley, detective, BCSO. Rosie is with the FBI, currently assigned to the National JTTF, out of New Orleans."

Rosie and Aaron greeted each other with a professional handshake.

"How are you, Aaron?" asked Joseph.

"I don't know, Joseph," replied Aaron. "I don't know what is going on around me anymore. I'm plucked out of a boat storage yard by an unmarked helicopter, which I'm guessing is an FBI helicopter, and we fly to a hangar on Tyndall."

"Two shoot-outs in two weeks. And you're still here with us. I can only imagine," added Rosie with more suspicion than concern in her voice.

"I know. I know. And my only case is a missing person case. A missing person case is causing all the mayhem around me. Two people dead in what appears to be targeted assassinations. Two people are targeted because of their association with me."

"It seems that way," added Rosie, again with a tone of suspicion.

"Only Harry Harper was working on the case with me, so why Sonny? Dear Sonny, only provided information local to his patrol area."

"Joseph, where are you taking her?" asked Rosie.

"I don't know."

Joseph paused, then quickly decided.

"My place. Let's all just go to my place. At least we will all be together to watch each other's backs."

The three slid into the specially equipped SUV. Aaron the rear passenger, Joseph the front passenger, and Rosie, the driver. Rosie maneuvered the SUV out of the hangar, down the tarmac, and to the security gate. Cleared of westbound traffic, Rosie turned right onto SR 98 and continued west.

CHAPTER 47

"Wait here, I'll be right back," said Gheorghi.

Petar was agitated by not knowing what Gheorghi was going to do, he said, "No. Stay here. Don't do anything; you're too close to it being over. Just stay here."

"Yeah. Be better than her. Just ignore them," added Penka.

"See, this is why I didn't stay in Bay County," said Gheorghi. "I didn't want to run into her."

Penka encouraged, "Just ignore her, Gheorghi."

"No. I had enough of Nerezza's control. I had enough of it all. I'm going to end this now. Just watch," replied Gheorghi. "She thinks she's all that. And look at him. He has to go too."

"What are you going to do," asked Petar still agitated from the uncertainty of Gheorghi's actions. "What are you going to do here in the restaurant?"

"You just watch," sounded Gheorghi. "I'll be right back."

Gheorghi stood and walked away from the table and out the front door. He walked to his car, opened the trunk, and rummaged through the contents. He pulled out his gun, released the magazine, checked to ensure it had the lone bullet, and slammed the magazine back in. He worked the slide and chambered the single cartridge marked for the task and stuck the gun into his waistband. He searched more and retrieved two more magazines filled with thirty rounds each. He closed the hatch and walked off as he slid the fully loaded magazines into his left rear pants pocket.

Gheorghi, as he walked back inside the restaurant, contemplated,

This must be done. This needs to end, today. Enough of her procrastination. Her control. And should I take him out too? Why not, he doesn't deserve to live either. He's a homewrecker. They want to be together; they can go together.

Six feet from the target's table, Gheorghi reached under his shirt to his waistband, fixed his grip on his gun, and drew it. He quickly hid the gun alongside his right thigh.

Gheorghi walked five more feet to the cohabitants' table and stopped. He stared first at her, then at him. He looked back at her, raised his gun with one hand, and fired the lone bullet. The bullet hit its mark, the center of the Petitioner's forehead. She rocketed backward as her skull and brain matter expanded out the rear of her head and onto the customers at the nearby tables and onto the floor. She came to rest sitting straight up, eyes wide-open, and jaw slightly lowered.

Gheorghi adjusted his gun left and with one hand, held it on the second target. He looked down the sights and saw the homewrecker shaking. The foul smell of feces permeated from the cohabitant whose eyes were wide-open. He too sat straight up and motionless. He tried to speak, but no words came out. Gheorghi squeezed the trigger, and the gun sounded click. Gheorghi lowered the firearm and laughed at the homewrecker as he balled up and begged for his life.

Gheorghi ejected the empty magazine, withdrew one from his rear pocket that was fully loaded, slammed it into the magazine receiver, and released the slide lock. The slide slammed forward and chambered a bullet. All this activity kept the crybaby cohabitant balled up in his chair as he bespoke for his life.

Gheorghi said nothing in reply to the homewrecker but smiled as he continued to execute his mission. He raised his gun and pushed it in the direction of the crying cohabitant who continued to plead for his life. Gheorghi ignored the sobbing pleas and calmly squeezed the trigger until a surprise shot sounded and the bullet hit its mark. Gheorghi continued to pull the trigger twenty-nine more times until the slide locked back and signaled the weapon was dry. All thirty shots hit the homewrecking cohabitant. Somewhere between the eighteenth and twenty-first shots, the bullet-ridden cohabitant fell backward in his chair and lay lifeless on the floor of the restaurant next to his cult lover.

Gheorghi raised his focus from the targets and scanned the restaurant in a 360-degree pan. He saw no threats; all the patrons were stunned by the completed task. Gheorghi calmly ejected the empty magazine and caught it in his hand and slid it into his pocket. From his rear pocket, he retrieved the other fully loaded magazine and slammed it into his gun. He worked the receiver, and it slung forward and charged the weapon.

Gheorghi, with his fully loaded and charged gun, looked one last time at his completed task. The lone nickel-coated casing, from the lone bullet, lay on the tablecloth. The glow of the candle illuminated the word *Petitioner* inscribed on the casing. The Petitioner's face had morphed from her present aged looks to her past youthful looks when first married. The bullet hole and blood remained.

He tactically shuffle-stepped closer, reached with his left hand and opened the Petitioner's purse. The Respondent was looking for a small voodoo doll. Gheorghi pulled out a baggie of drugs and threw them onto the Petitioner's plate. He searched the bag further and retracted his hand that held a doll. He took the doll with him as he limped and pulled his right leg making his way back to his table.

Gheorghi sat down and laid his gun on the table to his right. To his left, he put the doll. With both hands on the table, he expanded a deep breath and announced,

"I feel much better now. See, what did I tell you? The doll, see where the pins are."

Gheorghi pointed to a pin in the right leg of the doll and another in the lower back. He pulled out the pin from the right leg, and immediately, the pain in his right leg went away. He pulled the pin out of the doll's lower back, and his lower back pain ceased. He threw the stuffed toy down on the table, stood up and said to Petar and Penka,

"Now watch me walk."

Gheorghi walked around the table once. A second time, quicker. And a third time, even faster. He reached out and took hold of his brother's hands. He raised his still shocked brother up and started to dance around the table with him. He released his brother who immediately sat down as Gheorghi made his way back to his seat and sat.

"Did you all see? Did you see my movements were no longer restricted?"

Petar and Penka, still in shock from the unrestrained double homicide their little brother/brother-in-law just committed in front of a restaurant full of witnesses, nodded their heads yes. They both saw when Gheorghi took the pins out of the doll, the spell was gone, and he moved carefree, which also added to Petar's and Penka's state of shock.

Gheorghi said, "Oh, excuse me. How rude of me. I'm sorry I put my gun on the table."

Gheorghi reached for the gun and removed it from the table. He placed it into his waistband. Out of the corner of his eye, he noticed someone seated in the fourth chair at the table. Spooked, he jerked his head left and saw Angel.

Angel slowly said, "Gheorghi. Gheorghi."

She paused a moment while she gazed deep into Gheorghi's bright blue eyes.

Angel continued, "Why did you do that? You didn't have to do that. Why didn't you call me? I told you I would be there for you if you let me. Why didn't you let me help you?"

Sweating profusely and groggy from being woken from a nap on the beach, he looked around to determine where he was and slowly remembered he went to the sugar-white sand beach of PCB to sun himself. He fumbled the phone to see the message, a text from Petar. It was an invitation to dinner; to join them at a local upscale restaurant across the bridge.

The invitation to dinner took Gheorghi to a remembrance of a dream. Gheorghi sat in the sand and recalled a part of one of the dreams with Angel. He remembered the part where he and Angel were dining on Angel's parents' yacht in the middle of the Caribbean after watching the sunset and then dancing to "Morning" by Poncho Sanchez and His Latin Jazz Band, the live version. Gheorghi knew it was just a fantasy, but it comforted him.

Gheorghi, forced to be the Respondent, thought to himself,

A dream. Another dream. It was only a dream, but what if it really happened like in the dream? What if the Petitioner is found dead? Motorman might just do it. He's crazy enough to do it. Did he? Are these prophetic dreams?

CHAPTER 48

Joey, Rosie, and Aaron arrived at Joey's apartment on the beach. All three had a long, sleepless night.

"I just called Prat. Everything is set for the shipment. I'm to meet him at the state park at noon."

"Are you going alone, Joey?" asked Aaron.

"Yes. I don't see any other option."

"What if I go with you?" said Rosie.

"I don't know," replied Joey. "I think you should stay here with Aaron. I'll be fine."

"No one has to stay with me. I appreciate all the help, but no one has to babysit me," said Aaron with the tone of a macho law enforcement officer.

"This isn't babysitting, Aaron. This is officer safety," replied Joey.

"Who's going to back you up for officer's safety, Joey?" asked Rosie.

"I'll be fine," replied Joey.

"How are you going to stay alert with no sleep all night," asked Rosie.

"Maybe all three of us should go?" added Aaron.

"Aaron, how are we going to do that?" responded Joey with a quizzical tone.

"Wait. That won't work. Prat knows me. He knows I'm a detective. We have talked a few times," said Aaron. "We can't risk Prat questioning me and then Joey."

"Okay. I'll go by myself. You two stay here. That's all we have to play. If nothing stupid happens like last time, I'll be back by nine. I have to go."

"You be careful, Joey," said Rosie. "Make sure you're back by nine."

Aaron said, "See you at nine, Joey."

Joey checked himself to make sure he had the necessary equipment and notably the microtape recorder. He checked to make sure the black electrical tape was tight over the red recording light, so it didn't shine through his clothing. Joey first looked to Aaron and then to Rosie, holding his look on Rosie longer. Then he walked out the door.

As soon as the door closed behind Joey, Aaron asked, "Rosie, what's with you and Joey?"

"Nothing. What do you mean? Why do you ask?" replied Rosie.

"To get a response like you just gave, I have my answer. So, you're hot on Joey? Cool. That's cool."

"I don't know what you're talking about."

"Yeah. That's the other typical response when someone is interested in someone, but they don't know if the person is interested in them."

There was brief silence before Aaron sounded,

"I'll ask him when he gets back. I'll ask him for you?"

"No. Don't do that. Just leave it be."

Aaron laughed and then continued,

"I'm just joking with you. I'm just trying to break the worry. But that is the third response that announces someone's romantic interest in a person."

Aaron continued to laugh, and Rosie joined in.

As their laughter slowed, Rosie asked, "Would you like some coffee?"

"No, I need something stronger than that. Is there any whiskey?" replied Aaron.

"I don't know. This is my first time here. I'll look."

Aaron went into the living room and sat on a chair. She looked around the apartment and observed it was sparsely decorated. Though she didn't expect much for an undercover apartment. It had two bedrooms. One of the bedroom doors was slightly opened, and when Aaron looked carefully, she saw someone lying in bed. She realized no one conducted a security sweep of the apartment in the haste of Joseph leaving to meet Prat.

The sight startled her, but Aaron quickly composed herself, rose from the chair, and walked back into the kitchen. When Aaron put her arm around Rosie, Rosie jumped away.

Aaron drew back and said, "There's a man in the back bedroom, laying on the bed."

Rosie moved to the kitchen table, picked up the P90, and said, "Let's go."

She raised it to her shoulder, locked it in, and looked down the gun as she shuffle-stepped to advance on the bedroom.

Aaron drew Sonny's duty weapon and tactically followed Rosie to the bedroom door.

At the door, both on the same side of the doorjamb, Rosie positioned herself standing and motioned for Aaron to go low. When they were both positioned, Aaron pushed the door open, and Rosie shouted,

"Hands. Let me see your hands."

Nothing. There was no answer to the command to control the unknown individual. The man did not move or reply.

Rosie shouted a second time, "Hands. Let me see your hands."

Again, nothing. The man did not move or say anything.

Rosie motioned for Aaron to advance on the man. In a crouched position, Aaron moved forward. When she reached the foot of the bed, she popped up and grabbed the man's legs and pulled him halfway off the bed, dropped his legs, and retreated to concealment on the right side of the doorjamb.

From there, Aaron studied the man and exclaimed, "That's Sid. That's Sid."

Rosie, at the same time, exclaimed, "Sid. No. Oh, my God. Sid."

Rosie looked at Aaron and asked, "How do you know Sid?"

"He's Joey's handler. He also works for USDA's OIG," answered Aaron.

They both looked back at the man. With the man twisted a little, they saw he had three bullet wounds to the chest and one to the head.

Rosie shuffle-stepped to Sid, reached out her hand and checked for a pulse. She did not feel a pulse and declared, "Sid's dead."

"Do you know Sid too?" asked Aaron.

"Yes. Sid and I were in the same mixed Criminal Investigative Training Program at the Federal Law

Enforcement Training Center. I was from Customs and Sid was from OIG Agriculture. He stayed with the IG, and I moved from Customs to the FBI."

"Now what do we do?" asked Aaron.

"He's dead. Let's move into the room and think this through."

Rosie led the way to two chairs. She sat on one and Aaron sat on the other.

Aaron immediately began, "Rosie, I must tell you something. I must explain the events of two days ago."

Rosie said nothing, and her professional experiences blocked any emotions. She just listened.

"Two days ago, Sid called me and asked me to meet him at the White Star in Lynn Haven. When he arrived, he was in a hurry, and he instructed me to get into his car. He had a FISA warrant for Harper's office at the county emergency center. We went to Harper's office and found it had been searched, and the duty deputy was murdered and placed in Harper's office."

"Why didn't you report the murder?" asked Rosie.

"Sid said we couldn't because that would compromise the use of a FISA warrant and all the secrecy of the warrant. And I assumed the secrecy was paramount to his, to Joey's case and undercover safety. When we were walking out of the last placed we searched, Sid was hit on the head first, and when I went to his aid, I was hit on the head too. I woke up in the hospital, and Boudar was in my room. The next day Sonny took me out. We were starting to retrace the events when Sonny was murdered."

"Okay," said Rosie. "We saw the rest captured by a White Star security camera. That is why we came to get you out. But you know, I'm concerned here. Every time you're with someone, that someone gets killed."

"That's not funny, Rosie."

"I don't say it as a joke. I think someone is playing with you."

"What do you mean?"

"I saw the video footage from White Star. As one of our analysts said, I could have shot and killed you when you ran across the parking lot to the alley."

"Hmm."

"But a shot wasn't even taken."

There was a brief silence before Rosie continued,

"Why did you wake up in the hospital, but Sid was missing until tonight?"

"I don't know," answered Aaron.

"Why didn't you disappear?" asked Rosie.

Again, Aaron answered, "I don't know."

"See, it looks like someone is playing with you. Like they could kill you whenever they want to, but they don't."

"I see. Yes, I see what you mean."

"Who is this Boudar?"

"He's the BCSO commander of the CID. My supervisor. The father of my adult son."

"What? You and Boudar had an affair?"

"No. It's a long story. The short version, Boudar and I were romantically involved in high school. For ten years or so, we lived together. He could not commit to me; you know how some men are. Our relationship produced one child."

Rosie gave the impression she was not listening to Aaron when she commanded Aaron,

"Help me. Help me move Sid back to where he was."

"Why?"

"I'm going to take a picture of him and send it to Boudar and the sheriff."

"They'll trace your phone."

"Not this throwaway phone. Not my undercover phone."

The FBI agent and the BCSO detective positioned Sid back to his original position. Rosie took a picture and typed a message to send with it.

HI THERE. I WAS BURGLARIZING THIS PLACE, AND TO MY SURPRISE I FOUND THIS MAN DEAD IN BED WITH FOUR BULLET HOLES. HE DOESN'T LIVE HERE AS BOUDAR KNOWS. SHERIFF, YOU HAVE A PROBLEM IN YOUR DEPARTMENT. I HOPE YOU'RE NOT INVOLVED. I VOTED FOR YOU. SINCERELY, A CONCERNED CITIZEN OF BAY COUNTY.

"Look, how does this sound?"

Aaron read the message and commented, "Good. But are local police going to set up Joey for this?"

"No. Joey has a gay grill owner and me as an alibi. If they don't believe me, they will believe the gay guy. Who's going to risk a backlash from the gay community? Sometimes, a straight white male has to make political correctness work in his favor."

Rosie mashed the send button, and her cellphone sounded confirmation the email was sent correctly.

"Let's get out of here."

"What about Sid?"

"What about the deputy at the emergency command center?" answered Rosie.

"I see," said Aaron. "Let's go. But where are we going?"

"I don't know; it'll come to us as we go."

CHAPTER 49

Joey peddled past the park entrance and continued the park roads to the parking lot and then to his truck. As he was loading the bicycle into the back of his pickup, Jack pulled up.

"What are you doing with the bicycle, Joey?"

"The last time we did this, I left my truck here and went with you. Then we ended up in New Orleans in your truck. You left my ass stranded in New Orleans; you piece of shit."

Joey slammed his tailgate shut.

"Now I'm going to punch you in the head, asshole."

Joey walked up to the driver side window, and Jack sat in the driver's seat, laughing. Joey punched him in the head.

"Hey. Ouch. Come on. You can't take a joke?"

"A joke."

Joey punched Jack in the head again then sounded,

"No. I guess I can't take a joke."

Joey hit Jack a third time.

"You're an ass, Joey. That really hurt."

Joey said, "You're nothing but a baby. A piece of shit. You're not even man enough to keep a woman. Did you find Sandy yet?"

Jack said nothing.

"I didn't think so," continued Joey. "But you left me in New Orleans because the grill owner said he saw Sandy."

Jack continued his silence.

Joey went on with his rant, "Sandy was there, and that's why you left me at the grill. Sandy was in New Orleans, and you didn't want anyone to know."

Jack finally broke his silence and replied in a defensive tone, "You don't know what you're talking about."

"Oh yes, I do," argued Joey. "Why don't you want anyone to know where Sandy's at? And you don't want her back in Bay County, do you?"

"Are we going to make the pickup or not?"

"I don't know, Jack. Are we?"

"Get in."

"I don't know that I want to."

"You don't want to make money?"

"I have enough money, and this is small stuff compared to what I usually do."

"Come on, get in. I'm sorry about New Orleans. I'll explain it to you when I can, just not right now. We have business to take care of, and we can't be late."

Joey walked around the back of the white Tundra to the front passenger door, opened it, and got in. He shut the door and turned to Jack to find Jack had a gun pointed at him.

"Really, Jack. Are you going to use that thing?" asked Joey.

"Maybe. You hit me three times. It hurts."

"Asshole put the gun away and drive. You don't want to be late, do you?"

"There's something about you, Joey. You're a likable guy. You're cool. Your style, I like your style, Joey. Let's go."

Jack reached down and put the gun in a holster that was attached low on the driver side console hub.

"Yeah, drive asshole. Where're we going this time?"

"Same place for the pickup."

After Jack eased away from the boat launch parking lot in the state park, he drove in the direction of the front gate.

"Now where are we going for the delivery?"

"We aren't going anywhere. I'm taking you back to your truck."

Jack turned left shortly before the main park entrance and continued to the parking lot. At Joey's truck, Jack stopped and placed the gear selector in Park. He reached under his seat, which made Joey nervous, and Joey gripped his undercover gun and readied himself to draw down on Jack if he came up with a gun again. Jack only came up with a white envelope retrieved from under the driver's seat. He threw it at Joey who caught it with his gun hand and said,

"What's this?"

"Your payment. It's only half the amount of last time. You only do half the work; you only get half the pay. Fair, right?"

"Whatever. This is the last time I'm going to help you, anyway. There's too much drama with you."

"We'll see. I hope you don't have any pain tomorrow or the next day."

"What do you mean pain?"

"You'll see. Sandy will send a sample your way. A sample of what will happen if you don't do what I say."

"What did you say? Did you say, Sandy? You know where she is at?"

"Joey, you're mine now. I have enough information to turn you into Five-O. Sure, false information. But Five-O will believe it. They aren't the sharpest tacks in the box here in Bay County."

"What are you talking about?"

"Get out, Joey. I'll call you when I need you. Make sure you answer by three rings."

"What did you say about Sandy?" demanded Joey. "Did you say Sandy will do something to me? So, you know where Sandy is, you know how to contact her?"

Bluntly, Jack replied, "I didn't say anything about Sandy. Get out."

Joey was taken aback. He slid out of the truck, and Jack drove off in a high rate of acceleration. Joey moved to his truck, entered, and sat thinking about what he should do. He finally drove off, still thinking puzzling questions.

Is Sandy alive? Is Sandy in New Orleans? Why? Or is there something wrong with Prat? Perhaps a mental ailment that caused him to be flippant. Given all that had happened to Presley since she was assigned the case, is there any more concern by the BCSO about the missing person?

Joey continued to drive in the direction of his apartment to meet back up with Rosie and Aaron. As Joey drove, he concluded his thoughts,

The thing I know for sure, Sid as a missing person case is now my priority, not the BCSO case involving Sandy Diddler. I need to find Sid.

CHAPTER 50

Joey turned right onto the street that led to his apartment
building. In the distance, he saw blue flashing emergency
lights. As he got closer to the building, he saw the BCSO
deputies were focused on his apartment and were going in
and out. Two sheriff's office crime scene investigation
trucks were parked in the parking lot. And the sheriff
himself was there, which was odd to Joey. Highly unusual
thought Joey for the top law enforcement officer of the
county to be out at night, at what appeared to be a crime
scene from all the activity. Also, odd, there was no media
presence. Joey became concerned and turned left on a cross
street and continued to drive west to avoid the police
activity.

As Joey drove, he spoke out loud to himself, "A crime at
my apartment. What is going on? What happened in my
apartment? Did some type of harm come to Rosie or
Aaron?"

The thought that it could be Rosie or Aaron, or both made
Joey restless. He retrieved his cellphone from his pocket,
searched the contacts and dialed Rosie's number. It rang
seven times, but there was no answer. Joey ended the call
and continued to drive west.

Once again, Joey spoke out loud to himself, "Is someone
setting me up? Is it Jackass Prat? Maybe it's Boudar."

About two hundred yards farther down the road, two
women jumped onto the roadway in front of Joey's truck.

Joey jammed on the brakes, and the wheels locked up and caused the tires to squeal, but he brought the truck to a stop without hitting either individual. Stopped and under control, Joey flicked the high beams on and saw Rosie and Aaron standing in front of the truck. Joey slapped the console shifter into Park, opened the driver's door, slid out, and ran up to them.

"What's going on? Why are you here? Is someone chasing you guys?" rambled Joey. "Rosie, you okay?"

"We're okay," replied Rosie. "We had to get out of your place."

"Why? I saw all the police activity at the apartment. What was going on?"

"We need to go now. Right now. I'll explain everything as you drive."

Everyone got into Joey's truck. Aaron in the right rear, Rosie in the front right, and Joey in the driver's seat. Joey drove along, and Rosie explained what happened at the apartment after Joey left to meet Prat.

"Sid! Sid's dead? No. No way," muttered Joey.

Rosie reached her hand out and placed it on Joey's shoulder.

"Yes, Joey. Sorry."

"Aaron, are you sure it was Sid? You only saw him a few times."

"Sorry, Joey. Rosie and I both identified him as Sid."

Joey did not know what that meant and looked to Rosie.

"What? What do you mean you both identified him? Rosie, how do you know Sid?"

"Sid and I were in the same Criminal Investigative Training Program at the Federal Law Enforcement Training Center. It was a mixed class. I was from Customs, and he was from OIG Agriculture. He stayed with the IG, and I moved from Customs to the FBI. We stayed in touch for a while, but not in the past few years or so. I thought he was retired."

Joey turned his attention back to the road and continued west.

"What's our plan?" asked Rosie.

Joey answered, "We have to get rid of my truck, first and fast. BCSO probably put out an all-points bulletin on it. If they know where I live; they know my vehicle. Where's the SUV from the hanger?"

"It's not available," replied Rosie quick and short.

"What do you mean not available?" queried Joey again.

There was a brief silence before Rosie said, "It's out of gas, okay. I parked it out of sight."

The three went silent until Rosie asserted, "Just get us back to the hanger. Back to the hangar, Joey. In my haste, I didn't check the gas. There's another car at the hanger."

Joey turned right and sped to the traffic control light. He braked lightly, visually cleared the intersection and without stopping, turned right onto SR 98. He accelerated the truck to expedite the travel to Tyndall.

"When we get the other car, then what?" asked Aaron.

"We need someplace to hole up and slow this whole thing down. It's starting to move too fast, and the speed is being controlled by others. That will cause mistakes. Fatal mistakes. We already lost Harry, Sonny, and Sid. We need to get someplace and slow this down. Everyone agree?" answered Joey.

"Yes, Joey," replied Rosie. "We need to slow this down and come up with a plan to finalize this investigation."

"I agree," added Aaron. "Where, though? We can't use any place within a five-county area because of the possible connivance of neighboring law enforcement agencies."

The truck went silent as Joey continued to drive east. All three law enforcement officers, each from a different law enforcement organization, each with a separate investigative mission and objective, thought of options specific to the completion of their investigation. They did not realize how they and their inquiries were entangled; how they and their investigations were entwined.

CHAPTER 51

The three law enforcement officers – Joey, Rosie, and Aaron – continued in Joey's truck. As they passed through Callaway, a ringing cellphone broke the silent thoughts of the three. All three instinctively grabbed their phones, but Joey was the only one to pull his to his ear.

"Hello," greeted Joey.

"Joey?" asked the caller.

"Yes," responded Joey.

"Where the hell is Sid?" said the caller.

"What?"

"Where is Sid? I have been trying to get a hold of him for three days. I have some interesting information to give him."

Joey moved the phone from his ear and looked at the screen. Nothing was identifying the caller. He put the phone back to his ear and stuttered a response to buy time to think about how he would reply to someone unknown to him.

"I don't know?"

"What do you mean you don't know? He's your handler. When was the last time you talked to him?"

Rosie and Aaron heard Joey's side of the conversation and were now looking at Joey. His comments puzzled them. Joey shrugged his shoulders to respond to their stares.

"What information do you have for Sid?"

"I have the results from the tests on the feathers you guys have been submitting to the lab."

Now Joey knew who he was talking to. It was Big Sam from USAMRIID.

"Oh, great. What did you find out, Sam? What were the results of the tests?"

Joey tapped his chest to get the attention of Rosie and Aaron. He motioned to them, then to his ear, then to them again, and put his phone on speaker.

"You're not going to like this," sounded Sam.

"Why?"

"You'll have to shut down your investigation, immediately. That per USDA's directives, of which I'm sure you're aware of the Animal, Plant, and Health Inspection Service directives, you the OIG's biological security program manager and all. This is some bad stuff."

"Sam, what do you have? What is it?"

"Something unusual enough to cause panic to the public if this gets out. All the agencies responsible for anti-terrorism are concerned. Really concerned."

"Joseph, this is Lenore Smith," sounded a second voice from the telephone's speaker.

"Yes, ma'am," sounded Joey as he sat up straighter in his seat, a nonverbal sign of talking to someone of authority.

"Sam is correct. All the federal agencies responsible for anti-terrorism are concerned about this. Of course, USDA leads that list since APHIS is responsible for detecting and intercepting such things. OIG is lucky you're in place, and we can say we are working on it."

"Of course," replied Joey.

"Joseph, you need to come to Washington, immediately."

"Okay."

"And don't say anything about this to anyone. Anyone. You hear me?"

"Yes, ma'am."

"I'll see you tomorrow. One o'clock. In the IG's office. Everyone will be there to debrief you."

"Debrief me? Everyone?" repeated Joey.

"Yes, we need to know what you know. We need to figure out how to handle this within the department."

"Yes," replied Joseph.

"Sam, give Joseph the highlights," instructed Lenore.

"Yes, ma'am. Joey, the chicken feathers are contaminated with psittacosis, which is also known as parrot fever or ornithosis. The latter term describes the infectious disease in chickens. Psittacosis is a term used for the condition when associated with parrots such as cockatiels, parakeets, cockatoos, macaws, and other parrots. Other birds, such as turkeys, chickens, doves, pigeons, finches, seabirds, and birds of prey can also be infected.

People can become infected when they breathe in the dust from dried bird droppings or nasal secretions. And, the contaminated dust can be stirred into the air from feathers and litter in birdcages. Within five to fourteen days after exposure, the symptoms begin, but the incubation period could be longer. The symptoms include: sudden fever, chills, headache, general discomfort, muscle pain, a dry cough usually occurs and can be followed by shortness of breath and pneumonia. Treatment requires two to three weeks of antibiotics."

"I see," replied Joey.

"So, you can see how this has the potential to be airborne," added Lenore. "Or I should say, the possibility to make this infectious disease airborne has not been ruled out."

"Yes, Lenore. I understand," answered Joey.

"We'll see you tomorrow," commanded Lenore.

"Yes, you will," agreed Joey. "Anything else for now?"

"No," sounded Lenore.

"Sam, anything else?"

"No, Joey, not for now," sounded Sam.

"Enjoy your evenings. I have a plane to catch."

Joey ended the call and gave a long sigh. He turned to Rosie and Aaron.

"I need to get to the airport."

"We'll take you," replied Aaron.

"Easy, everyone. I have to inform Leo," said Rosie.

"This is starting to get complicated," added Joey.

"Now I'm glad I'm not a federal agent," added Aaron. "Who was that?"

"That was the deputy inspector general for USDA," replied Joey.

"Oh. She sounds important."

Joey expelled a deep breath, then continued,

"She's number two in command at the OIG, and the IG assigned her as the OIG's point person for the Biological Security Program. She makes all the final decisions to combat biological events involving the agriculture sector. She's important, alright."

Joey adjusted himself in the driver's seat and continued,

"I don't know what else to do. Leo is going to have to come with me," said Joey. "And Rosie, I don't want you or him to think I'm trying to shut you all out."

"Let me call Leo."

Rosie tapped on her cellphone and then pushed the speaker button. The phone rang four times, and then a voice sounded,

"Hello, Rosie. How are you?"

"Good, thank you, Leo. How are you?"

"Doing well. Why do you call?"

"We have a situation, Leo. You're on speaker with Joey and Aaron."

"Good evening, people. Okay, Rosie, what's the situation?"

"The DIG from Agriculture just called Joey and Joey has to be in Washington tomorrow for a one o'clock meeting with the DIG and IG and others unknown. The meeting is about chickens. Apparently, what we discussed seems to be a real possibility."

"Really."

"Yes. We just talked to Big Sam at **USAMRIID, and he confirmed the chickens were contaminated with** psittacosis, ornithosis, in this case."

"Hmm."

"We are calling to see if you want to go with Joey to the meeting?"

"Was I invited?"

"Not by Agriculture's DIG, but she didn't know we were listening. I'm sure Lenore doesn't know how involved we are in this matter."

"Good old Lenore; she probably doesn't know. Well. No. I better not go if I wasn't invited. I know Joey won't shut us out. Right, Joey?"

"No, Leo. I won't unless I'm ordered to. But then you will know that too."

"Thanks, Joey. Then no. Joey, if you need something from me, just call. I can conference call the meeting at that point."

"As you wish. I'll call you after the meeting."

"Good. Thank you. Anything else, Rosie?"

"No."

"Rosie, take Joey to the plane at Armstrong. I'll clear it for him to use the National JTTF jet, the military plane. This is JTTF business. The jet will be ready by the time you all get to the airport. And for officer safety, and protection of a National JTTF witness, take Aaron. I'm sure the three of you will be discussing case strategy the whole way to D.C. Right?"

"Yes, sir. We will, and it will be in a secure environment."

"You all have a good evening."

Rosie ended the call.

"Okay, let's get to the airport. We are going to have a long night even though we are taking a private jet."

CHAPTER 52

"People, I think I'm done here," said Aaron. "I started with a missing person case. That's all. And only that one case because Boudar reassigned the other cases I was working on. Hindsight shows that to be very unusual."

"What do you mean you're done?" interrupted Rosie.

Joey turned his attention to the conversation.

"I have nothing else to contribute to either of you. From a missing person case to an undercover operative for the Agriculture OIG, to losing a friend, Sonny, and losing a professional counterpart, Harry. The missing person case is going nowhere, it will be placed in the cold case files. That is what happens to all the missing person or homicide cases involving members of the OWO, as I see now. I need to get back to the county and develop leads. I need to get back to the sheriff's office to work on it. I don't know who I can trust there now, and I don't know how I will interact with Boudar who is complicit in the animal smuggling and the OWO's extortion involving rich women who come to the county for the bliss of coastal living. Not to mention Boudar is also involved in a national security investigation. I have some challenges ahead of me."

"We'll help you, Aaron," replied Rosie.

Joseph moved his head and signaled agreement with Rosie.

"I'm sure, but I don't have a good feeling about this missing Sandy Diddler. Though almost all missing person cases are solved…"

Aaron paused from the stir of professional emotions as a dedicated detective. Composed, she continued,

"… the fact remains the person is still missing, perhaps to escape something or maybe she is dead. I suspect the same with all the other missing person cases involving members of the OWO.

Aaron paused again before she exclaimed Rosie's offer, "Help me!" and continued, "I should have moved from this county a long time ago. The good old boy system, nepotism, corruption, and racism."

"Aaron, I believe Diddler is alive and living in New Orleans," said Joseph.

Aaron did not hear Joseph because her attention was directed on an object that she felt in her pocket. She pulled it out and saw it was a thumb drive. She thought,

What's this? Why do I have it in my pocket?

Then she remembered and spoke loudly,

"This is from Harry's office."

Rosie and Joseph looked at each other and then looked to Aaron.

Aaron rested back in her seat and continued to look at the thumb drive.

Joseph's attention was directed to Aaron, and he excitedly asked, "What do you think is on it?"

Aaron replied, "I don't know. I have no idea."

"You got it from Harry Harper's office when you and Sid searched it?" inquired Joseph.

"Yes. Harry hid it in the men's room garbage can."

The truck went silent until Aaron spoke again,

"I need to see what's on this drive."

Joseph and Rosie moved their heads in agreement and said in unison, "Yes, we do."

The three law enforcement officers arrived at the hangar on Tyndall. All three slid out of the truck and swiftly moved to the office area to use the FBI computer. Rosie stood in front of the desk, tapped on the keyboard, and entered her passwords. The computer booted up, and Rosie moved back to Joey. They waited away from the computer to allow Aaron privacy to review the documents on the thumb drive.

Aaron rolled her chair to the desk, placed the drive in the port, and operated the computer to open it. The storage device had one file on it, a video file. Aaron moved the cursor over it and clicked the mouse. The computer hummed, and the recording opened. She paused it.

"There is one file on the drive," Aaron announced to Joey and Rosie.

"Just one?" Rosie and Joseph replied in unison.

"Yes. It's a video. Are you two going to watch this with me?" asked Aaron.

"If you want us to. We would understand if you want to watch it by yourself first," replied Joey for both him and Rosie.

"No. Pull some chairs over here."

Rosie and Joey moved to Aaron, and the three positioned themselves to watch the video together. Aaron clicked the arrow button, and the video started.

"Hello. My name is Harry Harper. I'm an intelligence analyst for the BCSO. I am holding this newspaper up to show the date of this self-made video.

During work on a missing person case with BCSO Detective Aaron Presley, my research disclosed disturbing information about the BCSO CID commander, Henry Boudar. Mr. Boudar is collaborating with a home-grown terrorist cell out of New Orleans. The terrorist group is plotting to kill a high-ranking government official in Washington, D.C. The name, specific level, or position, I did not develop. Also, Mr. Boudar conspired to commit murder with members of the OWO; they killed members of the OWO. And he, along with co-conspirators from the OWO, devised a scheme to defraud unsuspecting wealthy women of their money, forcing some into divorce to get funds that the OWO cheated from them and use to finance domestic terrorism."

Harry went silent. His face showed signs of concern. He fidgeted with the newspaper with his left hand and rubbed his neck with his right hand.

"My discovery of this information and the evidence to prove my allegations against Mr. Boudar will place me in harm's way. I know that, and that is why I made this video, saved it to a thumb drive, and hid the thumb drive in the garbage can in the men's room of the emergency command center. I suspect Sid Archer, ASAIC, USDA, Office of Inspector General, Investigations, Gainsville Sub-office is watching now, as the person who found it.

Likewise, I placed all the documents to prove the allegations against Mr. Boudar in envelopes and sent them to a courier service in the nation's capital. I instructed the courier service to deliver the packages to the OIG, USDA headquarters, Washington, D.C. if I failed to check in with them by email for five consecutive days.

Sid, since you are watching this video, things must have escalated to the point you more than likely obtained a FISA warrant and you and Aaron searched my office. Sid, help Aaron, please. Aaron, if something happened to Sid and you are watching this alone, you need to contact the Agriculture OIG undercover operative for assistance or go to New Orleans to the FBI National JTTF satellite office and show them this video. It should provide credibility to you, and the federal government should be able to protect you from Boudar until they take him off the street. I know of your investigative abilities, Aaron, and it would not be a surprise to me that Joey and Rosie are watching this video with you because you all are working together now."

Harry went silent again. He rubbed his neck.

"That's all I have to report. That's all I have to say. For the love of God, country, and humankind, please stop Boudar and the terrorist plot."

The video ended, and the computer screen went black. Aaron, Joey, and Rosie sat back in their chairs. No one said anything; they continued to digest what Harry told them from his grave.

Joseph finally broke the silence,

"Okay, I need to get to the airport."

"Right," replied Rosie. "I'll get the helicopter pilot."

Rosie walked away from Joseph and Aaron.

"Aaron, are you sure you don't want to go with us?" asked Joseph. "We could use your help."

"Yes, I'm sure. I have work to finish here."

"Okay, take my truck."

"Thank you, Joseph."

"We're ready to go, Joseph," said Rosie as she walked back to Joseph and Aaron.

"All right," replied Joseph.

"Aaron, you sure you don't want to come with us?" asked Rosie.

"No. I have to finish this," replied Aaron.

Joseph and Rosie said goodbye to Aaron and walked out of the hangar to the helicopter and entered. The helicopter engine labored, the four-blade propeller rotated faster and faster, and the aircraft lifted straight up. It hovered for a moment, then turned to the west and accelerated.

Aaron walked to Joseph's truck, entered, and drove off.

In flight, Rosie asked Joey, "Do you think Aaron meant anything when she said, 'I have to finish this.'"

Joseph raised his head and looked at Rosie.

"I don't know," replied Joseph.

"We should have brought her with us."

"How? We can't force her to come with us."

Silence took the passenger compartment of the JTTF helicopter as it continued westward to the Armstrong airport.

CHAPTER *53*

"Sir, we're ready."

"You've completed all the testing?"

"Yes, everything down here has been completed."

"You're ready to move the operation north and engage the target?"

"Yes, we are. The team is packed and ready. We're waiting for your directions."

"Get up here. Get up here now. Let's move this operation forward. The party needs this."

"Yes, sir. If you have nothing else, I will hang up, and we'll move out."

"Great, are you coming on the campaign plane too?"

"Yes, sir."

"When you get here, call me."

"Yes, sir."

The short, well-groomed, heavyset, gentleman dressed in stylish Cuban clothing, stowed his cellphone in his pocket as he turned to the group of men and looked at each one. Then he spoke,

"It's time. It's time to go and get this done. It's time to be in motion with a purpose, and we all know the purpose."

The heavyset leader paused briefly, then without gestures added,

"This is for our country. In us, we trust."

The group of men, also absent gestures, repeated back in unison,

"For our country. In us, we trust."

The heavyset leader turned and started up the steps of the private jet. He struggled and moved slowly up the narrow steps because of his size, but he made it without assistance. The other men followed in turn. The last man aboard raised the steps and closed and sealed the door.

The private jet moved down the tarmac to the runway and prepared for takeoff.

The air traffic control tower broadcasted: "HBX100 next for takeoff."

The pilot broadcasted: "10-4 tower. HBX100 next."

Stopped at the end of the runway, the pilot continued to check the instruments of the jet and made a few necessary adjustments.

The tower broadcasted: "HBX100 cleared for takeoff."

The pilot broadcasted: "10-4 tower. Cleared for takeoff."

The pilot flexed his hand on the throttle, gripped it and eased it forward. The private jet, per its declared flight plan, took off from Louis Armstrong New Orleans International Airport en route to the Ronald Reagan Washington National Airport.

At the VIP side of the Armstrong airport where private planes and charters arrived and departed, Rosie and Joey disembarked the agency helicopter, walked across the tarmac, and boarded the agency jet still in the hangar. They prepared for their flight to Reagan national and Washington, D.C. to attend the Agriculture OIG meeting.

CHAPTER 54

Aaron parked Joey's truck in her driveway, slid out, and walked to the front door of her house. She juggled her keys to find the right one, unlocked the door, and entered. Inside, Aaron closed the door behind her and locked it. When she turned to walk back to her bedroom, a gunshot rang out. Aaron reached for her duty weapon as her chest exploded. She felt the hot lead move through her body as she redirected her hands to her chest. Aaron's body buckled, and then fell to the floor, bounced once and came to rest on the hardwood. She clutched her chest with both hands and started to cough as she felt her warm blood on her hands. Her dark house was getting darker as she struggled to breathe while she applied limp pressure to her sucking chest wound. Aaron, weak from the gunshot wound, struggled to see a pair of tactical boots in front of her. She started to fade in and out when she heard the second shot and felt the hot lead enter her forehead from which Aaron expired.

The shooter knelt on one knee next to Aaron. He stared at his now lifeless former lover and confessed, "I loved you, Aaron. I loved you so much. I never stopped loving you. It didn't have to be this way. You just kept digging and digging. You and Harper. It was just a missing person case, only a member of the OWO, a transplant from the north. A damn Yankee. As typical, an unsuspecting member of a homegrown terrorist group. I planned all along to suspend the case indefinitely due to the lack of leads. And then, you cooperated with the feds. You were too dedicated to the job. A job that became a wedge in our relationship and the reason for my indecision and womanizing when we were together. I never told you that, perhaps if I had. Perhaps."

Henry held his gun in his right hand and reached out with his left. He slid his index and middle finger onto Aaron's neck and gently pressed, but no pulse was felt. He studied Aaron and observed no signs of life. He withdrew his hand, raised it to his eyes, and wiped his tears. He stood, shuffle-stepped around Aaron out of respect and walked out the front door. He paused on the porch and mumbled to himself,

"Two more."

Then Henry struck a match, threw it inside and shut the door behind him.

CHAPTER 55

It was Saturday, early morning, and the pain was not subsiding as usual. Gheorghi tossed and turned all night trying to get comfortable, but he found no position that reduced the pain. He finally sat straight up in bed, slid to the edge, and slowly stood. His legs buckled, and he fell back to the bed. He sat for a while, contemplating why he experienced severe pain every Friday night and randomly during the week. He stood again, and this time was able to remain standing before he walked off to the kitchen to get a glass of water.

Seated at the kitchen table, Gheorghi sipped his water and noticed he had not opened all his mail from the day before, which included a small box. He set his glass down and picked up the box. He looked at the address label and recognized it as the address to which he mailed the Petitioner's monthly court-ordered payments. He shook the box, and it felt like only one snug object inside. He carefully opened the box and immediately dropped it to the floor when he saw the contents. He sat back in his chair and mumbled softly,

"What is she doing? What is she doing to me?"

Gheorghi looked closer and saw the doll had his likeness and it had a needle in its right leg. He kicked the box, and the doll rolled out. When it came to rest, he saw a needle in the doll's back and to scale, a small sack attached.

Gheorghi tightly closed his eyes to make the pain go away or at least subside. The pain was more intense now, and his attempt was unsuccessful. When he opened his eyes, the doll was standing upright and stared at Gheorghi. When Gheorghi moved, the doll's eyes rolled with him.

Gheorghi started to panic. He rose from the chair and moved to the cupboard. He retrieved a large freezer zip bag, moved to the doll, and quickly reached down and picked it up with the bag like he was picking up dog droppings. He shook the plastic bag to force the doll into it, which caused the contents of the doll's sack to empty into the plastic bag. He pressed all the air out, zipped it closed and studied what had fallen to the bottom of the bag. Gheorghi froze, and the bag dropped out of his hand to the floor. He spoke out loud with a stutter,

"The casings. The casings inscribed Petitioner. Four of them."

It became difficult for Gheorghi to breathe, and it felt like he was suffocating. He calmed himself enough to breathe steady and to pick up the plastic bag. He held the bag at arm's length to keep the doll as far away from him as possible. He walked to the trash can and threw it in.

Gheorghi stared down at the doll and sighed deeply before he closed the garbage can lid and went back and sat in the kitchen chair. He turned slightly to reach his water glass, and he saw the doll was sitting upright on the table. It was now holding the sack, which appeared to have the inscribed casings back in it.

Gheorghi jumped up, moved to the counter, and retrieved a large cutting knife from the magnetic holder. He moved back to the table, and the doll was gone. Gheorghi looked around the table, on the floor, and in the garbage can. Nothing. The voodoo doll was nowhere to be found. He sat back down and worked to stop himself from shaking.

Gheorghi's cellphone rang. He slowly changed the knife from his right hand to his left as the phone progressively rang louder.

A little groggy, but awake, Gheorghi picked up his cellphone and saw the caller was Petar. Gheorghi answered in a shallow, shaky, weak voice.

"Hey."

"Hey," replied Petar. "Did I catch you at a bad time? You sound out of breath."

"No. You just woke me up from a dream."

"Was it a dream about you and a lady? You sound out of breath. You know."

Petar laughed at his joke suggestive of a sexual dream.

"No. Not quite. It was about that damn voodoo shit again."

"Oh. You just ate the wrong thing, again."

"Maybe, but the doll had my likeness."

"Get out."

"And it carried four shell casings in a sack on its back. Shell casings inscribed Petitioner."

"Really."

"Penka injected, "I think you should go see a doctor to get something to relax you. The procrastinated litigation is messing with you."

"No, I don't want any drugs."

"Well, we're concerned about you," continued Penka.

"Thanks for the concern, but I'll handle it."

"You're still having those dreams," commented Penka. "How are you handling it?"

"I'll handle it," replied Gheorghi.

"How are you going to handle it?" asked Petar.

"Just like Motorman suggested."

Gheorghi laughed at his joke, not realizing the call had been dropped.

"What?" said Petar.

Petar too did not realize the cell call went dead, nor did he hear Gheorghi laugh at his own joke.

"You better call your brother back," sounded Penka. "I'm concerned about him."

"You don't think he's off to do it?" said Petar. "You know, do what Motorman suggested."

"No way. But I don't know. I just don't know. Sometimes I think I wouldn't blame him. Five years is a long time. A long time to deal with the stress and uncertainty. He has no control over any of it."

"You shouldn't say that, Penka."

"Hell, the detective wanted to talk to him about Rezza. What did he have to do with her for the past five years? Why did the detective want to talk to him? Did she talk to the asshole who drove Rezza's truck for the past five years? Did she speak to anyone from the pier? Those people."

Petar's cellphone rang through the truck's speakers, and the screen identified the caller as unknown. He pressed the answer button.

"Hello."

"There you are. What happened?"

"The call dropped. Where you at?"

"I just called back, so you didn't think I was rude and just ended the call."

"No. Where you at?"

"I have to go. I have some things to take care of. I'll talk to you all later."

"Wait. Where are you? What do you have to take care of?"

"Gheorghi hung up," said Penka.

"Shit. Gheorghi doesn't need to do anything stupid. This thing is almost over for him. He has the final hearing coming up soon."

CHAPTER 56

Jack waited in his truck in the dark parking lot of St. Andrews State Park. He came as quick as he could; Jack thought Henry was already in the park, and he did not want to keep him waiting. Jack knew from past experiences that the narcissistic Henry was not one to keep waiting. That was not the case, as Jack sat in the Tundra and waited for Henry.

About twenty minutes later, a vehicle flashed its lights at Jack as it made its way through the empty, dark parking lot. The vehicle had its high beams on, and Jack could not see if it was Henry. The vehicle pulled alongside the Tundra and stopped. Henry alighted from his unmarked sheriff's office cruiser and walked up to Jack's truck.

"Thanks for meeting me here, Jack."

"Not a problem, Henry. What do you need from me?"

"Your silence."

Before Jack said or did anything, Henry reached through the driver's window and grabbed Jack's arm and pulled it out the window. Henry wedged Jack's arm in the lower right corner of the window frame and bent it down and to the back to control the arm and in turn to control Jack. Jack resisted, but his strength was no match for Henry's.

As Henry continued to control Jack's arm, Henry pulled a syringe out of his pocket, removed the needle's cap with his teeth, and stuck it in the bulging vein of Jack's arm. Jack's resistance started to diminish, and his arm finally went limp. Henry slowly released control and it hung loosely out the window with the syringe still firmly stuck in the vein. Henry reached into the truck and checked Jack for a pulse, but none was found. The pure heroin had the effect Henry wanted, the quick death, and subsequent silence of Jack.

Henry tucked Jack's arm back into the Tundra and positioned it to look like Jack injected himself. Henry turned to walk away but jerked back around, walked back to the window of the Tundra, and threw the red needle cap onto the driver's side floorboard.

Henry turned, walked to his truck, and retrieved a five-gallon plastic gas container from the bed. He returned and doused the interior of the white Toyota Tundra with the gasoline and threw the empty container into the cab of Jack's truck. Henry paused, struck the flare, and tossed it into the cab of the truck, which exploded into flames.

Henry quickly slid into his unmarked cruiser and drove off. He watched the Tundra burn in his mirrors until it disappeared out of sight. Henry continued to the main entrance. As he waited for the gate to rise, he spoke to himself,

"One more. I have one more, and everyone will be silenced."

Henry stopped at the red light in the left-hand turn lane. He clicked on his left signal, and when the turn arrow showed, he turned left and proceeded to his task of silencing all possible witnesses to the animal smuggling.

Two miles on North Lagoon Drive, Henry turned right and eased down the street. He found Joey's apartment cordoned off with yellow police tape. Henry continued beyond the residence and brought his cruiser to a stop at the four-way intersection. He moved through the intersection and pulled to the side of the road.

In the darkness, the glow from the onboard computer screen highlighted Henry's face as he concentrated on clicking the computer keys to command the computer to display BCSO files from the server. As a commander, he had access to all records from all divisions.

The computer sounded receipt of the patrol report from the first patrol deputy who responded to a dispatched call from an anonymous complainant who sent an email. The full message was pasted into the report, and Henry read the email complaint about himself.

HI THERE. I WAS BURGLARIZING THIS PLACE, AND TO MY SURPRISE I FOUND THIS MAN DEAD IN BED WITH FOUR BULLET HOLES. HE DOESN'T LIVE HERE AS BOUDAR KNOWS. SHERIFF, YOU HAVE A PROBLEM IN YOUR DEPARTMENT. I HOPE YOU'RE NOT INVOLVED. I VOTED FOR YOU. SINCERELY, A CONCERNED CITIZEN OF BAY COUNTY.

Henry opened the attached picture file, and the picture was Sid Archer just as Henry had positioned Sid in the bed of Joey's apartment.

Henry raised his hand to his mouth and mumbled aloud,

"This isn't good. Who sent this? This isn't good for me. Too many people have seen this; I can't kill them all."

Henry scrolled through the file searching for the name of the anonymous complainant. He found no name or any leads to the identity of the concerned citizen.

Henry continued to stare at the photograph of Sid and recalled his plan to himself,

"I was going to kill Joey, undress them both, position them in a naked embrace with Sid holding the gun that shot them both. Then I was going to set the apartment on fire."

Henry closed the file, logged out of the BCSO file system, shut his computer down, and closed it. He rested his hand on his laptop as he sat in his vehicle, in the dark of night, on a side street of a small northwest Florida coastal town. His heart raced a bit as he contemplated his next move. He knew someone set him up, not just with law enforcement, but also with the people with whom he conspired during his years of lawlessness. He was consumed with concern about retaliation from the co-conspirators, and he was unaware of an individual approaching.

Soft popping sounds interrupted Henry's concentration. Henry did not twitch, he just slumped over the center console, and his hand remained on his closed BCSO computer.

The driver's door opened. A small, black-gloved hand, clenching a semi-automatic pistol, extended into Henry's vehicle and up to his head. One soft pop sounded, and the gun was retracted from the cruiser. It was replaced with an empty, small, black-gloved hand that reached to Henry's neck and searched for a pulse. No pulse confirmed the completion of the felonious task. The black-gloved hand withdrew, and the driver's door softly closed.

CHAPTER 57

"Your mail is in the car. I'll give it to you when we leave," said Penka.

"Thank you," replied Gheorghi.

"So, tomorrow is the big day," said Petar.

"Yes, it is. Though it won't be completed tomorrow," replied Gheorghi.

"Why not?" asked Petar.

"The judge will still have to sign the documents. Tomorrow is before the magistrate," explained Gheorghi.

"Really?"

"Yeah. Tomorrow, the opposing attorneys argue the points the Petitioner and Respondent could not agree on. Though the Petitioner never made any offers. She deflected the lack of negotiations to her attorney's way of handling the case. I guess it was their case strategy not to negotiate and rely on the sympathy of a female magistrate."

"Hmm," sounded Penka. "The magistrate is female? I don't like that. That could work against you."

"Yeah. At the last hearing, I was the only male in the room. The court deputy was even female. Boy, did I feel out of place."

The three laughed.

"Can I get anyone anything?" asked the waitress.

"No. Nothing now," replied Petar for the table.

After the waitress moved out of earshot to the conversation, Gheorghi said, "I called that BCSO detective."

"What did she say?" inquired Petar with a nervous twitch in his voice. "What did she ask you?

"She never called me back. I left a message and my contact information, but she never called back."

"That's unusual from the way she talked at the house that day. Huh, Penka? I thought she was going to haul me off to jail right then and there."

"I'll say," replied Penka.

"That's what I thought by the way you two described her demeanor. I thought she was an aggressive detective. But nothing. My call went unanswered."

Petar continued, "She sure wanted to talk to you when she visited us."

"And the detective was adamant to Maria that I was a person of interest. What does that even mean? A suspect, I suppose."

"The detective talked to your daughter. All your daughters?" inquired Petar with the nervous twitch still in his voice.

"Only Maria. And according to Maria, Maria put the detective in her place. With no words minced, Maria told the detective I had nothing to do with her mother being missing."

Silence came over the table until Gheorghi continued,

"So, I don't even know if the Petitioner will be in court tomorrow."

"Does she have to be there?" asked Petar.

"Yes," replied Gheorghi. "How can my attorney ask her questions if she is not there? And I assume she is the chief witness for the Petitioner, for herself, for her case."

"This thing could be continued again," asked Penka.

"Sure could," replied Gheorghi.

Everyone stopped talking until the waitress cleared the table.

Gheorghi smiled and said, "I should have spent the twenty cents like Motorman joked."

"Sometimes I think you should have too," said Petar and Penka in unison.

"I should have given you the twenty cents," said Petar with laughter.

The three laughed then Gheorghi became serious when he spoke,

"Maybe someone did spend the twenty cents. She is missing."

Petar began to fidget with his coffee cup.

Gheorghi stopped sipping his coffee, looked over his cup, and stared at Petar. When Petar noticed Gheorghi staring at him, he looked down and continued to fidget with his coffee cup. Penka dropped her eyes down to the table in unison with Petar.

Suddenly, Penka raised her head and injected, "Well, she's missing. That was obvious from the detective's visit and inquiry. Apparently, she's still missing, and it makes no matter who made her go missing."

Penka quickly lowered her eyes back down to the table. Petar continued to watch himself fidget with his coffee cup. Gheorghi turned and glared at Penka.

Penka felt Gheorghi's glare and raised her head and continued with a stutter.

"What? I'm just saying. Why are you looking at me? She's missing, according to the detective. That's all I know; that's what I mean."

Gheorghi continued to stare at Penka and Petar jerked his head and directed his stare to Penka. Seeing Petar's reaction, Penka said nothing more and lowered her eyes back down to the table.

Gheorghi started to become suspicious about Petar's and Penka's irregular manner of talking. He thought, *Did they do something? I can't ask.*

Gheorghi spoke aloud,

"Yeah. You're right, Penka. I've said all along, I couldn't care less if she was dead."

Petar redirected his glare to Gheorghi and Penka raised her head and stared at Gheorghi. Their shifty eyes, which indicated deceit or evasion, continued to feed Gheorghi's imagination of possible retaliatory actions by them.

Gheorghi took one last sip of his coffee, set the cup down and sounded,

"She's missing. I'm hoping that will help my case. That's all I'm saying."

"Yeah. And Motorman has experience with these matters. That's all I'm saying," added Petar.

The three smiled at each other and laughed at the situation.

Composed of their laughter, Gheorghi, Petar, and Penka rose from their table and left the restaurant. As the threesome walked out, Gheorghi thoughts wondered again. This time to Motorman.

Maybe Petar and Penka knew more about the missing Petitioner than they told me. Maybe Motorman did something and told them but not me. Or maybe Motorman had something done by someone else. Maybe that Private Eye he hangs out with.

Gheorghi, back from his conspiracy thoughts, reminded Penka, "I have to get my mail."

"Yes. Let me get it from the car. There's only one piece, a small box."

Penka retrieved the small box from her car and handed it to Gheorghi.

"Thank you. I'll open it later."

"We got two of those same small boxes too. One was addressed to me, and one to Petar," said Penka.

"Yeah," replied Gheorghi.

"Yeah. I haven't opened mine yet either. Have you opened yours, Petar?" asked Penka.

"No. Not yet," replied Petar.

"I wonder what's in the boxes?" asked Penka.

"I'll open mine later. I'm going. Talk to you all later," replied Gheorghi.

Gheorghi drove off from the restaurant, and before he went any distance, his curiosity got the best of him. At the first steady red light, without inspecting the box, he opened it and pulled out the contents. It was a small doll with a pin in the lower back and one in the right leg. Gheorghi stared at the doll that bore his likeness. There was no mistake, it was a voodoo doll carrying a hex to him.

Gheorghi, in a state of mental numbness, did not move. Nor did he drive off when the traffic light cycled green. He just sat in the driver's seat of his sports car and held the doll and stared at it as the traffic control signal continued to cycle through its recurring sequence – green, yellow, and red – which reflected into Gheorghi's car.

Gheorghi impeded traffic by not driving off. Other motorists reported a parked car in the middle of Twenty-Third Street near the college, which summoned the Panama City Police to the scene.

The sergeant first on the scene tried to communicate with Gheorghi, but he was nonresponsive. The sergeant directed a uniformed patrol officer to call emergency services to transport the nonresponsive driver to the hospital.

CHAPTER 58

"How is he today, Doc?" asked Petar.

"No change," replied the doctor without looking up from the chart."

The doctor continued to review Gheorghi's chart stored at the end of his bed. Finished, the doctor placed it back in the holder. As he walked to the head of the bed, he looked to Petar and Penka and broke the silence.

"It's a good thing his daughters finally agreed and committed him when they did. People in his condition, people exposed to a prolonged stressful event, they need help. They need medication. Extreme cases like your brother's – five years of constant stress – the last resort is a self-induced coma. It lets the brain rest. His daughters made a wise decision to move forward with the procedure."

The doctor went silent once again as he checked about the head of Gheorghi. When he finished his brief examination, he continued,

"When the police found him sitting in his car on Twenty-third Street, just staring off, that was the final sign for his daughters that he needed medical care."

"That's what we thought too," said Penka. "That's what my research on the internet disclosed, and we're glad his children agreed with you."

The doctor added, "I think the self-induced coma will help and he's showing signs of improving. But, as I explained to you both, there is no way to determine how long this procedure will take. It could be a week, a month, or maybe a year. I just don't know. I can't say."

"What is the longest time you're familiar with, Doc?" asked Petar.

"I have read of a case that the patient never came out of the coma. Unfortunately, the family had to make another decision, keep the patient on the machines, or relieve him of mechanical life."

"I see, doc. I understand," replied Petar.

"I explained this all, I explained this same prognosis to his daughters. They too said they understood, which was good," said the doctor.

"That's good to know," replied Petar.

"It won't happen tomorrow or the next day. Nor in a week. We have longer than that. You all will have time to take in the worst-case scenario, the worst results," added the doctor.

"Thank you, sir," replied Penka.

"And, I explained the same prognosis to the lady who visits your brother," said the doctor.

Petar snapped his head in the direction of the doctor and with a stutter asked, "What? A lady comes to visit Gheorghi?"

"Yes. The lady comes here once a week. Every Friday evening."

"What's her name?" asked Petar.

"She never said, and I never asked," replied the doctor. "As we talk about it now, there is one strange thing about her."

"What's that?" demanded Petar.

"She wears black leather gloves," replied the doctor.

"And you never asked her name? You never asked anything about her?"

Petar started to shake but inquired further,

"Is it your policy to let visitors in without knowing their names?"

Petar paused a moment, composed himself and continued,

"I assumed Gheorghi's daughters told you Gheorghi's demand. I reminded them to tell you."

"His desire to be or not to be sustained on life support?" asked the doctor.

"No, his demand that the Petitioner is not around him, no matter what happens to him. Sick, dying, or dead."

"Petitioner? What do you mean, Petitioner?" asked the doctor.

"Gheorghi is in the process of a divorce. A divorce that is into its sixth year. He believes the prolonged divorce was the source of his stress. He doesn't want to ever be in the same room with the Petitioner."

"You mean his ex-wife?" asked the doctor.

"Petitioner, doctor. Petitioner. Gheorghi doesn't have an *ex*. I respect his wishes never to mention the money-grabbing..."

Penka cut Petar off and comforted him by rubbing his shoulder and softly said,

"Easy, Petar. It's okay. That's enough. The doctor will accommodate your requests."

Penka looked deep into the eyes of the doctor and added, "Right, Doctor?"

"If it upsets you, I'll ask her name next Friday."

The doctor paused and looked away from Petar before he continued,

"She was concerned, and she knew a lot about Gheorghi. I assumed she was his sister. She placed a doll with his likeness under his pillow, and she gave me a doll too. She asked me to carry it in my pocket to my white lab coat and said it was part of her religion."

The doctor paused and studied the concern on Petar's and Penka's faces.

"Here, I'll show you," added the doctor. "I thought it was a good luck piece."

The doctor reached into the pocket of his heavily starched white lab coat and retrieved the doll. He held it up to Petar and Penka. It was in the likeness of Gheorghi, right down to his thick, brown, slicked-back hair. And there were pins in the doll. One in the lower back of the doll and one in the doll's right leg.

Penka exclaimed, "Petar, that's just like the dolls sent to us in the boxes."

Petar started to shake again, and Penka guided him back to a chair.

"Here, sit down. Sit back down," consoled Penka.

Penka reached out and shook Petar as she said, "Wake up. Wake up. You're dreaming again, and I can't hear the television because you're talking in your sleep too."

Petar looked at Penka with a blank stare. Still groggy from his nap, he said, "Where did you put those dolls?"
He slowly worked his way up from his chair with the aid of his cane.

"We have to get rid of those dolls now. I don't want them in the house. You have to burn them."

"What are you talking about, Petar?" asked Penka.

"The dolls we received in the mail."

"Did you have another dream like the ones I have?"

Petar did not say anything; he just stood there. The television programming was interrupted by breaking news, and Petar fixed his attention to the TV.

CHAPTER **59**

The television showed a still picture of the words *Breaking News* in white letters on a red background and a pre-recorded voice sounded,

"We interrupt your regular schedule of programs to bring a news update."

Petar continued to stand and watched the television as the still picture turned to a live news broadcast.

"We interrupt tonight's regular schedule of programs to bring you an update on the criminal activities in Bay County."

The newscaster paused as he shuffled papers in front of him.

"I reported by special programming that Bay County continues to have many violent crimes but continues to remain off any listing highlighting such information.

Tonight, I report four violent crimes in the county.

The first violent crime occurred in Millville. After a house fire was put out, and county fire personnel searched the structure, a lone body was discovered on the living room floor. The body was believed to be the owner of the house, Aaron Presley, a respected and decorated detective with the Bay County Sheriff's Office. The body was transported by the Bay County Medical Examiner's Office to their facility for a full autopsy. We were told the medical examiner's office will report the results to the public after their completed autopsy. The spokesperson for the medical examiner's office declined to comment on the cause of death at this time and without the autopsy results.

The second violent crime was a fully engulfed pickup truck in the parking lot of the St. Andrews State Park on the beach. Emergency personnel responded to the fire, quickly extinguished it and found a charred body in the driver's seat. The body was transported by the medical examiner's office to their facility for an autopsy. The spokesperson said they will report the results when they conclude their examination.

The third violent crime was a homicide victim at an apartment on the beach. The victim remains unidentified. Due to the ongoing investigation and need to first notify next of kin, the BCSO spokesperson declined to comment.

The fourth violent crime was another homicide. This victim was the commander of the Criminal Investigation Division of the BCSO, Henry Boudar. Mr. Boudar was found in his assigned sheriff's office vehicle three blocks from the third unidentified homicide victim I reported on. Mr. Boudar's body had six gunshot wounds. One gunshot wound was to the back of his head, a universal sign of an execution-style killing, a gangland murder. This all according to the BCSO spokesperson who confirmed Mr. Boudar did not have any next of kin.

The BCSO spokesperson declined to comment on whether tonight's four victims were separate, or if the violent acts were related.

That is all we have to report about the four deaths until we receive updates.

Violence has riddled the county this evening. I remind viewers, these incidences of violence are in addition to the numerous incidents I report through the program series, *Violence in Bay County*. I will be working on compiling another segment that will highlight the pier cult, the OWO, and its connection to the rise of crime in the county. Please continue to watch for the date and time it will air. Thank you."

The television showed a still picture of the words *Breaking News* in white letters on a red background and a pre-recorded voice sounded,

"We now return you to our regular schedule of programs."

CHAPTER 60

One month later.

Silence held the four ladies, all sisters, as they sat and watched the *Special Program, Violence in Bay County – The Other World Order*. The ladies were transfixed by what they were seeing and hearing during the locally produced and televised program. During the entire two hours of the broadcast, the four sisters said nothing. As the credits scrolled up the screen, the small apartment's living room remained silent.

Finally, Maria exclaimed, "Wow!"

"Wow! is right," sounded one of Maria's three sisters, the conservative sister.

Silence retook the small room until Maria asked,

"Do you think mom is missing because of that violence? Do you think somehow, someway, she was involved in the hideous violence in the county as reported in that program? Maybe something bigger as alluded to in the program?"

Again, silence took the room until the conservative sister spoke,

"She's missing. She doesn't return any of our telephone calls or text messages. We don't even know how long she has been missing. I don't want to believe she's involved with that level of violence, but the facts are the facts."

Another sister, the pragmatic sister, noted, "We knew she was involved with Jack Prat. A relationship that was much more than just a caregiver as she purported to dad. According to the program, Prat died when he was injected with a lethal dose of heroin, and then the truck was burned with him in it. The program exposed the OWO for what it was, a cult that extorted money from women, unsuspecting women who moved to Bay County for the bliss of beach living and became caught up in the rhetoric of the pier people. I suspected mom similarly met her fate because she was involved with Prat and therefore, most likely with the OWO. The divorce fit the cult's model, and mom fit the profile of women on whom the cult preyed."

The other three sisters, silent but in unison, moved their heads in agreement with their pragmatic sister's comments that assessed their mother's now prolonged absence and lack of contact.

"Must be," mumbled Maria, who sighed deeply and continued, "I suppose we will never know the truth about it all. We just have to move on until mom comes back. What are we going to do, investigate it ourselves?"

The conservative sister added, "The deputy said, *no leads, it's a cold case.*"

The pragmatic sister sounded, "And dad is still in the hospital with a stress-related illness. Still in a coma induced by the doctor. We don't even know if that therapy will work. We still face the possibility of losing him."

The room fell silent as the sisters contemplated the possibility of losing both parents. The ruin of a family unit because of the finality of divorce was one thing. The loss of the family unit to the death of both parents was a much worse outlook for the four sisters as they silently thought about life with neither father nor mother around anymore. It was this unknown that the four sisters grappled with the most. Occasionally as a foursome. Typically, as strong, independent women, in their own solitude.

The pragmatic sister continued, "And when the doctor brings dad out of the coma, he faces the same stressful event, the procrastinated divorce, now with a missing petitioner. That will complicate things."

"Dad didn't kill mom," announced the conservative sister who paused and sighed deeply, then continued, "One, that's not who he is. Two, he just wants the matter to end. He wants the final order signed by the judge so he can get on with his life like mom did six years ago."

The more aloof sister chimed a rhetorical question, "Has it been six years? No way."

The pragmatic sister sounded, "This conversation needs to end."

The four sisters agreed, and they stopped talking. Rare for the four sisters, with themselves or anyone, they moved together, even the aloof sister, and hugged each other at the same time.

What the four, strong, independent women knew for sure, they still had the embrace of each other.

* 9 7 8 0 9 9 7 1 5 0 6 5 0 *